To Geoffrey
Best Wishes

WOMEN IN
AIR FORCE BLUE

Beryl E. Escott

WRAF Airwomen in the First World War.

WOMEN IN
AIR FORCE BLUE

The Story of Women in the Royal Air Force
from 1918 to the Present Day

SQUADRON LEADER BERYL E.ESCOTT

Patrick Stephens Limited

British Library Cataloguing in Publication Data

Escott, Beryl E.
 Women in air force blue : the history of the
 WRAF/WAAF 1918 to the present day.
 1. Great Britain. Royal Air Force. Women's
 Auxiliary Air Force & Great Britain. Royal Air
 Force. Women's Royal Air Force, to 1988
 I. Title
 358.4'1348'0941

 ISBN 1-85260-066-7

Patrick Stephens is part of the
Thorsons Publishing Group, Wellingborough,
Northamptonshire, NN8 2RQ England

Printed in Great Britain by Biddles Limited,
Guildford, Surrey

10 9 8 7 6 5 4 3 2 1

Contents

Foreword

by

Air Commodore S. A. Jones ADC WRAF
Director of the Women's Royal Air Force

I am delighted to be associated with the publication of this book. It is most appropriate that the final editorial polishing took place in the 70th Anniversary year of the formation of the Royal Air Force, and that the book is published during the year of the 50th Anniversary of the outbreak of the Second World War. Both World Wars changed the course of history and with it the lives of so many women.

The author received a very great response to her requests for personal recollections from former members of the WRAF (1918 to 1919), the WAAF (1939-49) and the WRAF (1949 onwards). The material has been painstakingly pieced together to paint a vivid picture of the work and life of women in the Royal Air Force.

From the outset the book emphasizes the women's integration into the parent Service. Those of us serving today may reflect on the dedication of our predecessors who paved the way for the opportunities we now enjoy in the branches and trades of the RAF in which we are employed.

Author's Introduction

W hen I was near the end of this book, Air Commodore Probert of the Air Historical Branch asked me, 'Did you realize when you took on this task that it would be so long and hard?' My response was 'Yes and no.' Yes, I knew it would take a long time, but no, I never thought it would take over three years. Yes, I knew it would be difficult breaking so much new ground, but no, not as difficult as it proved in combining the results of research with the Pandora's box of information unleashed by the thousands of ex-WAAF/WRAF from all parts of the world when I appealed for help through the press. I was practically submerged. And how they wrote – warm, enthusiastic, endearing letters, with an irreplaceable fund of first-hand stories, wise, funny and sometimes heartachingly sad, showing what wonderful people they are. The result was a constant battle with length, dictating not so much what I should put in, but rather what I had to leave out — often the best bits! I could more easily have filled 20 books rather than one.

What has been largely forgotten by the public and the services over the years is the less glamorous work of airwomen and their women officers. In many accounts it is hard to believe that they ever existed, and yet without them the RAF would be the poorer. I intend that their contribution here outlined will provide a reminder and reassessment of their role. I must also assure the men and women of the other services, alongside whom we often served, that their work is not forgotten; but they are better documented elsewhere.

For the non-service readers, I have done my best to convey a flavour of a life and time strange to them, so that they can 'piece out the picture with their thoughts'. I want them to enjoy browsing through these pages and in so doing come to an understanding of the extraordinary efforts and sacrifices made by quite ordinary women to keep the RAF flying in war and peace, in their efforts to create a safer and more ideal world for us all.

Servicewomen, I believe, will recognize something of the picture, for whose omissions and imperfections I apologise ahead. This is their story, often in their own words and usually in their unmarried names of the time. Square brackets [ ] indicate my additions.

It would take many pages to thank everyone who has helped me, so let me only express here my special gratitude to my main sources of help.

Without the suggestion of the former Director of the WRAF, Air Commodore Renton, and the support and encouragement throughout this project of the Air Historical Branch (RAF), with all its staff and in particular Air Commodore Probert, my great tower of strength, I would never have contemplated this task. I must also give special thanks to the resourceful Mr Lake of Adastral Library, who sought out the most abstruse references, as did the Keepers of the RAF Museum at Hendon, who gave me an almost free run of their archives. Part of my thanks will be expressed in a gift to the RAF Benevolent Fund.

I could not have managed without Queenie Hierons, who early answered my plea, and despite the sad loss of her husband, continued to liaise with me from London, over the long years. Nor would the book have been completed without Barbara Barrie, who puzzled out my untidy manuscripts, gently prevented my enthusiastic attempts to outrun the pages, typed them impeccably and then checked them with her patient, ex–RAF husband.

I am also grateful to my long-suffering mother for her moral support and her distractions when she felt sure the sunshine would do me more good than writing.

Additionally, I must not forget to thank the vast body of ex-WAAF/WRAF who, because they loved the RAF, freely shared their reminiscences in the hope that I would make their story reflect them truly. Without them this would have been a different book. I hope they will not be disappointed.

My thanks also, for help over and above the call of duty, to : Basil Beagent, Rosemary Boot, Norman Chandler, Janet Dudley, Monica Dunbar, Peggy Heard, Paula Irwin, Olivia Kingsbury, Wing Commander and Dr Lewis, Lady Llewellyn, Cyril Ludlow, Joy McArthur, Yvonne Pateman (USAF), Dr Putley, Dee Scandrett, Patricia Stephenson, Pat Sturgeon, Daphne Veitch-Wilson, Jim Wilson, Eileen Younghusband, and many RAF Stations and Sections.

I cannot end without my own tribute to the RAF, with whom I have served for many years. Please accept this as my attempt to repay in a small measure something of the debt that I owe to this fine service.

Finally, I commend this history to you, my reader. May you gently hear and kindly judge our story.

Beryl E. Escott

Chapter 1

Time To Fly

I t may come as a surprise to many, not least those who served in the Second World War, to discover that airwomen first appeared during the First World War. The story of the Women's Royal Air Force therefore goes back to the earliest years of the twentieth century, and the cornerstones of its creation were the emergence of the Women's Services and the formation of the Royal Air Force.

*   *   *

Flying has always fascinated mankind. Centuries BC, Daedalus may have flown. In the fifteenth century, Leonardo da Vinci designed an air vehicle. Over the ages, kites, balloons, gliders and airships took to the air with growing success and sophistication, carrying people, messages and supplies. Weather permitting, all that happened on the ground below was fully revealed to those eyes in the sky. A third dimension had been added to land and sea.

In the nineteenth century, balloons were increasingly utilized over battlefields in many parts of the world, and consequently, in the 1880s, the British Army established a special Balloon Section in the Corps of the Royal Engineers. There was one snag, however. Balloons were dependent on wind. Man was not in control. Even lighter-than-air airships were an unsatisfactory answer.

Then in the twentieth century came the breakthrough. The Wright brothers of America designed and flew a heavier-than-air, man-carrying, powered machine. By 1904, the first flimsy aeroplane had arrived, and man's dreams of flight had become reality. From that point, the aeroplane's progress was breathtaking, as private aviators and craftsmen seized its challenge with enthusiasm.

Unfortunately the twentieth century, as well as ushering in the era of the aeroplane, also brought a growing German threat to the peace of Europe. So, might this new toy have some military application if war came? In 1910, Lord Haldane, whose reforms had modernized the army, seemed unconcerned.

PER·ARDUA·AD·ASTRA

~The Dawn of Aviation~

(*From* Eight Months with the WRAF, *Gertrude A. George, c1920*)

'When a new invention like the submarine or the motor comes to light, the Englishman is usually behind. Give him a few years and he has not only taken care of himself in the meantime, but is generally leading. As it was with these inventions, so, I suspect, it will prove to be with aircraft.' But were there to be enough years?

The Royal Engineers were also doubtful of the value of this new machine, but they agreed to replace their Balloon Section with an Air Battalion containing two companies, one of which was to specialize in military aircraft. The date was now 1 April 1911.

Scarcely had the Air Battalion had time to draw breath than the Chairman of a Defence Committee was reporting:

'At the present time in this country we have, so far as I know, of actual flying men in the army about eleven, and of actual flying men in the navy about eight, and France has about two hundred and sixty-three — so we are, what you might call, behind!'

With the threat of war looming ever nearer, this report galvanized the military into action. On 13 April 1912, the Royal Flying Corps (RFC) was created, replacing the short–lived Air Battalion and dissolving its link with the Royal Engineers. It was to concentrate on training pilots at a Central Flying School and to develop the use of aircraft in two wings, military and naval. Nevertheless, its Royal Warrant stressed that the RFC was to be regarded as a single force, although the wings were to be administered separately by the War Office and the Admiralty. The Naval Wing, however, anxious to develop flying for its own different needs, severed its connection with the RFC and became the Royal Naval Air Service (RNAS) on the eve of war in 1914.

The role of the aeroplane evolved rapidly during the First World War, turning it into a weapon so powerful that it was ultimately recognized that mastery of the air was essential to victory. It also brought war and destruction to the homes of hitherto safe, civilian populations, and it was public reaction to German air raids on the south coast of Britain — attacks culminating in the bombing of an inadequately defended London — that finally swept away both the RFC and the RNAS. In their place was established a new unified body answerable neither to War Office nor Admiralty, but to a newly-constituted Air Ministry. Thus on 1 April 1918, the Royal Air Force (RAF) came into existence, the third and youngest of our Armed Services.

* * *

The First World War changed everything. The mud and blood of trench warfare in France and Belgium sucked up millions of lives, and yet the area over which armies were hurled at one another, like pawns in some demonic chess game, varied by no more than 50 miles in four years. The war drew in countries from all parts of the globe, its tentacles reaching into peaceful civilian homes where many lace-curtained parlours cherished a fading photograph surrounded by black ribbons.

1916 was the worst year of that war. After two years of fighting on this scale the Empire and Britain were being drained of men, with losses in front-line troops on an enormous scale. They threatened to outstrip the resources not only of the Regular Army and Kitchener's Volunteer Army but also the desperate new expedient of conscripting ordinary men, plucked from all walks of civil life and not in otherwise vital 'reserved' occupations.

There was only one further untapped source — women.

* * *

10 December 1916
From Field Marshal Sir Douglas Haig, Commander in Chief (C in C), British Armies in France:

'I am prepared to accept the principle of the employment of women in substitution of men, as Clerks in certain offices at General Headquarters and in the Lines of Communication.'

18 December 1916
After visiting France, Lieutenant Colonel Geddes grumbles at over-optimistic female staffing figures. They must be raised by at least 20 per cent as women cannot stand as much strain as men. He also wants to add women in Administrative and Disciplinary posts, as well as Cooks and Domestics.

15 January 1917
The Commander in Chief starts talking about employing women as Telegraphists and Telephone Switchboard Operators in the rear of the British Army in France.

February 1917
The War Office is occupied in laying down conditions for service for women Drivers with the Royal Flying Corps and the Army Service Corps.

11 March 1917
From the Commander in Chief:

'The principle of employing women in this country (France) is accepted and they will be made use of wherever conditions admit.'

While the paperwork flew to and fro, a London Conference of Women's Societies was convened on 26 February 1917 by the Secretary of State for War, Lord Derby, to evaluate their reactions. To it came representatives from voluntary bodies up and down Britain. The Women's Legion, whose Military Cookery Section had been one of the first to be accepted and whose Drivers were not far behind, was present, together with the First Aid Nursing Yeomanry (FANY) with its well organized Transport and Nursing services, and the Voluntary Aid Detachments (VADs) who would turn their hands to any work, no matter how unpleasant. These and many similar voluntary bodies were bursting with women eager and anxious to help in their country's war effort, many of whom were already doing wartime work in civilian life. Others were already working behind the lines, often to the annoyance of established authorities. They crowded into

A 1917 recruitment poster (RAF Museum).

the hall and listened to the speakers, including Mrs Chalmers Watson, sister of Lieutenant Colonel Geddes, as they learned what it was hoped to do. The meeting was an overwhelming success. Later, in February, delegates learned that Mrs Chalmers Watson had been engaged by the War Office to raise and command a new organization of which she was to be Chief Controller. The Women's Army Auxiliary Corps (WAAC) was under way.

Shortly Mrs Watson was joined by the woman who was to become her second-in-command, then one of the Commandants of the Women's Royal Air Force, Mrs Helen Gwynne-Vaughan. With the assistance of this indomitable woman and through a series of trials and errors, after the incredibly short preparation time of just over a month, a small unit of 14 Cooks and Waitresses crossed the Channel to serve with the army in France. The date was 31 March 1917. In this short space of time, history was made and the first uniformed women's service appeared.

So successful was this first venture and so urgent the need to release more manpower that volunteers to serve in the WAAC abroad were rapidly followed, in the summer of 1917, by girls enrolled for service within the United Kingdom. On 9 April 1918, the Queen allowed her name to be added to its title so that it became the Queen Mary's Army Auxiliary Corps, the QMAAC.

The navy had also come to its own conclusions. On the day that the first WAAC had landed in France, the Admiralty was looking at a report headed *Female Labour on Air Stations*. By November 1917, it had decided to employ women in naval establishments ashore, officially creating the Women's Royal Naval Service (WRNS) in February of 1918.

*　*　*

On any air station of the RFC or RNAS you were likely to see women. In the early days most were civilians. Some did voluntary work in their spare time, cooking and scrubbing, others did regular paid jobs, usually clerical, employed in the capacity of 'civilian subordinates' as they were quaintly termed, while women Drivers from the Women's Legion had been with the services since September 1916. Later these were joined by the khaki-clad WAAC and still later by a few navy-uniformed WRNS. As their numbers increased, it was inevitable that the brighter and more adventurous types would find their way into the workshops.

Women in RFC workshops, 1917 (Mr Cole).

Air stations were a headache both to the War Office and the Admiralty. They were very much *ad hoc* and independent, their unorthodox organization not fitting easily into any normal pattern. By August 1917 the War Cabinet had decided to form an independent air service out of the RFC and RNAS.

Details of the new force took time to work out, and during these months flying stations did all they could not to lose any female workers they were employing. Complaints appeared from places like Lincoln, Reading and Peterborough, that stations were recruiting women as Clerks and Drivers for the army, and then not enrolling them in the WAAC, on the pretext that they were only filling emergency appointments. An adjutant from RFC Headquarters, Stamford, was more specific. He would not draft his women into the WAAC until he received a guarantee that they would not be removed from the town. The impasse was resolved on 28 December when the RFC was finally allowed to recruit women officially for itself.

It was, however, only the beginning of the difficult process of creating the Women's Royal Air Force out of such disparate elements. Foremost was getting the new male flying service organized, so a woman's service came very low in the priorities. Arguments shuttled back and forth. Was a new women's service really necessary? Why shouldn't the women already serving on air bases continue to do so without change? It would be far cheaper and less complicated! Closer examination showed the flaws. There were too many organizations involved, and the advent of RFC women and WRNS only further complicated the picture. Also, women on air stations did much specialized work, completely different from that required for the other two services. In any case, direct attachment to an individual body produced better work, loyalty and morale. There must be a new women's air service!

On 29 January 1918, the Air Council agreed to a Women's Auxiliary Air Force Corps to work with the forthcoming male service, provided the Treasury, who would have to find the extra money, approved. It did, and with this point achieved there seemed little hurry in formulating regulations for the women, and no difficulties were anticipated. How comforting to have the examples of the other two sister services to follow!

Many items had still to be settled in the male service. The War Office, Admiralty and new Air Ministry were meeting regularly to thrash out everything ranging from the transfer of air contracts — another important reason for forming a separate air service — to the ultimate demobilization of air service personnel.

Enough time was spared, however, to make two noteworthy decisions in February. On the 12th, all agreed that WAAC and WRNS presently working on air stations should be given the option of transfer to the new women's service, at a yet unspecified date. On 19 February this date was officially announced as 1 April 1918.

Rumours began circulating on stations. Those most involved often understood least and reallocation to the new service seemed almost accidental. In March 1918 Topsy Austen thought she was joining the WRNS at Dover.

'We could not understand why we were not issued with uniform, and were told that the RNAS and RFC were amalgamating and that we should possibly be going into an Air Force Corps. In the meantime we wore khaki WAAC uniform

Women in RFC workshops, 1917 (Mr Cole).

THE FLYING GROUND

From the Dope Shop door

(*From* Eight Months with the WRAF)

and after a while we were given wings, which we could sew on our felt hats and shoulders of our dresses.'

Louise Dalglish-Bellasis kept a very full diary of events from the time she joined the RFC in January 1918. An extract shows the effect on stations:

'2 March 1918
The Shawbury we know will soon be no more. Captain Philips broke the news to us that he will be moving on in April. All the squadrons are going from here and Ternhill is to make room for the Handley Pages and the de Havilland 9's. Ternhill and Shawbury are to become a TDS and not only that but there are to be naval flying men here as well as RFC.'

March, in fact, saw many difficulties and doubts about the April deadline for both services, and a degree of panic seemed to set in. The Air Council was treating as a matter of urgency the distribution to stations of pamphlets detailing the conditions of transfer for the men from the older services to the new. Still there was no news of the conditions of service for women. However, in March a name was announced. The King graciously called the new service the Royal Air Force (RAF) and on 5 March 1918 agreed to the female service being called the Women's Royal Air Force, the WRAF. Now, at least, people knew how to refer to them!

As the final date drew still nearer, stations already knee-deep in changes of role, aircraft and men, begged for transfer details for the women. There was a strong feeling that the WRAF should be delayed until other changes had been absorbed. Then at the final hour came two blows that rocked and nearly finished both RAF and WRAF.

Major General Trenchard, the presiding genius and Chief of Air Staff, fretting over disagreements and waste, offered his resignation; and the Germans threw everything into a big push in France, which caught the Allies napping and nearly had them on the run. During this furore, and with three days to go before 1 April, the urgently–needed Field Service Publication Number 14 (FS Pub 14) at last was approved giving the Constitution and Regulations for the WRAF. It is a particular tribute to the determination of all concerned that it then appeared.

Thus, against this background of catastrophe, the WRAF came into existence, the only occasion that a women's service has been created alongside its male counterpart at one and the same time.

The change took place overnight. Stations which had gone to bed on 31 March 1918 as RNAS or RFC, woke up next morning to the new designation of RAF. Louise Dalglish-Bellasis mentions reading various regulations and signing some papers, but the actual significance of the 1 April passed by unnoticed. Dora Pacey joined the RFC in January 1918 and was kitted out in khaki. She recalls, 'On April 1st, a startling item of news passed along the grapevine — the RFC and RNAS were to be joined and become one unit and the new title was to be the Royal Air Force. We [girls] would have a separate identity and be the Women's Royal Air Force, and most startling of all, both [services] would have a new uniform and it would be blue.'

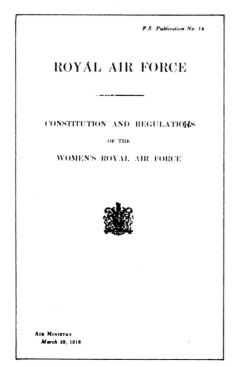

Constitution & Regulations WRAF F S Pub 14.

Louise Dalglish-Bellasis notes the effect a little later:

'30 April 1918
The camp is beginning to fill up gradually but there is hardly any flying done, as there are so few instructors. My new CO is a very large and woolly Canadian. Shawbury is being made so smart now. All round the Wing and other Headquarters, flower beds and little lawns are being laid out. There are tremendous numbers of RNAS men in the camp now and they look so quaint among the khaki.'

Basic conditions of joining the RAF differed between men and women. Men were enlisted under the terms of military law, with military discipline, medical care and compensation for injury all covered. Women, on the other hand, were enrolled and not enlisted. This made them little more than civilians in uniform, though the civil contract which they signed was strengthened by the Defence of the Realm Act, or DORA, for time of war. This handicapped them in terms of discipline, leave and pay, while important matters like sick care, injury compensation and in some cases unemployment cover, were woefully inadequate except overseas, where the men's military law took over.

Fortunately the WRAF rank structure was simpler than the RAF. Women were divided into a small number of Officers — mainly managers — and members, who were all the rest. Of course there were further subdivisions for those of more or less authority in both groups.

Transfer from army and navy to the RAF also differed for men and women. Men were given a month to decide, later extended to six to encourage them to make up their minds; women were only allowed the month, and if by 1 May they had not applied to join the WRAF, the women were then to be reposted to an army or navy station on 1 July 1918. Thus the small WRNS force lost 2,867 women to the WRAF and the WAAC had a proportionately greater exodus of 6,805.

Members of the Women's Legion Motor Drivers, attached to what were to become RAF stations, were given the choice of joining the WRAF too, but they were allowed even less time, in fact only until 14 April, after which they could be immediately whisked away. Perhaps this date was too premature, since it was shortly amended to 23 April 1918. Here, 496 women elected to transfer. There was to be trouble later over their status, as they had previously been treated as Officers, and now found themselves demoted to ordinary members. Transfers also were offered to civilian subordinates on air stations. A prim little note on their terms of transfer reminds stations that no form of pressure was to be used to

A historic moment in late 1918. The men are in Army/RFC uniforms. The girls in front wear WAAC khaki coat-dress and hat with RFC shoulder badges and WRAF hat badge. The girl standing on the right wears a 1918 WRAF coat and cap (Mrs Porter).

bring them to a decision. Nonetheless these women were warned that it was intended to fill their posts with WRAF as soon as possible, on only a week's notice, if they did not elect to enrol.

These dates were obviously not adhered to rigidly, because of the scrambled start. There must have been misunderstandings as late as 8 May, when a War Office memorandum finds it necessary to point out that the right of transfer was only extended to women already working on a RAF unit, and not at any other service station. Indeed the conditions of transfer were still repeated in FS Pub 18 when it emerged in November 1918. Much the same happened with recruiting from the civilian population outside, which did not effectively begin until May 1918.

For this and other reasons, figures giving the exact size of the WRAF during the first few months of its existence are unreliable until 1 August 1918, when the transfers and the service had begun to settle down. On this date its strength is given as 15,433 — about 5,000 recruits added to around 10,000 women who had been transferred. The original intention in creating the WRAF had been to raise a force of about 90,000 women. It proved to be nearly four times smaller, and at its maximum the WRAF never exceeded more than 25,000 in any one month.

However, this was all in the future. On 1 April 1918, the problem for the WRAF was that, having been born against all odds, its hasty birth had left a legacy of many difficulties to be overcome, and there was a war to be fought as well! The question then to be answered was, would it survive?

Left *An appealing recruitment poster* circa *1919* (RAF Museum).

SIGNING ON

We plunge into the Unknown

(*From* Eight Months with the WRAF)

Chapter 2

Against The Odds

'[The WRAF] believed in the future of the air and they were proud to serve it. The RAF accepted this attitude and the WRAF were no longer outsiders.'

Dame Helen Gwynne-Vaughan

From the first the WRAF was more integrated with its partner than the other services, and perhaps the bond was stronger, because the men and women of the RAF passed through a period of criticism and growth together. Certainly for the WRAF there was plenty of both!

Criticism was to be expected for anything new — particularly when it was a revolutionary new women's service — but the growing pains of the WRAF were almost enough to destroy it. Nineteenth-century thinking was hard to change. Women's place was in the home, sheltered from the harsh realities of life, and only the terrible man-shortage and the undeniable usefulness of the women, drove the experiment on. So how did the WRAF begin?

At the beginning, most of the planning by the Air Ministry had been concentrated on transfers from the other services. The ink was hardly dry on FS Pub 14, the booklet outlining such essential arrangements as the intended structure, pay, administration, ranks and accommodation scales for the new service, before the WRAF appeared. Almost immediately further details were introduced, so that 14 was quickly out-dated, overtaken by various amendments and additions, later reflected in Air Ministry Weekly Orders. Those who had to apply the rapidly-changing directives had a daunting task.

The question of leadership, too, was fraught with problems. At the top, the post, whose designation and rank changed numerous times in the first year, was filled by a rapid succession of ladies, a situation hardly calculated to give confidence to any new body.

As for the Officers transferred from the other services, they had a wholly understandable confusion of identities. 'Play it by ear, my dear' was their best advice. Fortunately, they at least brought some experience with them, which was not the case with the enrolments from the civil population who followed them. The most senior Officers were put to work straight away, postponing training until much later. For the rest, their training was sketchy, encompassed by about two weeks on a course followed by one on station. At the outset their numbers were reported as 73, but even if this was an under-estimation in the confusion, there were still many camps where no Officers appeared until late in the year.

At Air Ministry London, things were scarcely happier. The Air Council had arranged that WRAF matters should come into the Department of the Master General of Personnel, delegated to the Director of Manning as one of his many sections labelled M3. This section for WRAF was run, with no doubt the best of intentions, by men, who dealt with matters affecting the WRAF externally. They worked alongside the branch WM3, staffed by the Commandant, her deputy and a few civilians, who dealt with internal WRAF matters ranging from welfare to discharges. Because these were small sections they operated from cramped quarters in Mason's Yard, in the corner of Jermyn Street and Duke Street, while other Departments were mostly located at the nearby Hotel Cecil. This resulted in delays, loss of vital papers, misunderstandings through not always the most co-operative of intermediaries and — most trying of all — the greatest difficulty of getting the ear direct of the Director General of Personnel. It also made little of the very subordinate position of the WRAF Commandant, and therefore much depended on her personality and relationships, a clearly invidious situation. In the early stages, too, the Commandant's tiny staff proved only moderately capable and three members were so unhelpful as to resign together in July 1918.

Recruiting campaigns were normally not very strenuous or vociferous. In the early days recruiting was done by whoever was available at that moment. Alice Chauncey found herself speaking at a Recruiting Rally in Folkestone, planned and prepared well in advance by the Air Ministry, but for her at no more notice than the time it took to drive there.

No station was allowed to enrol WRAF for itself, even in dire emergency, unless sanctioned by Air Ministry. All applicants had to go through the Labour Exchange, a clearing agency for both men and women in most jobs, including munitions, teaching, agriculture, transport, government and private service. It also produced Selection Boards on whatever day of the week service applicants appeared. In the case of WRAF, the majority of the three to five selectors were women, who might come from any of the services and sometimes from none at all. Credit must, however, be given to those hard pressed interviewers in the Labour Exchanges, whose selections, for the most part, turned out so well. There was the girl who, when asked for her trade, answered hopefully, 'I can take orders'. She later became a more than competent Officer. Then there was the lady who, assigned to an aircraft repair section on her first day, marched out some hours later, saying that she had come to scrub and scrub she would.

Although the processing of recruits was pretty thorough, the occasional over- or under-age applicant slipped through. A Cook is on record at over 60, and Grace Bateson, a Telephonist, joined the RFC at 15 and was still that age on

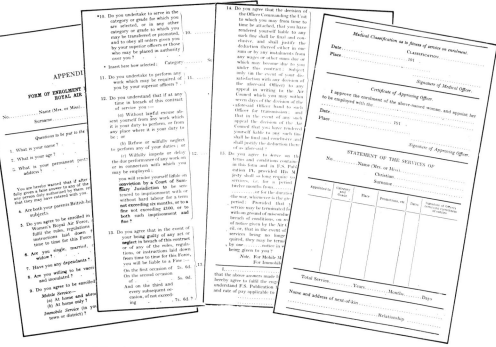

WRAF Form of Enrolment.

transferring to the WRAF, when the minimum was 18!

In fact, for the hopeful girls who flocked to join the new service, it was not easy to get in. There was a whole battery of forms, testimonials from people who had known them more than two years, questions, warnings and quite stringent medical tests. On this last hurdle many fell, for those born in the crowded industrial streets were prey to chronic ill-health. Where few failed was in literacy.

Properly speaking, all the girls who became members should have started in the WRAF with a course of Initial Training, designed to explain service terms, forms, discipline, drill and enough to manage in the new alien life they would encounter on a RAF camp. A WRAF Training Depot for this purpose was hastily nominated at Halton Camp — already busy training men and boys — but very few early WRAF actually attained the couple of days initiation there. As a consequence, station personnel reacted to them in different ways and frequently ignorance was mistaken for stupidity or awkwardness. At the beginning, much the same difficulty was encountered in the area of work, and except for a few, fully qualified before they were enrolled, most girls were put to work with no preliminary training whatsoever.

Difficulties in early planning, leadership, recruiting and training coalesced into welfare problems. Mistakes were corrected at a fantastic rate, but it took time, and that was what the WRAF lacked. Top of the list came accommodation. WRAF 'Mobiles' who lived on camp were supposed to have a set size, number and type of rooms and furnishings, including casement and muslin curtains,

Standard types of hutted accommodation, 1918 (Mr Cole).

candlesticks, tapestry-covered couches, rugs, wash-handstands complete with wares, painted chests of drawers, and mattresses. Scarcely any camps met these criteria, and as early as 1917, committees had warned that army and air camps were refusing to employ WAAC because they lacked suitable accommodation. Hardly a month before the WRAF appeared, 40 bricklayers were diverted from France to begin building WRAF accommodation at one camp, yet by May 1918, there were WRAF on over 500 camps.

The RAF addressed itself to do the best it could with the problem. Makeshift huts were taken over or built, later to be encircled rather ludicrously by barbed wire. Houses were requisitioned as residential Hostels, and approved lodgings arranged, even though they were more than the desirable one mile from the camp. Wherever possible, girls were encouraged to live at home, with lorries to pick them up daily to bring them to work. Inevitably in the hurry, some huts, buildings or hostels turned out to be cramped, draughty, insanitary, cold and wet.

Not that this was the only complaint. Another was food, and although some WRAF were fortunate, others, despite ration scales that were plentiful and generous, suffered badly. In lodgings food was often insufficient, while on many camps it varied from boring at best, to abysmally cooked at worst. 'Earwigs with everything — even in the rice pudding' was common.

Uniform — or rather the lack of it — caused further trouble. Promised full uniform when they joined, the girls frequently found they had to work in dirty, damp conditions in their own clothes and overalls, which were unsuitable and quickly ruined. Service uniform, when it was issued, often went to the last in, and then turned out to be old army-style khaki dresses and round hats. True, the question of money compensation for inadequate clothing provision was shortly tackled, but this did not fully make up for the discomfort and disappointment of many.

Dissatisfaction was not improved by misunderstandings about pay. FS Pub 14 promised gratuities to mobile members every quarter, on top of their pay. Perhaps some recruiters had been over-enthusiastic or had misread their information, but many new members believed that they were entitled to this bonus at the end of their first month. When this did not materialize, there were strikes and unrest at widespread camps, and in particular with the Drivers at Number 1 Depot, Hurst Park, who were always somewhat of a law unto themselves. In any case, the many different rates of pay needed sorting out and the payment system took time to stabilize.

There were other instances of confusion or worse, not least of which was the standstill on discharges. As the RAF Records Office was inundated with transfers and enlistments, it shelved such applications for the time being, causing real hardship in genuine cases.

Early arrangements for medical services were also most unsatisfactory. A sarcastic notice in a WRAF camp warned airwomen how *not* to get medical attention: 'If you wish to report sick, don't fiddle here in the Orderly Room, go direct to the CO about it. He will tell you what ails you.' Lodgers and living-out members had to make their own medical arrangements, and their numbers were increased by those earning over a certain sum. Similar difficulties with National Unemployment Insurance excluded a large number of girls from being insured, as they were considered not to be wholly employed on manual duties. In addition, the handover of air stations from Army and Navy to RAF was very slow. The process trailed through 1918, and was still going on in November of that year. Meanwhile in the general confusion, 200 WAAC wearing RFC badges and working at the RFC Maintenance Depot at Rouen since 1916 were somehow forgotten.

Little wonder, therefore, that there was much mismanagement in living and working conditions, not improved by a situation where girls of all types had to adjust to living at close quarters with unaccustomed work and discipline, under the control of many not as experienced and often not as old as they. There were complaints by WRAF, under- or over-employed, unfair discharges and appointments, various letters to the press, even questions in Parliament, and all the while the process of getting a new organization under way continued.

In a letter to a January 1919 *Daily Telegraph*, a disgruntled WRAF complains 'I joined up as a Carpenter and after six weeks I was called up and sent to a reformatory for a week near Birmingham, instead of some place for a "month's training in any trade" which we were promised. A few drills was all the training I received.

'I was then drafted to an aerodrome where a place was made for me in the carpenter's shop. I am tolerated by the men as another military nuisance. There I have been six weeks, spending eight hours a day (most days) in that shop, and have never yet done one single day's work. I should go on like the rest, enjoying my drills, physical and otherwise, and my hockey and dances, but I have a conscience.'

Nevertheless, while all these difficulties had to be sorted out by the WRAF, it must be emphasized that the RAF was encountering and solving similar problems, aside from the purely technical ones connected with the machines it flew. It was a time of trial for both sides of the service.

Once the first few months had passed, the worst was over and improvements appeared. Public confidence, which had been shaken by earlier tales, gradually returned and the initial hostility to women in uniform was dying down. This reversal of attitude to the WRAF appeared in proportion to the rise in morale among the girls. It neared its lowest point about June 1918 at the Hyde Park Celebration to mark the Silver Wedding of King George V and Queen Mary. To the chagrin of the WRAF their promised uniforms had not yet arrived, so their Commandant had the unenviable duty of watching the representatives of most women's organizations, in or out of uniform, marching by without a single WRAF.

At the beginning of September a Commandant was appointed who was to stay and difficulties with WM3 staff were resolved. The Commandant's awkward sub-department had been replaced by December 1918, when, in the name of economy, a more common sense structure had appeared. The Commandant moved and was put in charge of a Directorate, responsible only to the Master General of Personnel. This Directorate was known by the letter 'W' and contained five departments, four headed by a WRAF Assistant Commandant and one, the Inspectorate, controlled by the Deputy Commandant attached to the staff of the Inspector General RAF, under whose authority she carried out her inspections. The departments were W1 which dealt with Officers, W2 Inspections, W3 Training, W4 Discipline and Welfare, and W5 Airwomen in general.

Meanwhile, a workable system of administration had been evolved in the five areas into which the United Kingdom was divided. By autumn 1918, there was an Assistant Commandant WRAF with her deputy and a small staff in each area headquarters. She communicated upwards with the appropriate WRAF department at Air Ministry and downwards in the chain of command with the Group Administrators of her area. As no WRAF Officers were represented at Wing Headquarters, the chain then connected directly with the Administrators and their staff on the units. With the help of the new officers and the goodwill of stations, accommodation problems too were easing. Though conditions were still far from perfect, the airwomen were coming to terms with an environment so different from their homes and making the best of the improvements as they gradually appeared.

WRAF Depots at last began opening for reception, kitting and initial training of airwomen. True their appearance was piecemeal, but they were set up as quickly as a suitable place could be found. The first was at Handsworth College, Birmingham, in the Midlands, followed in August by Glasgow for the north-west, then later by Lindfield Gardens, Hampstead, in the south-east, Flowerdown, Winchester, in the south-west, and York in the north-east. Once the area depots were working well, the need to centralize and regularize the recruiting and intakes became apparent. The irregular system of selection boards and entry to the service at whatever time the recruit applied, was now replaced by preset dates of entry, and by March 1919, the whole business of selection was passed to a

Airwomen in front of an accommodation hut in late 1918. One wears RFC khaki coatdress, the other is in the khaki WRAF suit. Both wear soft-top WRAF caps with embroidered WRAF badges (Miss Simms).

Airwomen in full khaki WRAF uniform with RAF members of their family. Chief Section Leader with 3 chevrons on the left. Early 1919 (Mrs S. Davies for Mrs Webb).

single WRAF Officer at each Depot, to whom the girls applied and by whom they were chosen. As a consequence, course places, figures for postable members and trades were much easier to forecast and allocate. The WRAF also stopped providing uniforms and items of 'kit' from the WRAF Clothing Controller at Wellington Street in the Strand. It amalgamated with the RAF Clothing Distribution Depot at RAF Feltham, where all issues were centralized, although small holdings for foreseeable issues were held on stations.

The training machine, too, was learning fast, since it had soon become apparent that women were better at certain tasks if given a few weeks training. In October 1918 Berridge House, Hampstead, opened to fulfil this need, first to train in two weeks Cooks, General Domestics and Mess Orderlies, and later, two to three weeks on Physical Training, Patrol and refresher courses. Participants and those who received the trained women had nothing but praise for the results, and in December 1918, Berridge House received the accolade of being called the WRAF School of Instruction. It was not the only training school. Drivers were trained at Number 1 Mechanical Transport (MT) Depot School of Instruction, Hurst Park, and there were some other small, specialized centres. Most other trades still learned 'on the job', usually from a male NCO, who, starting hostile, remained to be proud and grateful for these unwanted, unlikely hands. Officer Training, too, improved. After six courses at Portland Place, training moved to Southwood Hostels, Eltham, and Hackney College, Hampstead,

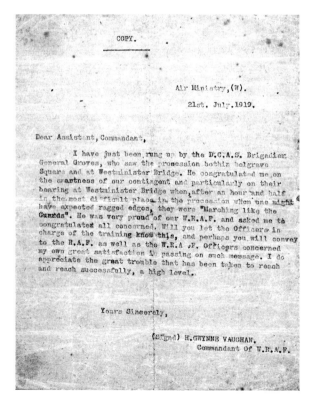

COPY.

Air Ministry,(W).

21st. July.1919.

Dear Assistant, Commandant,

I have just been rung up by the D.C.A.S. Brigadier
General Groves, who saw the procession bothin belgrave
Square and at Westminister Bridge. He congratulated me on
the smartness of our contingent and particularly on their
bearing at Westminister Bridge when, after an hour and half
in the most difficult place in the procession when one might
have expected ragged edges, they were "Marching like the
Gumrds". He was very proud of our W.R.A.F. and asked me to
congratulated all concerned. Will you let the Officers in
charge of the training know this, and perhaps you will convey
to the R.A.F. as well as the W.R.A .F. Officers concerned
my own great satisfaction in passing on such message. I do
appreciate the great trouble that has been taken to reach
and reach successfully, a high level.

Yours Sincerely,

(Signd) H.GWYNNE VAUGHAN.
Commandant Of W.R.A.F.

Above *Airwomen in a mixture of WRAF uniforms. Two on the right wear the final blue WRAF uniform and cap, with high collared tunic, buttoned on the left, and metal RAF cap badge. Mid 1919 (Mrs S. E. Davies).*

Left *Congratulatory letter from the Director to the airwomen on the London Victory Parade (Mrs S. Davies for Mrs Webb).*

Above right *WRAF Subordinate Officers and members waiting on camp for transport. They include 2 Chief Section Leaders and a Sub Leader (1 chevron) (Flt Lt Beard).*

for two further courses each. By November 1918, when training ended, nearly 600 Officers had benefitted.

In the same way, medical organization altered for the better. After a trial period, the Royal Army Medical Corps relinquished its WRAF responsibilities to the RAF Medical Service, in everything except recruiting until WRAF Depot recruiting would be functional. A RAF Women's Medical Service came into being on 30 August 1918 and its women Doctors had the same rank as, and wore similar uniform to, their RAF counterparts. The Women's Branch hardly exceeded a dozen, but up to today it has always been RAF and never WRAF. By December 1919 all women Doctors were discharged, with the exception of their Medical Director who continued part-time for six days a month until the last airwomen had left the service.

The work of the women Doctors was not totally confined to the WRAF. Airwomen on stations could be medically examined by male or female Medical Officers on their monthly inspections and treated by male or female doctors when they were ill, depending on the medical staffing of their station.

At the start, WRAF cases were not allowed treatment in all-male service hospitals but as time passed, a small ward for service women was opened at Endell Street Military Hospital. Shortly afterwards the Area Depot Sick Quarters at Hampstead was converted into a WRAF Hospital, followed by wards for WRAF at Halton, Cranwell and Blandford. However, those unfortunates whose illness or injury fell between or beyond the care of a Sick Quarters and Hospital, often found that because of the limitations of the strictly civilian National Health Insurance and Workman's Compensation Act, they were to be discharged without resources. Trying to ameliorate or soften the results of these anomalies

SAVOY HOTEL - APRIL 7ᵗʰ 1919

Her Majesty the Queen presents prizes to winners in Women's War Service Competitions.

(*From* Eight Months with the WRAF)

caused the growth of complicated and time-wasting regulations, so that neither servicewomen nor the service gained in the outcome.

The RAF showed its growing confidence in the WRAF when in October 1918 it handed over the maintenance of WRAF Records to one WRAF Officer and her eight airwomen, a service never faulted, despite three moves, starting at Portland Place.

Christmas 1918 was a happy occasion as the WRAF marked their first Christmas in the service. They began to feel that improvements were appearing slowly but surely and their hard work was beginning to have an impact. The next day being Boxing Day, the women's services shared route-lining duties with the men in London for the State Visit of President Wilson of the USA, Britain's great ally in the latter part of the war.

The following year saw WRAF members taking an increasing part in public activities. They were at the Memorial Service for RAF dead held at Westminster Abbey on 19 February 1919, where Air Ministry RAF and WRAF made up most of the choir; with representatives from their two sister services, they met the Queen on 7 April in the magnificent setting of the ballroom of the Savoy Hotel; they gave displays in the Royal Tournament at Olympia, and marched in the London Lord Mayor's Show, the Thanksgiving Service at Westminster Abbey, and the Great Peace Parade in Central London. The latter was possibly the high spot of their public appearances, when 700 airwomen and six Officers, who had rehearsed for weeks beforehand, covered a route that took over four hours. Not one woman dropped out and the general feeling was that they could do it all over again. Only one mishap occurred when a male Staff Officer found himself unexpectedly marching ahead of the girls to the comments of 'Look at the Captain of the Lady Airmen'.

Airwomen also took part in an education scheme, designed to help the men and women of the RAF prepare for civilian life. The classes were mixed and covered mainly domestic, technical, clerical and general subjects, the most popular subjects among the WRAF being, perhaps not surprisingly, dressmaking and cookery, but they were closely followed by poultry-farming and carpentry.

During this time, the general reaction of the WRAF and the public for whom they served, was interest and pleasure. How unfortunate this was not to last much longer.

Chapter 3

'There's a lot of widows you'll be responsible for'

> 'Women have been enrolled in the WRAF with the object of enabling them to assist in the war by releasing men for duty at home and overseas.'
>
> *Air Ministry Weekly Order 1237*

'There's a lot of widows you'll be responsible for!' shouted one angry Corporal to a woman Clerk, whose coming was releasing him for the frontline. She had already met some civilians who looked down on women in uniform as immoral and unfeminine, because they believed the women formed a fighting service – in truth, a complete contradiction of their function. Opposition in the service she did not expect, but she did her best; all the WRAF did.

Few knew the trade to which they were allocated, usually in a fairly arbitrary fashion according to existing vacancies. It is something of an eye-opener today, to realize that as far back as 1918 airwomen were employed by the RAF in over 40 trades, rising to over 50 in a further two years. Nor were these only limited to work of a purely domestic, nursing or clerical nature. Given their limited education, particularly in the sciences, it is still surprising to find so many girls taking over the technical jobs more generally associated with men or the more skilled women of a later age.

On first joining the WRAF, a girl found herself directed into one of four basic trade categories. Clerks and Storewomen formed one, Household Workers comprised the second, while the technical and non-technical types made a third and fourth. Each category was divided into six sections, many of these being themselves sub-divided into smaller trade and pay groups, though pay rose with rank and experience.

Members who lived at home and were denominated 'Immobiles' were paid an extra 14 shillings a week for their keep, in what was termed a consolidated allowance. A 'Mobile' airwoman who lived on camp and whose food, clothes

CATEGORY "A"—CLERKS AND STOREWOMEN

Sub-Category	Employment	Grade	Pay	Consolidated Allowance	Weekly Total
1	Head Section Leader (at Record Office only 1–20 clerks) . .		31/-	14/-	45/-
2	*Clerks*				
	(a) Chief Section Leader . .	I	25/6	14/-	39/6
		II	24/6	14/-	38/6
		III	23/6	14/-	37/6
	(b) Shorthand Typist with speed of 100 words a minute .	I	31/-	14/-	45/-
	(c) Shorthand Typist with speed of less than 100 words a minute exceptionally employed	II	29/-	14/-	43/-
			23/6	14/-	37/6
	(d) General	I	19/6	14/-	33/6
	(e) Stores	II	17/6	14/-	31/6
	(f) Pay	III	15/6	14/-	29/6
		IV	13/6	14/-	27/6
3	*Storewomen* (for Technical Stores)				
	(a) Chief Section Leader . .	I	28/-	14/-	42/-
		II	26/-	14/-	40/-
		III	24/-	14/-	38/-
	(b) Section Leader . . .	I	22/-	14/-	36/-
		II	20/-	14/-	34/-
		III	18/-	14/-	32/-
		I	18/-	14/-	32/-
	(c) Worker . . .	II	16/-	14/-	30/-
		III	15/-	14/-	29/-
		IV	14/-	14/-	28/-

CATEGORY "B"—HOUSEHOLD

Sub-Category	Employment	Grade	Pay	Consolidated Allowance	Weekly Total
1	*Hostel* Chief Section Leader . .		17/6	14/-	31/6
2	*Cook*				
	(a) Chief Section Leader . .		17/6	14/-	31/6
	(b) Section Leader . . .	I	13/6	14/-	27/6
		II	11/6	14/-	25/6
	(c) Worker		10/-	14/-	24/-
3	*Waitress*				
	(a) Chief Section Leader . .		15/6	14/-	29/6
	(b) Worker		10/-	14/-	24/-
4	*Laundress*				
	(a) Chief Section Leader . .		15/6	14/-	29/6
	(b) Worker		10/-	14/-	24/-
5	*General*				
	(a) Housemaid . . .				
	(b) Vegetable Woman . .		10/-	14/-	24/-
	(c) By-Product Woman . .				
	(d) Pantrymaid . . .				
	(e) General Domestic Worker .		9/6	14/-	23/6

CATEGORY "C"—TECHNICAL

Sub-Category	Employment	Grade	Pay	Consolidated Allowance	Weekly Total
1	*Technical*				
	(a) Chief Section Leader . .	I	28/-	14/-	42/-
		II	26/-	14/-	40/-
		III	24/-	14/-	38/-
	(b) Section Leader . . .	I	22/-	14/-	36/-
		II	20/-	14/-	34/-
		III	18/-	14/-	32/-
	(c) Acetylene Welder . .				
	(d) Camera Repairer . .				
	(e) Coppersmith . . .				
	(f) Electrician . . .				
	(g) Fitter (Aero Engine) . .				
	(h) Fitter (General) . . .				
	(i) Instrument Repairer . .	I	18/-	14/-	32/-
	(j) Machinist . . .	II	16/-	14/-	30/-
	(k) Magneto Repairer . .	III	15/-	14/-	29/-
	(l) Rigger . . .	IV	14/-	14/-	28/-
	(m) Tinsmith and Sheet Metal workers . . .				
	(n) Turner . . .				
	(o) Vulcaniser . . .				
	(p) Wireless Mechanic . .				
	(q) Wireless Operator . .				
		I	16/-	14/-	30/-
	(r) Carpenter . . .	II	14/-	14/-	28/-
		III	12/-	14/-	26/-
		IV	11/-	14/-	25/-
2	*Motor Transport*				
	(a) Chief Section Leader (Head Driver)		31/-	14/-	45/-
	(b) Qualified Driver employed on special duty, including Ambulance and Van Drivers. .		27/-	14/-	41/-
	(c) Qualified Driver employed on general duties . . .		24/-	14/-	38/-
	(d) Probation Driver, i.e. those on one month's probation .		14/-	14/-	28/-
3	*Draughtswomen* (Tracers and Colourists)				
	(a) Chief Section Leader . .	I	28/-	14/-	42/-
		II	26/-	14/-	40/-
		III	24/-	14/-	38/-
	(b) Section Leader . . .	I	22/-	14/-	36/-
		II	20/-	14/-	34/-
		III	18/-	14/-	32/-
	(c) Worker	I	21/-	14/-	35/-
		II	18/-	14/-	32/-
		III	16/-	14/-	30/-
4	*Upholsterers*				
	(a) Chief Section Leader . .	I	20/-	14/-	34/-
		II	18/-	14/-	32/-
	(b) Section Leader . . .	I	16/-	14/-	30/-
		II	14/-	14/-	28/-
	(c) Worker	I	15/-	14/-	29/-
		II	13/-	14/-	27/-
		III	11/-	14/-	25/-
5	*Painters* (including Dopers and Sign Writers)				
	(a) Chief Section Leader . .	I	20/-	14/-	34/-
		II	18/-	14/-	32/-
	(b) Section Leader . . .	I	16/-	14/-	30/-
		II	14/-	14/-	28/-
		I	16/-	14/-	30/-
	(c) Worker	II	14/-	14/-	28/-
		III	12/-	14/-	26/-
		IV	11/-	14/-	25/-
6	*Photographers*	I	26/-	14/-	40/-
		II	24/-	14/-	38/-
		III	22/-	14/-	36/-
		IV	20/-	14/-	34/-
		V	18/-	14/-	32/-
		VI	16/-	14/-	30/-

This page and overleaf F S Pub 14. *Classes of Employment and Pay Rates 1918.*

Sub-Category	Employment	Grade	Weekly Rate of Pay and Allowance		
			Pay	Consolidated Allowance	Weekly Total
CATEGORY "D"—NON-TECHNICAL					
1	*Miscellaneous*				
	(a) Chief Section Leader	I	16/-	14/-	30/-
		II	14/-	14/-	28/-
		I	15/-	14/-	29/-
	(b) Shoemaker	II	13/-	14/-	27/-
		III	11/-	14/-	25/-
	(c) Assistant Armourer	I	12/-	14/-	26/-
	(d) Packer	II	11/-	14/-	25/-
	(e) Storewoman (Non-Technical)	III	10/-	14/-	24/-
		I	14/-	14/-	28/-
	(f) Tailor	II	12/-	14/-	26/-
		III	11/-	14/-	25/-
2	*Fabric Workers*				
	(a) Chief Section Leader	I	20/-	14/-	34/-
		II	18/-	14/-	32/-
	(b) Section Leader	I	16/-	14/-	30/-
		II	14/-	14/-	28/-
		I	15/-	14/-	29/-
	(c) Worker	II	13/-	14/-	27/-
		III	12/-	14/-	26/-
		IV	11/-	14/-	25/-
3	*Motor Cyclists*				
	(a) Chief Section Leader		31/-	14/-	45/-
	(b) Cyclist		24/-	14/-	38/-
	(c) Probation Cyclist, *i.e.* those on one month's probation		14/-	14/-	28/-
4	*Washers* (Motor-Car)	I	11/-	14/-	25/-
		II	10/-	14/-	24/-
5	*Telephone Operators*				
	(a) Chief Section Leader (Overseas)		26/-	14/-	40/-
	(b) Worker (Overseas)		21/-	14/-	35/-
		I	19/6	14/-	33/6
	(c) Worker (Home Service)	II	17/6	14/-	31/6
		III	15/6	14/-	29/6
		IV	13/6	14/-	27/6
6	*Labour* (General Unskilled)				
	(a) Chief Section Leader	I	16/-	14/-	30/-
		II	14/-	14/-	28/-
	(b) Worker	I	12/-	14/-	26/-
		II	11/-	14/-	25/-
		III	10/-	14/-	24/-

Below An Assistant Administrator (centre) with WRAF members of varied ranks and trades (including a nurse and 2 MT with goggles) at RAF Howden – an ex RNAS station – in 1919. Also note the mixture of uniforms (Mrs Gurowich).

and accommodation were all found, did not have this allowance, but she was given an extra one shilling a week bonus, which was added to her pay once every three months. To help equate today's money values with those of the First World War, a pre-war report estimated that the average person then needed about 15s a week on which to live, although women working in industry earned about 11s 7d.

In the WRAF on the other hand, expenses were not great. Scarcely any girls smoked, or took alcohol which was in any case forbidden to WRAF on camp unless under doctor's orders. Entertainments were largely home-based and a man still paid for a girl's outing (there was some dissension here after the Americans arrived with their generous gifts of candies, which the airmen could not match). Little was deducted from pay at source — 4d weekly 'for Lloyd George', as National Health Insurance was called, plus, for any unfortunate offenders, money collected for losses or disciplinary fines. The rest was more like pocket money or for 'sending home to mum'. There was also a fortnight's paid leave a year. By the standards of the day, therefore, and in comparison with her civilian opposite, the airwoman, with her full keep, and then her working wage on top of that, was extremely well paid, and there were not many complaints.

Category 'A' – Clerks and Storewomen

The largest proportion of girls, up to 11,000 of them, were employed as Clerks of one kind or another, perhaps predictably as these were the most obvious tasks from which men could be released. They included Clerks involved in book-keeping, filing, records and Unit Pay Offices, and they did all the paper work in Clothing and Equipment Stores, as well as doing general tasks in the thousand-and-one offices throughout the RAF.

Mildred Mather was the first to arrive at the building selected to be the head-quarters of the new Number 9 School of Aeronautics, Cheltenham. She sat on the stairs while lorries arrived with tables and chairs, under the eye of a Flight Sergeant who assured her, 'Nothing at all can be started in the RAF until the "Central Registry" is working and we must immediately get going on the files.' Rose Williams, who worked in the Orderly Room, dealt with leave and transfer papers, listing guard and fire piquets and compiling and delivering daily orders. Laura Ride, on the other hand, handled the Officers' Commuted Ration and Billeting Allowances in the Pay Office of the Pilot Central Despatch Pool. Another member filled in forms relating to repairs to be done to planes, took them around to the appropriate workshops, recorded and entered repairs completed in log books and then chased the test pilot and receiving pilot for signatures. Such was the multiplicity of tasks covered.

The élite among the Clerks were the Shorthand Typists, some with speeds exceeding 100 words per minute. They were much sought after, and were the highest paid airwomen at 29 - 31s per week without their allowances, but were only accepted if already fully trained. The RAF sometimes treated them strangely, however, Dorothy Howe being expected to stand to attention while taking shorthand from her Commanding Officer. Others like Marian

Hainsworth had the dubious and, after accidents, unpleasant duty of taking and typing minutes at Boards of Enquiry.

On 23 May 1919, Sergeant Schreiber wrote a testimonial for one of his airwomen:

'Miss A.D. Ritchie has been a capable member of the staff of this (23rd Wing) Headquarters for the past six months, and no better Shorthand Typist of her sex is in existence. Her knowledge of Pitman's shorthand is uncanny, the most mysterious hieroglyphics reading to her as real words in the English language, and what is more wonderful, reading in proper sequence and sentence. The hand power she develops when tapping the various keys on her typewriter would probably equal the driving-power of a Ford car when going downhill with full engine on and the brakes beyond repair.'

Women working in Technical Stores also formed part of the Clerical group. About 1,150 were employed in Number 3 Stores Depot, Milton, where they serviced the timber yard and sorted, stacked, packaged and despatched all kinds of aircraft parts, work that was dirty, difficult and heavy, but similarly duplicated by Storewomen who worked in RAF Technical Stores up and down the country. That the girls could turn their hands to whatever was needful was proved by the Clerical and Domestic trades working in Number 11 Group in Ireland, where they had to survive much civil provocation and on at least one occasion a few had physically to fight off an attack on their transport.

Category 'B' – Household

Most girls enrolling in the WRAF knew something about running a home, so about 9,000 of them found themselves in the Household section. They were unsung heroines, with long hours, unsocial shifts and hard, often unappreciated, back-breaking work. They were also the poorest paid.

'We are the little WRAFs weak –
We only get ten shillings a week,
The more we do the more we may,
It makes no difference to our pay!'

So wrote Mary Dempsey in Doris Simms' autograph album – a rare complaint similar to, and possibly borrowed from, the men!

Cooks worked in WRAF and RAF Messes and Cookhouses, usually under their own WRAF subordinate Officer. Before the introduction of training, the standard of cooked food was variable, according to how well the new Cooks bridged the gulf between cooking for single numbers and then dealing with hundreds. At Cranwell, Alice Morgan and her fellows found the food so bad that eventually they all marched to the Officers' Mess with their dinners. After that, it improved. Dorothy Howe at Marske-by-the-Sea, an Immobile, had permission granted to stay on camp overnight after a dance.

'On going to breakfast, I found on the table a plate of hard, very stale bread and a bowl of green mould. Was it jam or marmalade? Apparently the kitchen was anti-Office Staff and Motor Drivers, and refused to renew the bread and preserve whilst there was still some left. The members who regularly lived in always brought their own bread, butter and jam from a local shop.'

THE OFFICERS' MESS

Cooks in the Officers' Mess kitchens (from Eight Months with the WRAF)

The number of Cooks for a station was laid down in scales allocating 2 Cooks for 20 personnel eating on station, 3 for 75, and so on, up to 13 for about 600. Kitchen equipment also ranged widely from the most up-to-date to the most antiquated or primitive. The Cooks did their best, however, to improve the quality of their meals, extending their skills to butchery and even coping with the unpredictable eating hours on flying stations, where breakfast could be called for at three o'clock in the early morning. Despite difficulties, the Cooks' morale was remarkably high, and like Florence Maple, they 'had some of the happiest times with the RAF in those days'.

Alongside the Cooks worked the Pantrymaids, whose care was glass and food stocks, the women who prepared the mountains of vegetables, the General Domestics who assisted in the appalling amounts of washing-up and cleaning, and the girls who dealt with by-products such as pig-swill, from the left-overs after meals.

Waitresses or Mess Orderlies served meals and were in charge of the dining rooms of the Mess Huts or buildings where the Officers, Sergeants or Corporals ate. If not already trained in civil life, they again were given special training at the same time as the Cooks, and some Senior Waitresses acted as Managers in their Messes.

Laundresses were employed in larger camps, and WRAF contingents were entitled to the services of 1 per 20 girls. At RAF Uxbridge, then the School of Armament, an all-women Laundress Section worked for a station of about 1,250 men and women.

Housemaids and General Domestics looked after staff in both male and female Messes. They were the polishers, the cleaners, the heavers, the scrubbers, the tenders of temperamental smoky heating-stoves, the moppers-up of wind-blown rivers of rain which were swept under hut doors into newly-cleaned corridors and then trampled for the umpteenth time by a flock of muddy gumboots. Their spirit and patience was sorely tested, but apart from occasional justifiable grouses they did their work under difficult conditions with humour and even the odd snatch of song. Generally, those who gave personal attendance to one or two members of staff, as Batwomen, were the luckiest.

Category 'C' – Technical

Technical members covered a very wide spectrum of trades, many of them highly skilled. Weekly pay varied according to the degree of knowledge and the relative need for the trade. It could be as low as 11s for Painters and Dopers, or as high as 26s for Photographers.

In this group were the girls who in one way or another were connected with machines. Planes of the day were made of wood covered with tightly stretched fabric, with rubber wheels, wood propellers, metal engines, and wire cables used to secure many parts including the wings, usually two, one above the other. Already they were given cameras, armament, flying instruments and eventually rudimentary wireless telegraphy. In all these areas women could be found.

However, as none of them had done this kind of work before, the general practice was to start members in the Salvage Workshops, where men and women

Aircraft Repair Workshop (ARS) in a hangar at Cranwell (Mrs Brown).

dismantled wrecked aircraft down to the smallest nuts and bolts. The bins of refuse resulting were then scrutinized for reuse or destruction. Since the damaged planes were often the results of fatal accidents from the same station, the girls sometimes faced a grisly task.

Suitable candidates then moved on to the Aircraft Repair Shops (ARS) where crashed planes were rebuilt. New aircraft were also assembled from the parts delivered in crates from the factories where they were made. Here the Officer or SNCO in charge was always a man, and it was these men who trained the most skilful of the women for more specialized and individual tasks. Naturally numbers were fewer, but the fact that some were capable of doing such work and doing it very well, prepared the ground for the highly responsible technical work entrusted to the RAF women of the future.

In this manner, some women learned to be Welders, using acetylene torches on aircraft engines, Coppersmiths, Tinsmiths, Sheet-Metal Workers and Turners. They were Vulcanizers, treating rubber with sulphur at high temperatures to increase elasticity and strength. They repaired the magnetos that ignited the engines, the cameras for aerial photography and the instruments used in flying. Riggers dealt with the hemp and wire cables holding together vital pieces of aircraft or airship. Edith White's task was 'assembling the packed kits of DH9s and Avros, and repairing existing planes. Our work was thoroughly inspected by a Flight Sergeant and when passed went to a Fitter to be finished.'. As Engine Fitters, they helped clean and re-assemble aircraft engines and cylinders, which had to be fully checked after 48 hours' flying.

There were Machinists and women Carpenters who helped with the wooden aircraft frames. Although electricity and wireless were still in their infancy,

WRAF were soon working with these and they became competent Electricians. At Blandford, for instance, they manned the Power House which kept the whole camp supplied. They also trained as Wireless Operators and Mechanics, and a few Officers and airwomen were even employed on Wireless Experimental work at Biggin Hill and Oxford, where Grace Bateson thinks she was the first person to hear a pilot speak from the air to the ground.

On the skill of these girls, especially those working directly on aircraft, the life of the pilot depended, and they took this responsibility very seriously. Their tasks were often done in the open air and in all weathers, so it was therefore a sensible dispensation to allow them to wear trousers, to the scandal of many, and decades before they became fashionwear for women.

Linked with this work in the technical trades were other types of jobs. There were Upholsterers; Draughtswomen were employed as Tracers and Colourists on the maps and charts essential for pilot navigation; in London there was a Photo Centre, the precursor of the valuable aerial photographic intelligence work carried out in the Second World War. Here, during the first war, about 70 women, trained as Photographers before they joined the WRAF, processed reconnaissance and cine film material, and also went on to make lantern slides and film for training and photographic recognition.

THE DOPERS' TEA.

(from Eight Months with the WRAF)

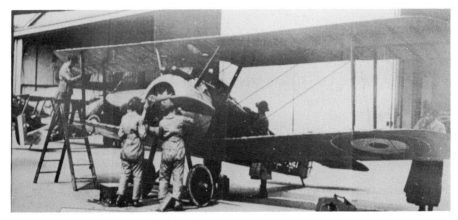

Airwomen servicing an aircraft (AHB).

One of the most popular technical trades was that of Painter, Sign-Writer and Doper. The RAF roundel and distinguishing letters found on aircraft wing and fuselage were the work of the Painter and the Sign-Writer respectively. The Doper on the other hand, painted differently mixed layers of a liquid cellulose varnish called dope over the fabric-covered aircraft frame. This was followed by further tape bindings and dope until the whole was tight, strong and gleaming. Girls enjoyed the work and the company, especially when visitors from other parts of the aerodrome dropped in to chat and share the mid-afternoon tea and toast provided on the instructions of medical authorities, to combat the poisonous 'pear-drop' fumes. The qualities of dope required temperatures of around 20°C (60-70°F) and doctors already knew that milk and fresh air were helpful in those surroundings. The workshops were therefore filled with the constant whirr of electric fans, while the vast sum of 2d per head, per day, was authorized for the extra meal.

Since Car Drivers were connected with machines, albeit the ones on land, they also were included in the technical trades. Their vehicles were chiefly Ford and Crossley cars and tenders, which did duty as Commanding Officers' cars, heavy transport vans, personnel-carrying lorries and crash tenders. Peggy Acton transported anything, 'from Officers, food, ambulance cases, coffins, messages and pig-swill' on Halton Camp, which kept pigs of its own. She worked a six day week with one late night until 10 pm.

Category 'D' – Non-Technical

Work not falling into the other categories was classified as non-technical. It tended to be lower paid than technical work but this did vary, for instance, Motor Cyclists had 24s, Telephonists abroad had 21s, while the poor unskilled General Labourer could receive as little as 10s.

Tailoresses and women Shoemakers did useful and necessary work, as did the Storewomen in Clothing, Furniture and other non-technical Stores, and the Packers who humped and dumped stores and equipment. Armament Assistants would be found at stations like Uxbridge, where women were employed at the

School of Armament, cleaning, greasing and testing guns and filling gun belts.

Sailmakers' Shops were normally noted for being clean, warm and cheerful places, where work proceeded in a methodical and efficient manner, accompanied by the whirr of sewing machines and the chatter of girls. Here the fabric was cut out, stitched and eyelets made, so that it might be laced tightly to the framework in the assembly shops, before the aircraft passed into the hands of the Dopers next door.

Fabric Workers were not limited to aircraft, but also worked on kite balloons and even airships. At Number 1 Scientific Aeronautical Research Depot (SARD), Farnborough, Riggers and Sailmakers made fittings for the rigid and non-rigid airships housed there and at Howden, Kathleen Appelbe was one of the wellington-clad WRAF contingent of all trades who was called upon to join landing parties when weather conditions made difficult the grounding of these unwieldy objects.

A greater contrast could not be found to the Motor Cyclists. With their knee-

Overalled airwomen sewing and putting fabric on to wooden aircraft frames in the Sailmakers Workshops next to the Dope Shop (AHB).

Howden airwomen hauling an airship into a hangar 1918 (AHB).

Confusion in uniforms: an RFC uniformed girl on an RAF motor cycle.

boots, goggles and breeches, their noisy and unpredictable machines, they hardly qualified for the most glamorous of trades, yet in an era when few men, let alone women, knew how to drive, this trade along with the MT Driver was much in demand. Hilda Ineson, an unrepentant Motor Cyclist, who also laid claim to be the first airwoman to wear the new blue WRAF uniform, recalled, 'In those days, planes flying at 70 miles per hour and women in trousers were regarded as "fast".' With their bone–shaking sidecars, girls on their motor bikes carried passengers, mail and messages on routes often too awkward and hazardous for other transport. Although in different categories — Motorists were 'technical' and Motor Cyclists 'non' — the RAF nevertheless appreciated their skills as both were paid virtually the same, although there was a two grade structure for Motor Cyclists.

If the excellent postal system was too slow for an urgent message, an alternative to a Dispatch Rider was the telegraph and telephone. A large proportion of Operators were women, to the extent that many station telephone switchboards were run entirely by them. They insisted on standards from users, however. 'They treated us well or we cut off their private calls,' comments Grace Bateson, who also remembers using a special type of telephone called a phonograph, which automatically recorded and reproduced sounds in a kind of shorthand. It was on this machine one day in November 1918 that she received the message, 'Hostilities will cease at 11 am on the 11th of the 11th'. It was, in fact, two days before the war ended.

The last of the trades designated as non-technical were the Motorcar Washers, and the unskilled General Workers. They were the lowest paid of all, although it was possible for them to move into another group if they subsequently acquired a craft.

*   *   *

Such were the categories and trades in which the first WRAF enrolled in early 1918, although in time more trades appeared. A few women arrived on coastal stations as Pigeon Keepers, like a school friend of Kathleen Appelbe who was 'in charge of Pigeon Lofts, as carrier pigeons were taken aboard airships in flight'. The girls cared for and logged the flights of the message-carrying pigeons.

Certain members of the WRAF were also detailed for nursing duties in WRAF hostels or camps where it was intended that one member of the staff should have VAD or nursing experience, but a trained Nurse had to be provided for numbers over 600. Six white aprons and six white caps were issued for them. These Nurses were officially enrolled in June 1918 as the Royal Air Force Nursing Service, and their main areas of work became Sick Quarters in camps and in Convalescent Centres. Towards the latter part of 1918, they were gradually replacing Army Nurses in RAF Hospitals. Then in 1921, their anomalous position was at last settled when they became a separate and independent branch of the RAF, two years later receiving the name of the Princess Mary's Royal Air Force Nursing Service, a title they have preserved to this day.

It was soon found for purposes of discipline that women needed a special type of Senior NCO to deal with more serious offences and prevent any breaches in the regulations. WRAF Patrols, as their red on blue armband announced, were therefore trained, and about 100 sent out on to stations for these duties. The girls, who were carefully chosen for this delicate and responsible task, had to be over 23 years of age, with an exceptional character and personality. They always went in twos, wore a lanyard and whistle, and worked so discreetly and efficiently that few outside the services knew they existed.

In mid-1919, the RAF called for a few selected airwomen to be given a month's training for the Meteorological Service. This done, the women were posted to various flying stations where they proved a great success.

Airwomen, therefore, had a wide variety of work open to them, and with over 32,000 members who passed through the service in just two years, it is clear that they took full advantage of their opportunities. WRAF Officers, however, had, on the face of it, very little choice of occupation. They were all 'Mobiles' and, for the most part, Administrators – there to look after the well-being, morale and discipline of their members, to intercede for them and often struggle on their behalf at all levels. For this reason, their work proved more varied than it first appeared. A few were Instructors, and a mere handful actually practised a trade, such as in Wireless Experimental work. Their pay was monthly, calculated on an annual basis, and, with keep, the lowest rank had 46s per week. The scales moved between this and the Director, who received a flat rate of £500 a year, without any allowances.

But all, Officers and airwomen alike, shared great enthusiasm and affection for their work in the RAF.

Chapter 4

'Wir fahren nach Deutschland'

'We are the only women other-ranks in Cologne so far and so I'll leave it to you to imagine how proud we are: and we are equally determined that the RAF and the Army of Occupation will be proud of us, before the watch on the Rhine is wound up for good and all.'

Extract from a member's letter

Not only was autumn 1918 the turning point for the WRAF in their conditions of employment and public acceptance, but the authorities also began to recognize the value of their work. Thus in October 1918, the Headquarters of the Independent Force, RAF, in the Nancy area of France was asking for a detachment of Domestic and Clerical workers to be sent out to join it. The WRAF Commandant lost no time in flying out to investigate and make arrangements. Plans were then drawn up to send the first contingent of WRAF overseas. Indeed the order was lying on the Commandant's desk ready for signature on the morning of that memorable day on 11 November 1918 when the Armistice ended the war.

It now seemed as if the hopes of the WRAF of serving overseas were to be dashed for ever. Indeed, there was a possibility that the WRAF itself would vanish, and recruitment, never vigorous, seemed about to end. The war was over and the reason for women in uniform no longer existed. As often happens in our history, all that hard work seemed doomed to be wasted. Then, fate took an unexpected turn, because in order to ensure that Germany would no longer pose a threat to Europe, an Army of Occupation was deemed necessary. Therefore, little demobilization of men or women took place, and as a consequence, by January 1919 there was great unrest among the troops. In the UK and abroad there were demonstrations, riots and mutinies, which even extended to the civil population, with strikes and public disorder. The Government was nervous, the example of the Russian Revolution still fresh in its mind. It was torn in two opposite directions. Demobilization for men must be speeded up and yet sufficient numbers of the forces must be retained to police Germany.

Women had not been involved in the troubles and since they had already shown that they could occupy men's jobs in many trades, the Government thankfully grasped at this unexpected source of relief. It decided to expand the Women's Services and use them to take over jobs at home and abroad, so that men could be released earlier from the forces.

Thus by a strange quirk of fortune the WRAF attained its dearest wish to serve overseas, and found itself needed even more in peace than in time of war. Nevertheless, uniformed women abroad were no novelty. Already there were women working in France — the French and Belgian Red Cross employed British Drivers, Nurses and Clerks, and there were also the VADs and the QMAAC.

The first selected group of WRAF set foot on French soil on 24 March 1919. Behind them was a frantic two months of organizing, with volunteers being called for, medicals, vaccinations, inoculations, issues of khaki RAF uniform, pay books, wills, leave and new regulations. A thousand and one things had to be done, and all in a hurry!

The initial four drafts were to comprise mainly girls from the Household Branch. The first departure was quite an occasion. According to Alice Chauncey, 'The girls detrained at Dover . . .[and] at 2.30 [40] women fell in to march to the boat . . . They formed fours on the narrow platform with their large kit bags and haversacks, and marched [so well that a QMAAC Officer] was heard to remark, "That was well done. They are smart!" 'There were at least three heads stuck out of each window, and as the boat left the dock, loud cheers rang out, and such songs as *Goodbyee* were sung lustily. About halfway over . . . it became rather rough . . . [but] anyone who dared to feel ill got little sympathy. Green-looking staff Officers were treated to . . . '*K K Katy, Give me the Air Force, Give*

Doctor and Administrator at Maresquel, April 1919 (AHB).

me the WRAF and . . . The WRAFs are Having a Jolly Good Time, Parlez-Vous.'

At Boulogne, a RAF Officer met them and saw them and their kit piled into the waiting lorries. After a cold drive of about 40 bumpy miles, they finally arrived at the WRAF Reinforcement Park, Maresquel, at 11.30 pm where they sat down to a meal of bully beef, bread and butter and tea, waited on and joined by their Officers who had arrived two hours earlier. Finally, the women were allotted beds and blankets, and silence once more reigned.

Accommodation was reasonable by standards of the day. Officers lived in Nissen huts. Helen Chappell describes her Adrian hut which slept 35 airwomen:

'With single iron beds with three straw biscuits for mattresses, which had to be placed one on top of the other at the foot of the bed. Blankets had to be folded neatly on top with the pillow, and all had to be ready before the girls left the hut in the morning. Floors were earthen, windows cut out of tin and blinds were pieces of sacking rolled up during the day. The coal-burning stove in the centre of the hut was attended to by German prisoners. Washing facilities were at the end of the hut — foot baths and cold water. When there was hot water for baths, three or four had to share. Dry toilets were some way from the accommodation, cleaned out by prisoners.'

There also was a large Recreation and Mess Hut with two huge fires. Duckboards, slippery in icy weather, led over the mud between huts. Indeed the weather at that time was so cold that the girls were issued with an extra cardigan each, and it remained unseasonably cold and wet until late May of 1919.

The huts did not remain bare for long, because the WRAF benefitted from many gifts including curtains, a piano, a raucous gramophone, cushions, novels and sports gear. When work was over, there was recreation in plenty, the chief difficulty being how to get transport. Once arranged, and if the WRAF Officer in charge approved, the airwomen were able to take advantage of the invitations to parties, dances and films, even at one point taking part in an obstacle race in and out of tanks under repair. The RAF and Army men made a great fuss of the new arrivals.

Maresquel, being the WRAF Depot, was to become a busy camp with constant arrivals and departures, most WRAF drafts passing through it on their way to other French stations. A residue of its permanent staff, however, went to work at the nearby Headquarters, RAF in the Field. This was three miles distant, at St André aux Bois. Part of the ruined château was used by the RAF but the majority of the girls worked as Cooks, Waitresses, General Domestics and Clerks in the many huts at the other side of the château, in the yard of which was a muddy pond inhabited by ducks and geese, and the sheds where vehicles were kept.

The WRAF were employed at 10 bases in France, including Number 1 MT Repair Depot St Omer, Number 2 MT Repair Depot Motteville, Number 1 Air Depot (AD) Arques, Number 1 Aeroplane Supply Depot (ASD) Marquise, the Pay Offices at Wimereux, and the Port Depots at Boulogne and Rouen.

Florence Maple, one of the early WRAF in France, found herself posted to

Aerial view of a typical RAF airfield in Germany (Mr Cole).

Number 2 Air Depot (AD) Vron in the Crécy Forest. Surroundings were very rural, and once a wild boar got into the camp and ran amok. Though small, this beast was very dangerous, so all the girls were ordered into one hut, its windows and doors barred, while the men chased the boar back into the forest and shot it.

All was settled in France now with nearly 1,000 airwomen fully employed there. The next question was, would they be allowed to join the Army of Occupation in Germany? Soon the exciting news swept through the camps that selected volunteers were going to be asked to join the RAF on the Rhine. Previously the only women there had been Nursing Sisters, VADs and women QMAAC Intelligence Officers, but now the WRAF were to have the honour of being the first women's other ranks to enter Germany.

On 1 May 1919, an advance party of 16 set off by lorry in the pouring rain and, crossing the German border, travelled to Marienburg in Cologne. Wherever the girls stopped they were the subject of curiosity to the Germans and of delighted welcome by the mass of khaki-clad men who swarmed round the tenders.

Marienburg, described as more like country than town, had large villas set in pretty gardens, wide streets lined with tall white-flowering acacia trees and every kind of flowering shrub. There the WRAF inhabited several houses. One larger building, formerly a public house, the grounds of which adjoined the RAF Headquarters, was used for the main WRAF kitchen, dining room, recreation rooms and some bedrooms, and was regarded by all WRAF as their Mess. It benefitted by having a large garden, more like a park, beyond which was open country stretching away into the distance.

When the Germans first vacated the Bierhaus, it was found to be filled with broken chairs, tables, crockery, rubbish and beer mugs of every shape and size — most unlike normal German orderliness and cleanliness. Helen Chappell thought it the most beautiful house in Cologne, but she took part in its cleaning, '. . . and very dirty it was too, with loads of beer mugs to get rid of. It had a lovely kitchen and other facilities. The maids were a bit hostile to us at first, but later became quite friendly.'

Soon large huts were erected in the grounds to take further drafts of airwomen and it might eventually have become their permanent headquarters.

Although at first the military had wanted to surround the place with barbed wire, this was thought unnecessary until the avid curiosity of the resident German population for these strange women in khaki, forced this to be done. No girls were allowed out on their own anywhere in the town, and a strict curfew kept everyone, German or otherwise, at home after 9.30 at night.

Most of the WRAF in Germany worked as Domestics, Clerks, Telephonists, Storewomen, Motor-Drivers (although there were only two vehicles in Cologne for their use), Sick-Quarter Nurses and Patrols.

The women from the French Headquarters, RAF in the Field, were mainly based at RAF on the Rhine Cologne, while the women from Number 1 ASD Marquise went to the Advanced Number 1 ASD Merheim, and those from Number 1 AD Arques went to the Advanced Number 1 AD Dormagen. All these camps were in or around Cologne.

For the girls the days usually started with breakfast at about 7.30 am, sometimes prefaced by a route march. After either drill or physical training at 8-8.30, work continued for the rest of the day, the girls marching back for meals, ending with tea at about 5.00 pm. This did not necessarily mean that work was at an end, however, because there were often tasks to finish or clear up, since by now the RAF was so short-handed that many girls returned to work until nine or so, and of course there were shift workers. It was a long day, but at the end of the evening they marched back to their billets singing. In the early days, in many sections, work seemed unending and there was little free time or energy for much leisure. But the girls had come prepared to work and they were not complaining. Gradually, sections began to run smoothly, the pressure eased, and there was at last time to relax and enjoy themselves.

The long light summer evenings encouraged, among other diversions, sport — tennis, netball, golf or cricket, team games being much more popular than individual ones. Occasional events provided a welcome diversion, as when the girls and men met for 'friendly' cricket matches, where the men bowled left-handed and still won!

In August, WRAF helped with teas and refreshments in the RAF enclosure at the Army Horse Show, the weather now having obligingly turned blazingly hot. Girls, in one station, went from 'oceans of mud' into drought and water restrictions.

Most camps found time to hold station sports days and on another broiling hot afternoon on 9 August 1919, the RAF of the Rhine Athletic Championships were held. Airwomen not only took part in races but also sold programmes, worked the field telephones and served tea. The outcome was that airwomen went back to the UK to represent the WRAF overseas, at the RAF Athletic Association Meeting at Stamford Bridge. The girls wore sashes or bands of their

Above *Aerial view of a typical RAF camp in Germany* (Mr Cole).

A

FORM OF THANKSGIVING AND PRAYER

TO BE USED

In all Churches and Chapels in England and Wales, and in the Town of Berwick-upon-Tweed

On SUNDAY, the 6th JULY, 1919

Being the Day appointed for Thanksgiving to Almighty God on the occasion of the signing of the

TREATY OF PEACE

By His Majesty's Special Command.

London:
Printed by EYRE & SPOTTISWOODE, Ltd.
Printers to the King's Most Excellent Majesty
and published at 33 Paternoster Row, E.C.

Right *Leaflet of Thanksgiving Service for Peace* (Mrs Graham).

overseas colours on tunics and knickers or white skirts, and black shoes and stockings. They did not break any records or bring back any medals, but they did themselves and the new service they represented great credit.

Out of the 1,064 women overseas on 1 September 1919, over 600 were serving in Germany, with 162 at Dormagen, around 300 at Merheim and probably well in excess of 130 at Marienburg, excluding numbers of Senior NCOs and Officers at all three locations.

Naturally, there was much public interest in how the girls were fitting into service life in Germany, so the Commandant paid two visits, one in May, the second in August 1919, and the Army Council and Winston Churchill also came to review the women's services. This latter occasion also saw the first official appearance overseas of the new bolo-blue WRAF uniform buttoned along the left side up to the high collar. Its appearance was mainly due to the heroic exertions of the WRAF Officers and Senior NCOs who, by August 1919, had been driven almost frantic by the non-existence of supplies of WRAF uniform generally. By somewhat unofficial channels, a quartermistress on leave in England finally tracked down and all but escorted the needful articles safely to their destination.

As the airwomen became established, so other things began to happen. An education scheme was introduced, partly to assist those who were anxious to learn the German language and partly to prepare the women in useful subjects for future demobilization. An Education Section was set up with classrooms and equipment. A small bookstore run by WRAF personnel was opened, which contained library and reading facilities as well as a bookshop. The WRAF Education Scheme in Germany employed two WRAF Officers and one Chief Section Leader as instructors, and lasted from June to mid-August 1919.

Religion was not forgotten either, and in an age when the outward trappings of religion at least were mandatory, it was found that overseas and in the forces it took a more serious and profound character. At first, Sunday services for the girls were held at the Bierhaus on a voluntary basis, but later there were Church parades, attended by both men and women at Churches set up on the camps. Even here, some sly comments escaped, to the effect that the girls scored points off the men in their drill.

Another venture that succeeded from its inception was the introduction in June 1919 of a monthly magazine called *The WRAF on the Rhine*. Written by and for WRAF, and professionally produced, it ran into four well-thumbed editions, the last issue in particular selling 'like ices on a hot summer's day!'. Articles ranging from the serious to the comic were sometimes of very high literary quality both in poetry and prose, but it also boasted articles on questions of behaviour and the then current shortages of uniform.

The airwomen's activities were limited in the early days by the curiosity of the Germans for these strange women 'pilots' and later, in the suspenseful period when it seemed that the Germans would refuse to ratify the peace, by the latent hostility of the populace which exploded into more violent forms. On more than one occasion a flight of airwomen had to march straight into and through a demonstrating crowd. Strangely, as one of the girls put it, the Germans 'hated the

Inter-Service relay race. Note the sensible dress of the WRAF winning (AHB).

Mr Churchill inspects the WRAF of the Rhine (Mrs Brown).

WRAF at RAF Headquarters, Cologne, June 1919 (Mrs Brown).

women in uniform much more than the men'.

At about this time the RAF seriously considered taking the airwomen with them on active service should war again break out and certain sections expected hourly to be called away. Fortunately, the Peace Treaty was signed, relations returned to normal, restrictions to camp were raised, the former curfew was restored and life returned to something resembling what it had been before. However, this had been a salutary reminder to the WRAF that they were living in enemy territory following a particularly cruel war.

Inevitably, among the troops themselves the airwomen were popular, there being so few English-speaking females in Cologne. The authorities had been finding it hard to enforce the non-fraternization rule on men who had not seen their homes and families for too long. The appearance of the mostly young, fresh-faced girls was a welcome distraction and helped greatly with morale. Though the airwomen were well chaperoned, the behaviour of the troops was also commendable, so that despite gloomy forecasts of immorality and worse, only one unmarried pregnancy appears on record for the whole overseas episode.

It was often hard for the airwomen to choose between the invitations which swamped their Administrator's office almost as soon as their unromantically flat, black-laced shoes settled on German soil. There were dances, balls, visits to plays by the Rhine Army Dramatic Society, visits to the zoo, walks through the magnificent Flora Gardens, a peace ball and fancy dress balls in plenty. Shortly after their arrival in Cologne, the airwomen instituted a guest night in their Recreation Hut on Tuesday evenings, to return some of the many invitations with which they had been showered. This soon became a regular feature.

Shopping in the locality was discouraged in the early days. In any case, war had left its legacy of empty shelves, ruined buildings, collapsed businesses and terrible housing and poverty. Here again, as time passed, with proverbial German determination and efficiency, the country and the contents of its shops vastly improved. It was certainly an attractive proposition to airwomen with an exchange rate at DM160 to the pound.

Sightseeing was very popular, particularly among girls who had previously never travelled beyond the confines of their own home town. It was as if they knew that time was short and they wanted to make the most of every minute. As it proved, it was, and they did. Sometimes, outings were arranged at weekends so that they could visit interesting places such as Bonn, Godesberg, Coblenz and the vineyards. They were not allowed out in groups of less than two, and although travel on trains and trams for the British Forces was free, the girls preferred to go together in tenders. Sailing down the Rhine was another unusual experience. Boats were often booked by a section or Mess, very often with a band on board, so that the WRAF and the servicemen could dance, talk, play whist or watch as the boat glided by storied cliffs, historic castles, legendary caves, fearsome rocks and breathtaking scenery.

The airwomen also found time to form a jazz band, much in demand at many functions and with a reserved slot, once a week, at the WRAF teashop which had been set up in Cologne for airwomen to have tea in informal surroundings with their male or female friends. No one could enter, however, without an invitation from an escorting WRAF, so needless to say this was a much sought-after honour.

It occupied the top two floors of a shoe shop, standing in the arcade off Hohe Strasse, on the ground floor of which the Education Department and Book Store were situated. Its six rooms had been filled with shoe racks, obligingly removed by a RAF party. With a loan of DM1,000, the airwomen scrubbed, whitewashed and painted the place. Finally, it was furnished with white painted chairs and tables from the Bierhaus, covered with white cloths, and cushions and curtains were dyed old-rose, green and blue. The lampshades were pink and flowers, matching the curtains, decorated every table, while pictures lent by *Vogue* added colour to the walls. A small room in black and white, with black and white check-ed table-cloths, yellow lampshades, curtains and table-flowers, was reserved on three days for Officers. In another room there was a little kitchen equipped with gas stove and washing-up facilities. Helen Chappell helped with the only extras the airwomen could add to the tea and scones — eggs, poached in a dixie-lid, boiled or scrambled. The menu was thus rather restricted! Later, further enticements were added, such as salads, soft drinks, little iced cakes and ice-cream. 'The girls prepared and served everything themselves and worked on a voluntary basis.' The shop opened on 12 July and was a roaring success from the beginning. When it closed, just over a month later, the venture was able to repay its loan and hand over a cheque for £2,000 to the WRAF Old Comrades

Some WRAF revellers in hired costumes outside the Bierhaus (Mrs Brown).

Association.

In early August, a rumour began to circulate that the WRAF contingent on the Rhine was closing down and this soon proved true. The RAF in Germany was to be reduced from 44 squadrons to one and the WRAF would not be needed after October. This meant that sections, just brought into order, must be closed forthwith, and the multitudinous task of running down all the camps began. As a farewell gesture, the airwomen decided to throw one big fair for everyone, the profits also to go to the WRAF Old Comrades Association. Accordingly, the 'Revelry' was held on 14 September 1919 at the Bierhaus, and men and women from all the services were invited. The trees had been hung with coloured lanterns, inside which the candles melted in the great heat of the day. The grounds were gay with bunting and covered with stalls, hoopla, hand-work, a fortune teller's tent and a merry-go-round. Music was provided by an army band, a local jazz band and a pipe-band. Starting at two in the afternoon it continued at night with a searchlight tattoo, limelight country dancers and a fireworks display. Such 'Revelry' was long remembered.

Then the drafts to Britain began, not without difficulties, as no section was willing to release their particular airwomen until the latest possible moment, and WRAF transport was held up in early October by a railway strike in England. However, by 1 November 1919, the WRAF had left Germany, following a momentous six months. Meanwhile, the run-down in France was also taking place, though in many units this started earlier and ended later than in Germany. Last were the six airwomen and their Officer at the Port Depot, Boulogne, who had supervised the final embarkation of all airwomen returning to Britain. This 'magnificent seven', their work done, now embarked themselves on 12 March 1920. The final WRAF had departed from Europe; their *annus mirabilis* was at an end.

As he contemplated the departure of the WRAF from Europe, Sir John Salmond wrote, 'I can remember how any doubts that any of us may have had on the advisability of the course, were completely dispelled by the manner in which the WRAF justified their position on the Rhine. The discipline of the force was at once an example to all, of what a well-organised, well-trained women's force can do. Their work was strenuous and in many cases long, yet, wherever they went, they astonished everyone by their willingness, capability and by their efficiency.'

Chapter 5

At Home With The WRAF

'I loved it. We all felt we were doing something worthwhile and the comradeship was so good, you felt life was good even with a war.'

Dorothy Porter

I t was early morning in Britain and already the huts in the camp were beginning to come alive. In the distance were large huts used for workshops and the huge squat shapes of the hangars, their corrugated iron roofs crouched protectively over their aircraft.

Reveille sounded as faint light crept between the closed curtains of the WRAF hut. Slowly, first one and then another of the pyjama-clad girls awoke. They shivered as the curtains were drawn, and they felt the blast of cold air from the two windows which the Commandant had instructed should always be open overnight in the dormitory for ventilation. Soon a procession of greatcoat-clad figures dashed into the cold outside air, down the duck-boards — a good deal better than cinders — to the ablution hut or the latrine. Then back to finish dressing, to brush long hair into a reasonably acceptable bun, to strip the iron bedstead and stack the bedclothes upon it neatly folded, and afterwards to polish and dust down the bedspace and any other part of the hut that had been detailed for the cleaning duties of the day. This was the time often chosen for roll-call, when the Section Leader or even the Chief Section Leader (CSL) forsook her room in the hut and her many other duties, to check the individuals and cast an eye over what would be more closely inspected later.

Dormitory huts usually contained several rooms with eight girls to a room. On large stations there was a flock of black huts where they slept. WRAF living accommodation generally comprised of sleeping, dining and recreation huts with their own cookhouse and stores, an isolation hut for sickness and Officers' Quarters. All these quarters were always kept well away from the RAF, often to the extent of being surrounded by a fence with guard and duty WRAF. The RAF

Left *'The Abode of the Unsquashables.'* *WRAF dormitory with bedding (including one-piece mattresses) stacked for the day (Miss Garfitt).*

Left *Fenced entrance to WRAF Quarters at RAF Cranwell (Miss Garfitt).*

Below *Morning parade (Miss Garfitt).*

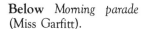

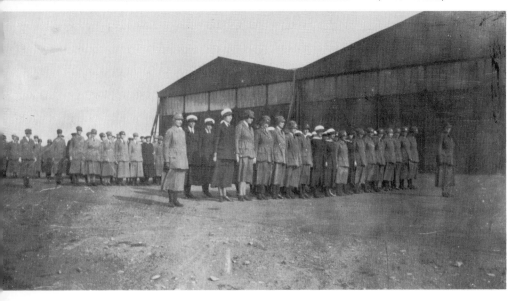

saw itself as *in loco parentis*, the guardian of the morals and behaviour of all girls entrusted to its care, so no RAF were allowed entry into WRAF lines except with a signed pass. An airwoman's only meeting with the men on camp was at work, or in organized events such as games or dances. Even off duty and off camp, on those rare special-pass nights, when her destination and escort was vetted beforehand, opportunities to meet were limited, for the girl was often under the watchful eye of the WRAF Patrol and had to dash back to camp in time for the 9.30 nightly roll-call. The WRAF therefore lived in the rather sheltered female environment that conformed to the standards of the day. The fact that so many girls, then and subsequently, married RAF, often from their own squadron, proved that the restrictions could not have been too hard.

If the dining hut was some distance from their sleeping huts, the airwomen would usually march to breakfast before 8 am — porridge, followed, if the ration for the week was sufficient by a little bacon, fried bread, if very lucky an egg, and the old standby bread and plum jam. Of bread, despite rationing, there seemed no shortage, although the Messing Officer had to juggle with very tight figures when it came to things like meat and sugar. Nevertheless, she was probably better off than the suburban housewife or her cook, who having smaller numbers to feed, found her ration books yielded an insufficiency of everything except garden produce.

Meanwhile transport converged on the camp carrying the living-at-home Immobiles, and Mobiles from outside lodgings or hostels. Some Immobiles came by train but most were picked up at central collecting points by tender. There, standing under a canvas awning, liable to be thrown off their feet by jolts and sudden turns, the airwomen chattered, laughed and sang on their journey, their high spirits not quelled by scorching sun, driven snow or frequent break-downs. Others, like Lilian Marshall, travelled from Harwich to Felixstowe by government boat, without cabins or much seating, so that 'in rough weather or fog we got wet. The skipper was short, fat and round, so we called him Butterball.'

Roll-call and reading the Orders for the Day often followed the airwomen's arrival on camp, when they reported for duty. Fitted in, before or after work, were fatigues such as collecting coal or cleaning. Depending on the camp and the WRAF timetable, some morning or afternoon time was devoted to drill and physical training, so it was around 9 am when Immobiles usually joined the live-on-camp Mobiles to remain with them for the rest of the day. Dora Toplis assembled with others on the Parade square at Spitalgate.

'At 9 o'clock, the Station Drill Sergeant took over. When the Lady Administrator appeared, the Drill Sergeant bawled, 'Get fell in!'. Then followed roll-call after which 'Madam' slowly walked along the ranks and inspected us with a keen eye. No jewellery other than a wedding ring could be worn, no hair on view — our buns had to be pushed well inside our caps — and our shoes and buttons had to be shining.'

Unenviable was the lot of the girl who failed to come up to standard. An appointment to attend an Orderly Room later in the day generally followed. After the inspection came drill. Marching, turning, forming fours, demanded concentrated attention and quick, instinctive reaction.

'In a voice like the crack o'doom the Drill Sergeant put us through our paces, as though we were candidates or recruits for the Brigade of Guards, but he was forbidden to swear at us.'

After a special WRAF Parade and Inspection by a visiting Officer, Ivy Austen was detailed to report to the Station Commander's Office. Fearing trouble —she had a brother in the Royal Marines, whose standard of drill she was constantly being reminded to keep up — she was relieved to find herself confronted by the visitor who congratulated her on being the smartest girl on parade. Once a week Dora Toplis's squad '. . . went for a march through the camp and on to the main road. As the heavy fatties in the squad began to puff, we had the command, "March Easy", and we would burst into song, accompanied by a girl who could produce any tune with an ordinary comb covered with tissue paper — a favourite was *The Bells are Ringing for Me and My Girl*.'

Though most girls grew to tolerate or even enjoy drill, route marches were not popular and more than one girl, marching in the rear, would slip into the Guard-room as the contingent passed, wait until it returned and then fall in again. Discipline, drill, games, physical training and hygiene were all actively encouraged by the Commandant, who was also very insistent on saluting. At first it was an uphill struggle, because although the girls were perfectly willing, many Commanding Officers of the old school disliked women saluting. They also opposed their girls doing drill or any work other than in cookhouse or office. Supported by a more practical majority, the Commandant gradually won her way, though the work and behaviour of the airwomen was her strongest pretext.

Work then took over shortly after 9 am, the girls being constantly reminded to 'Jump to it. Remember there's a war on'. In Dora Toplis' Sailmaking Workshop

Left *The WRAF, a cartoon and poem* (Miss Simms).

Right *Dining room in a WRAF hut* (Mrs Brown).

there were 24 women and 2 men; one man was the Sergeant in charge and the other was an airman who acted as general dogsbody, lifting the main wings, sweeping, and stoking the round coke-burning stove which supposedly heated the workshops.

'At 10.30 an urn of hot cocoa was brought in from the cookhouse and doled out in thick mugs, with one hard army biscuit, which had to be broken with a hammer before we ate it. The lunch break was at 12.30 and of 1¼ hours duration. We provided our own food, our own crockery and cutlery. The Mess room allocated to us Immobiles was a bare hut and we sat on backless benches at long bare tables — everything crude and exceedingly primitive. There was a free-standing iron range to heat our little dishes of meagre rations. For washing-up afterwards there was no wash basin and no hot water, just a stone sink, and the towels were rejected scraps of sailmaker's off-cuts.'

Conditions for Mobiles were similar, where girls sat in serried rows at long tables in their Mess hut, often in several sittings. They wore their caps all day, while on duty, even at meals, except when in overalls. Eating in such large numbers was not conducive to good manners at the table. Nancy Ritchie had a copy of a poem on Etiquette, possibly composed by a member of the Land Army, but which, she comments, 'could equally well have applied to the WRAF'. It includes such gems as:

'Don't smell the milk or bloater paste, however bad you think it,
And though your tea is horrid, unprotesting you must drink it . . .
And if to get your wants supplied, you seem to be unable,
Don't grasp the handle of your knife and hammer on the table.'

W.R.A.F. Mess, Cranwell

THE REST ROOM !!

(*From* Eight Months with the WRAF)

Dorothy Porter recalls Wednesdays.

'Our ration issue was large, brick-hard biscuits — similar to what we feed our dog with. A kind lady who lived in a small cottage near Headquarters, made a few of us girls cakes, and cooked vegetables from her garden, to eke out the ration. What an angel! We couldn't eat those hard biscuits. They wouldn't even soak.'

Others, like Laura Smith, remember the corned beef and sausages. After the midday meal the airwomen went back to work, a few with a tea-break to lighten the long day. Work usually ended around six o'clock, when the girls went back to the dining hut for their evening meal. Then some went back to do a fatigue as punishment, or to finish off some section work.

For most however, except the Immobiles who shortly returned home by transport, the day was over, and they were able to retire to the WRAF Rest Room. This was a misnomer, it being nothing as peaceful as the name implies, rather a happy hubbub which normally prevailed. Recreation Room might be nearer the mark.

To Gertrude George, coming 'out of a cold driving rain into a place of shelter and warmth, where dripping overcoats could be temporarily abandoned, where tea flowed in rivers and a cheerful pandemonium ever reigned . . . it was an experience calculated to revive the most depressed.'

It may have started as a bare hut with a single temperamental pot-bellied iron stove, but it was soon transformed with cushions and curtains, flowers and pictures and all the little touches for which the WRAF were noted. A gramophone or a piano was usually to be found there, and the girls were known for their

Airwomen in a corner of their Rest Room (AHB).

music, be it singing at work or play, learning the latest dance steps or picking out one-fingered melodies.

Sometimes the hut was deserted for a cinema showing a silent film, a play by the dramatic society or a dance at one of the Messes on camp or in the local town; sometimes it was filled to overflowing when the WRAF had a hockey tea or supper dance, or more rarely threw a party when they were allowed to invite men. Otherwise, under the gas lights, the airwomen talked and sewed, neatly darned their black stockings, cleaned shoes and buttons, told their fortunes, entertained one another or read and wrote letters. Time flashed by before roll-call at 9.30, and, in at least one London camp, prayers before bed, ending with lights out at 10 o'clock, save in the rooms of Officers still wrestling with their daily load of paperwork.

In this way, a typical day passed. Most airwomen worked weekdays and weekends and had one day off a fortnight; a few had one day a week and thought it generous. Shift workers had long hours and cancelled days off, but complaints came more from the Officers on behalf of their airwomen, rather than the girls themselves.

The highlight of the week was Friday, pay-day, when airwomen were paid weekly and Officers monthly in arrears. For this, Dora Toplis recalls, 'Army issue [overalls], which we had to wash at home, had to be off and our full uniform had to be worn. We lined up outside a small hut used as the Pay Office. When our number and name was called, we stepped inside to where Madam and the pay clerk sat at a table. A salute for the former and we were handed our wages — loose coins, no packets or paper money. Another salute for Ma'am, a smart about turn and back to work, to be greeted as ever with, "Jump to it, there's a war on".'

There were days, too, which were not so welcome. Woe betide the airwoman who had committed some misdemeanor or had been caught wrongdoing by an WRAF Patrol.

After breakfast she would consult the Orders for the Day and if her name was down for the Orderly Room she would present herself outside the room of the WRAF Officer in Charge of the airwomen at the given time, more often than not in tears. Here the WRAF CSL would smarten her up and remove her cap. Then she would be marched into the office at the command of the CSL, between two airwomen witnesses. At the Administrator's table she was halted while the CSL read the charge against her. The witnesses next each gave their evidence, after which she was asked if she had anything to say in her own defence. The Administrator then considered the charge and the sentence.

If it was serious, the Administrator then had to pass the offender to a more senior Officer, but for a minor offence, the Administrator would either fine the girl a sum, varying from 2s 6d to 7s 6d, confine her to camp and take away any privileges like late passes, or award a number of days extra duties or fatigues of scrubbing floors and peeling potatoes. Later this was noted on her conduct sheet. After a few wise words of advice from the Administrator, often far more lowering than any punishment, the offender was marched out, the door closed, her cap restored and everyone dismissed.

PAY PARADE

(*From* Eight Months with the WRAF)

(*From* Eight Months with the WRAF)

The commonest offences were trivial things like wearing jewellery, using different coloured shoes or stockings, or lowering the neckline of the uniform. Others posted absent without leave (AWOL) may have misread the date on their Leave Pass. Airwomen, unused to service regulations and discipline, did not consider themselves offending if they bent the rules just a little, and were surprised to be picked up for it. It very much depended on the discipline of their particular camp. While they were under training it was usually stiff and punctilious, although afterwards it often became more relaxed.

A good Officer or Senior Non-Commissioned Officer (SNCO) encouraged entertainments for her Mobile airwomen. Dora Pacey was fortunate.

'In June 1918, a new Lady Administrator came. She was more tolerant of the capers of youth and more concerned with our welfare. Among other things she organized as a special treat, a cruise of eight miles along the Grantham Canal. At the appointed time we assembled at the wharf, where a large horse-drawn barge was waiting. A brass band from a nearby village had been laid on to do the musical honours. When all were aboard, the groom took up the reins, the horse took up the strain of the tow-rope, the band struck up *Colonel Bogie* and we were under way. The birds, feathered and otherwise, were singing, the sun shining and all was so jolly. We disembarked at Woolsthorpe Locke, at a pub known throughout the Vale of Belvoir as the Dirty Duck. We filed into the inn, where tea awaited us, not the eagerly anticipated ham and eggs, but the traditional wartime standby of plum 'n' apple jam!

'The return voyage in the twilight was equally delightful. The huge carthorse swayed its hindquarters in time with *Nights of Gladness*, as it plodded along the tow-path homeward bound. What a lovely day!'

Further popular activities were acting and singing. On camps where there was little to do, airwomen like Barbara Prosser would borrow a bicycle from the station to ride around the countryside. Some girls enjoyed sports, particularly tennis, hockey and athletics. Topsy Austen was in the tug-of-war team and used to go to places like Calshot and Warsash to compete. Dora Toplis 'had another giddy-up at the Annual Station Sports Day. I entered the Sergeants' Chariot Race. Two Sergeants had to pull a heavy truck with a WRAF as passenger. My drivers had such a rare turn of speed that I, only a light-weight, was almost pitched overboard, as they raced to become the first at the winning post. The prize was 5 shillings.'

The Commandant won permission for airwomen on duty to travel in aircraft and there were other opportunities to fly, albeit strictly off the record. Louise Dalglish-Bellasis describes one such occasion in her diary for 22 May 1918.

'Captain Davidson, my new CO, asked me if I would care for a fly in a DH 9. Of course I said "yes" but thought no more about it, when to my surprise, the next morning, into my office he came, with a coat and helmet, and told me he had fixed it all up with someone called James and that he was coming for me. A few minutes later, the DH 9 appeared outside my office, so I slipped out of the side door and into the machine and was up 25 minutes. It was a lovely day, sunny but with big patches of cloud. The world looked so lovely.'

Sometimes things went wrong. A Balloon Section visited Evelyne Leslie's airfield at Number 9 Aircraft Acceptance Park, Newcastle-upon-Tyne.

'As my turn to go up in the balloon fell on my twenty-first birthday, I went home instead. The Officer's Orderly took my turn. Two of our test pilots, bored, went up for a flip. The wing of their aircraft caught the wire of the balloon and the plane crashed, killing both pilots. The balloon wire itself was almost severed and the four WRAF aboard were trapped up there for eight hours, because, although they had parachutes, it was a windy day and they were too near the sea. Help was finally sent from another station, which had the machinery to clasp the balloon wire above the break and draw it down.'

There were also air raids, chiefly by Zeppelin airships on the south, when the girls took cover, as best they might, in corridors or basements.

So to the great day, the Armistice ending the war on 11 November 1918. Dora Toplis was 'at work, when at 10.50 the station buzzer sounded and we were ordered on Parade. The Camp Padre conducted a short service, the Station Commander gave a brief talk, then the lorry arrived to take us Immobiles home, but the driver with gay abandon took us for a 20 mile joyride along the Vale of Belvoir. Heavy rain fell and we were glad to get home. Next day, it was business as usual.'

Mildred Mather's service was cut short by the terrible flu epidemic which swept the country in the winter of 1918-19. Men and women, both in the forces and civilian life, weakened by the stress and privation of war, went down like skittles, and there were long illnesses and many deaths, not least among the WRAF, whose medical care was rarely above a few days in bed at the WRAF Sick Quarters. Many girls who survived but took too long to recuperate were given their discharge on medical grounds with two months' sick pay. It was a sad ending to many bright young lives.

Then came the first Christmas in the WRAF. Despite continued rationing, the cooks managed to save enough food to make a special Christmas dinner, as existing menus prove. 'Soup. A choice of Turkey, Goose or Pork, potatoes and sprouts. Plum Pudding, Mince Pies. Celery, cheese and biscuits.' Afterwards there were parties, presents and celebrations.

In the new year, Laura Ride went to Bond Street and sacrificed her long tresses for the short bob, the 'flapper' hairstyle, so much easier to manage under a service cap. Officers' bolo blue uniform, first authorized in September 1918 and partly paid for with a grant, now carried RAF rank badges. By 1919, airwomen's free issues of khaki dresses and then khaki suits were replaced for the lucky ones by air force blue suits, with skirts 12 in from the ground. Dora Toplis, an Immobile, living at home, changed into 'civvies' at evenings and weekends, 'but on this particular Sunday, my girl friend and I couldn't resist wearing our new uniform to Church. Proud as peacocks, we strutted down the aisle and sat in the front pew to give the choir an eyeful of our glamour! Oh the rarity of youth!

'At the end of June 1919, another startling announcement shook us. The Immobiles were to be disbanded. We were given the option of signing on for service anywhere in the United Kingdom and perhaps abroad, or accepting demobilization. The final day of my service for King and Country was 7 July 1919. We were given a week's pay, work and demobilization certificates, a copy

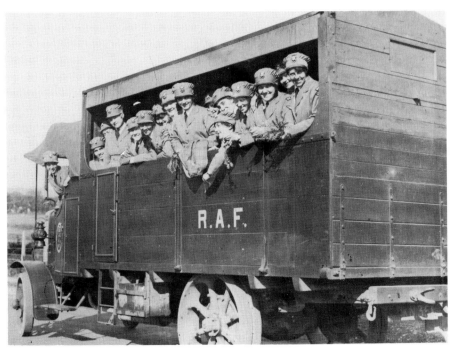

Above *RAF Transport* (RAF Museum).

Below *The new hairstyle, 1919* (Mrs Smith).

Below *The King's Message to the RAF 1918* (Mrs Porter).

The King's Message to the Royal Air Force.

To the Right Hon. Lord Weir, Secretary of State and President of the Air Council.

IN this supreme hour of victory I send greetings and heartfelt congratulations to all ranks of the Royal Air Force. Our aircraft have been ever in the forefront of the battle; pilots and observers have consistently maintained the offensive throughout the ever-changing fortunes of the day, and in the war zones our gallant dead have lain always beyond the enemies' lines or far out to sea.

OUR far-flung squadrons have flown over home waters and foreign seas, the Western and Italian battle lines, Rhineland, the mountains of Macedonia, Gallipoli, Palestine, the plains of Mesopotamia, the forests and swamps of East Africa, the North-West frontier of India, and the deserts of Arabia, Sinai, and Darfur.

THE birth of the Royal Air Force, with its wonderful expansion and development, will ever remain one of the most remarkable achievements of the Great War.

EVERYWHERE, by God's help, officers, men and women of the Royal Air Force have splendidly maintained our just cause, and the value of their assistance to the Navy, the Army, and to Home Defence has been incalculable. For all their magnificent work, self-sacrifice, and devotion to duty, I ask you on behalf of the Empire to thank them.

November 11th, 1918   George R. I.

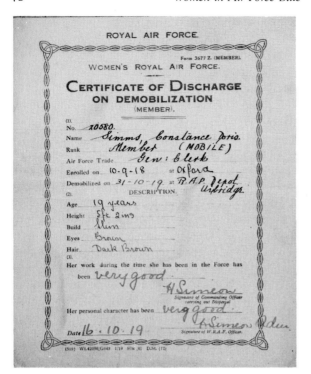

Certificate of Discharge, 1919 (Miss Simms).

of the King's Message and our uniforms.'

For a while the fate of the Mobiles hung in the balance as tentative plans for a small peacetime force were considered. But post-war reductions and economies left the RAF itself fighting for existence and so the WRAF was sacrificed. They were to be replaced and demobilized by 8 November 1919, except for a few sections required in the winding up, such as the newly-formed WRAF Hospital, Hampstead, and the WRAF Records Office, moving shortly to RAF Blandford. The girls left with sadness and the stations saw them off with regret.

The rapid falls in monthly returns from September 1919 tell their own story. At one point WRAF Records discharged about 12,000 girls within six weeks. In addition to any pay due for lost leave or lack of uniform, all Immobiles were given seven days' dispersal leave with pay, and could use their uniform while on leave. This privilege, extended to a month, was most useful to the Mobiles, who had spent the greater part of their service on station wearing uniform day and night with little or no civilian clothes. Mobiles were given four weeks' paid leave, as well as their quarterly gratuity, a clothing renewal grant and various allowances, plus their National Health Insurance card paid up-to-date, and a claim to unemployment pay for up to six months (Immobiles for three). The RAF also set up a Memorial Fund to help those bereaved, sick or unemployed, in which they included the WRAF.

Officers were treated similarly, except that they had a gratuity of the equivalent of two months' paid leave, but no entitlement to unemployment pay. In addition they all received a Demobilization Certificate, the message from King

George V, and a railway warrant to their homes, first class for Officers and third for airwomen.

Thus it was at Blandford that most of the remaining WRAF spent their second and last Christmas in the service. For Alice Chauncey, 'Christmas arrived and with it the usual festivities. A dance was held on Christmas day and a Christmas dinner; and on that afternoon the WRAF camp was closed, the women being entertained by the men. The following day the men were invited to a fancy dress dance and supper in the WRAF quarters, prizes being given for the best dresses. Most of these dresses were made of coloured paper and much difficulty was experienced by the wearers in reaching the Recreation Room without having their dresses rained and blown off them.'

Afterwards, work seemed to increase rather than decrease. WRAF from countries abroad had to be repatriated, while others took advantage of the Overseas Settlement arrangement to emigrate. In March 1920, the last women came from France and when on 28 March the RAF auditors arrived to check and close the books at WRAF Records, Blandford, only 20 girls were left.

On 1 April 1920, the last four sat on their luggage in the sunshine, awaiting transport to leave. Alice Chauncey was one.

'There was a great stillness in the camp; only the plaintive cry of some sea birds flown in from the coast, and the sound of the bugle borne on the wind across the downs from the RAF Records, broke the silence in the old WRAF Quarters. The huts that night were peopled with ghosts of the past — the spirits of success and failure, of honest effort and endeavour, also of comradeship, of loyalty and — best of all — service.'

Thus, honourably, but to the sorrow of most serving airwomen ended the first episode in the story of the WRAF.

Chapter 6

Trouble At The Top

'Tossed about in the ebbs and flows of political intrigue, the Air Service soon had an unenviable reputation for difficulty and intransigence.'

M. Izzard

Three Commandants in six months was surely something of a record anywhere. One of them indeed was to be the subject of a *cause célèbre* which was not to go away for over 20 years!

The first Chief Superintendent is a somewhat shadowy figure. She was Lady Gertrude Crawford, a daughter of the Earl of Sefton, a skilled craftswoman, whose last post had been in charge of women munition workers in a northern factory. She had been nominated by Sir Godfrey Paine, the Air Ministry Master General of Personnel, prior to the formation of the WRAF, and seemed to him the ideal person for the position.

When Lady Gertrude Crawford investigated her new responsibilities, what she found dismayed her. It seemed that she was expected to be little more than a figurehead, women not being deemed capable of leadership except with the guidance of a man, in this case Acting Lieutenant-Colonel Bersey of section M3 within the Directorate of Manning. He was delegated to act as her liaison officer between all the senior Officers and the maze of other Departments, and such limits were set on her every action that she was not even to be allowed to inspect WRAF units unless requested, with the solitary exception of one at Regent's Park.

Reports of her dissatisfaction were relayed to Sir Godfrey, who on 4 April 1918 asked for her resignation. With dignity, and no doubt relief, she stepped down, and without further comment slipped quietly out of the picture.

For this to happen to a new service was an unexpected blow, so Sir Godfrey searched around hastily for a replacement. On 19 April 1918, he was writing to the Secretary of State for Air.

'I have had the names of seven ladies sent to me by Miss Violet Markham, and all, or most of them, appear suitable for the post of Commandant of the WRAF.

'To make doubly sure, I have asked Miss Durham, Ministry of Labour, her opinion of these names and she has written recommending the name of Miss Violet Douglas-Pennant.'

This lady, a daughter of Lord Penrhyn, was a dark-eyed, fine-looking woman of fifty, with a silvery laugh and great charm. She had held high positions in the London County Council Education Committee, Girls' Youth Clubs and Hospital Units, helped in the founding of the WAAC, and latterly, she had been Commissioner for Wales in the National Health Insurance Commission.

'I was asked to take over the position on May 13th — unlucky day — and at first declined,' [among other things, she was taking a drop in salary of £500], 'but afterwards I agreed to take a month's look around, and take up my duties officially on June 13th.'

In fact, after less than a month, her reaction was similar to that of Lady Gertrude Crawford, so that on 11 June she again declined the post, giving her reasons.

'You will remember that I accepted provisionally, on the clear understanding that I should be responsible to you for the general administration of the WRAFs. This was apparently not made clear to others concerned — I found myself in the difficult position of seeming to assume responsibilities to which I was not entitled, so I was blocked at every turn. . . I hope you will forgive me for saying that you will never get this force on to a sound footing unless the Commandant

The Hon Violet Blanche Douglas-Pennant. Lady Commandant June-August 1918. From a photograph taken during a royal visit 1884 (Lady Janet Douglas-Pennant and University, Bangor).

is treated with confidence and given due authority.'

To Sir Godfrey her clear assessment of the situation proved her worth, so that he set himself strenuously to change her mind, going so far as giving orders in her presence, when he saw her on 13 June, that the amended regulations for the WRAF should be reprinted, including a change of her title to Lady Commandant, her status to that equivalent to a Brigadier and the vital information that she was responsible only to the Master General himself. So she accepted. Unfortunately, the reprint of FS Pub 14, the key to her new authority, took six months, by which time the damage had been done and it was too late.

Meanwhile, Lady Commandant Violet Douglas-Pennant went back to her cramped quarters in Mason's Yard, where she was once more plunged into an atmosphere of intrigue, sensitive egos, and trivial squabbles between Departments and the three Services, which seemed to intensify after her appointment was confirmed. She had already complained of the awkwardness of many above her, and as early as 1 June Sir Godfrey had given instructions that the Equipment Department was to take immediate action on her demands. What she still had not appreciated was the slowness of Government Departments, and the divided loyalties of her staff.

Most important was her Deputy, Miss Edith Pratt, ex-Deputy Chief Controller of the WAAC in France, and previously a civil servant and personal clerk to the Minister of National Service. Below her were two Assistant Commandants — Miss Katharine Andrew, also ex-WAAC, and Mrs Rose Beatty, ex-WRNS. There were also some civilian clerks, most of whom were women friends and relatives of Officers and staff in M3.

During the earlier absence of a Commandant, Colonel Bersey of M3 and the clerks of her own office of WM3 had been free to work in their own way. In the face of almost insoluble problems they had come to adopt a cheerful, slapdash approach, and that they had contributed little to the solution and probably more to the confusion did not seem to concern them overmuch.

Consequently, shortly after her appointment, Miss Douglas-Pennant had occasion to reprimand three civilian clerks for 'hysterical horseplay in deshabille' after office hours. She was also horrified by one Station Commander's complaint that on requesting women Drivers, he had been told, 'What sort do you want — front row of the chorus or ladies of title? We stock them all. Take your choice.' Another embarrassment was the withdrawal en bloc of five ladies, again with connections in high places, whom she turned down as Area Superintendents, desiring them to acquire a few weeks' or months' experience first in lower positions. Then on 1 July, she was shattered to receive the resignations of her three principal officers, Miss Pratt, Miss Andrew, and Mrs Beatty, without their statutory month's notice, and for what seemed no good reason. Ingenuously, she brought in a clerk from her Insurance Commission and worked in her office late into the night with an Air Force Officer and his wife, her personal friends.

In this way she discovered that there were no transfer nor recruiting figures for the WRAF, no filing system, no office organization, letters were not being received or going unanswered; the list was endless. In addition, the promised WRAF uniforms did not exist because when reselected, the cloth chosen was not available, then it was unsuitable. When that was settled she was promised it would come, but when? At every turn obstacles appeared in her way.

But the core of her troubles was having a large body of airwomen and too few Officers. Without efficient Officers to watch, act as intermediaries and safeguard the women, complaints about and by the airwomen were common, with remedies too slow and ineffective. Morale is a delicate plant, easily lost. The answer was fast training of large numbers of well-selected Officers. To this end, Miss Douglas-Pennant arranged, through her own personal contacts, the loan of Berridge House, West Hampstead, a large building capable of housing several hundred trainees. All it needed was furnishing. To her face Colonel Bersey was helpful, but despite Sir Godfrey's instructions, no authorizations or equipment emerged and the house was still standing useless and empty in September 1918 as a symbol of monumental departmental obstruction. In desperation, she herself negotiated the loan of the Southwood Hostels, Eltham, for the summer holidays. Here at last, large-scale training of Officers took off so that she could point to nearly 300 Officers trained and passed out to stations during her time, whose effects would appear in the future. She also set up two new Depots for airwomen.

During the whole of this time she was involved in planning, meetings, negotiations, interviews, individual appointments and selections, correspondence and speeches. In the teeth of frequent discourtesy by Station Commanders and difficulties in obtaining staff cars for official journeys, she made visits to training schools and stations — particularly when trouble brewed, which she usually calmed, as in the case of at least one strike, exemplified by the stoppage by 1,000 women in a Berkshire Station over the lack of bonus pay and uniform. Then, amazingly after all this, she still managed to laugh and assure anxious inquirers that all would be well, once her Officers were trained.

Complaints about the WRAF and her capabilities were, however, piling up. The Ministry of Labour, responsible for WRAF recruiting, complained to the Secretary of State for Air, Lord Weir, who did a perfunctory investigation and dismissed the matter. Shortly after resigning, Miss Andrew personally complained about her to Lord Weir, who listened but did nothing. On 7 August, three questions were asked about Miss Douglas-Pennant and the WRAF in Parliament, and in Lord Weir's absence, his deputy said that they had every confidence in the lady. Rumours about immorality and insanity started to circulate, which if true would have rendered impossible all Miss Douglas-Pennant's achievements. So in the face of the gathering back-biting and criticism, and weary from overwork and strain, she again formally offered her resignation to Sir Godfrey, who indignantly refused it, telling her that she was doing a grand job, and that she had his full support and confidence. Significantly, a few days later, Colonel Bersey was replaced at the head of M3 by Colonel Powell, a much more helpful man who liked Miss Douglas-Pennant, and was later to say that if he had been in charge sooner, things would have turned out differently.

As it was, matters were slowly and steadily moving to a head against her. A Lady Rhondda had been asked to investigate details of the women's services, yet strangely, although part of her report dealt with the WRAF, Miss Violet

Douglas-Pennant was not consulted. Enough was known of the report on 22 August, for the Minister of National Service, who had commissioned it and in whose Ministry Lady Rhondda worked, to go to Lord Weir and tell him, 'I will, I am afraid, have to embargo recruiting for the WRAF, if things are not improved.'

On the next day, Miss Douglas-Pennant was to lose her chief supporter in Sir Godfrey when he introduced her to Sir Sefton Brancker, his replacement in office, and the former Master General of Equipment whose absence in America had caused such havoc with her plans for Berridge House and WRAF uniforms. She saw Sir Sefton three times and at this first interview with him raised the question of immorality in the mixed RAF and WRAF Motor Transport Depot at Hurst Park, not knowing that one of his friends was involved. His reaction was that she seemed both helpless and meddlesome. 'She did not seem to have any real grasp of the situation.'

Complaints accumulated, so that on 26 August, Lord Weir wrote to the Minister of National Service, 'Over the weekend I made up my mind to supersede Miss Violet Pennant, and she will be told of this tomorrow.' The interview with Sir Sefton Brancker was delayed until 28 August, since on 27 Miss Douglas-Pennant was away, trying to quell a WRAF revolt.

'As soon as I reached his room, he told me very abruptly that he had sent for me to tell me that I was to go. He seemed very angry and told me that though he understood I was very efficient, I was grossly unpopular with everyone who had ever seen me. He spoke in a bullying, blustering and contemptible manner.'

When the Lady Commandant, recovering her voice, asked when she was to go, he told her 'Now, at once, tomorrow morning.' Bowing stiffly and ignoring his outstretched hand, she left the room. Her woman Medical Director, seeing her come out of the office after this traumatic interview, related:

'She was as white as a sheet as she said, "I've been dismissed". Clearly it had been a great shock. By then I was already regarding her as mentally ill.'

Her dismissal had been tactless and cruel in the extreme, as even Lord Weir, confirming it on 2 September, agreed. It was also illegal. When she had accepted the post, a condition was that she could not be summarily dismissed except for misconduct or a breach of conditions, and then only on receipt of notice given by the Air Council. Service practice was that an individual must read an adverse report and be given the opportunity to rebut any charges. In any case she could only be discharged at a month's notice and then only with good reason.

It was no good saying, as a later report tried to insist, 'that Miss Douglas-Pennant had not been appointed to any office at all'. The official post to which she had been appointed existed but was merely unpublished through printing delays. Nor was it fair to add that 'the Minister could dispense with her services at any time, if, in the honest exercise of his discretion and in the interests of the public service, he thought he ought to do'. This changed the rules of the appointment after it had been made.

Miss Douglas-Pennant parted from the WRAF with tears, and the Officers in training, for whom she had fought so hard, gave her a violet writing case — in compliment to her name — and a photograph of the Eltham Training Centre as a

UNDER
THE SEARCH-LIGHT

A RECORD OF A GREAT SCANDAL

BY

VIOLET DOUGLAS-PENNANT

" *Y gwir yn erbyn y byd* "

WITH FOUR ILLUSTRATIONS

LONDON : GEORGE ALLEN & UNWIN LTD.
RUSKIN HOUSE, 40 MUSEUM STREET, W.C. 1

Title page of Under The Searchlight, 1922
(Unwin Hyman Ltd).

Lady Commandant The Hon Violet Blanche Douglas-Pennant (Mrs Mackeson-Sandbach).

farewell present. Although offered back her former post with the Insurance Commission, she rejected it until she had wiped the implied disgrace from her name. The injustice of her dismissal became an obsession.

Because of her wide and important connections, she was able to publicize the matter and stir up much public sympathy, Church support and Welsh National feeling. As a result, over the years, there followed a private enquiry for Prime Minister Lloyd George, three debates in the House of Lords, an eighteen-session Inquiry by a Select Committee, a Parliamentary blue book and a series of libel actions. A Fighting Committee of her supporters was formed and her case emerged regularly in Parliament. She produced a book justifying herself, and the matter was not allowed to rest until her death in October 1945. It is notable, however, that Lord Weir later resigned from the Government and Sir Sefton Brancker left the RAF rather suddenly to work in civil aviation.

Thus ended the story of the second WRAF Commandant, in which the elements of farce and tragedy were strangely mixed. That she had been the scapegoat for the teething troubles of the infant WRAF and was more sinned against than sinning, is evident; that just over three months in office may have temporarily distorted her mental balance, is not surprising, and it also ruined the rest of what could have been a long and productive life; that she should have let the matter rest after a disastrous Parliamentary Inquiry, cannot be denied; but — as Sir Godfrey Paine later testified — that 'any success the WRAF achieved was largely due to her spadework' is no less true and must remain as her finest memorial.

In 1939, the new Director, Air Commandant Trefusis-Forbes, recorded an encounter with Miss Douglas-Pennant. 'She came up to me at a public meeting and said the RAF had dismissed her and it would do the same to me. She spoke in a loud voice and lots of people heard her. Fortunately Dame Helen had warned me.' Unfortunately her words were to prove sadly prophetic.

It was this Dame Helen who took Miss Douglas-Pennant's place. Helen Gwynne-Vaughan was a strong woman in every sense of the word and seemed to flourish on opposition. Born a Fraser, from an impoverished Scottish aristocratic army family, she had early gone against convention by entering a university and taking a science degree. She had then remained as a lecturer, taken her doctorate, and finally risen to become Head of the Botany Department at Birkbeck Coeducational College. In 32 years she published 25 scientific papers. With Elizabeth Garrett Anderson she had founded the University of London Women's Suffrage Society in 1907. In her estimation, the university laboratory of her day was the one place where men and women could mix and work most productively as equals.

At her coming out ball in 1896 she was accounted as quite a beauty, but by 1911 her family had given up all hope of her marrying. Then to everyone's surprise, and perhaps her own, she married Professor Gwynne-Vaughan, a fellow scientist, who seemed set for a brilliant career. Helen idolized her husband but still continued her academic work. At the outbreak of war, she joined the Red Cross and VADs, but by this time her husband was showing signs of the illness which was to kill him in 1915.

Childless, working but still grieving, it was therefore a relief to her to offer herself to the challenge of a fully absorbing job in forming the new women's army and such was her worth that in March 1917 she was posted to France, on indefinite loan from her university, as Chief Controller (France) WAAC. There she seemed to find her true vocation, revelling in the work and the contact with all ranks of men and women.

It was therefore a nasty shock when, having answered a summons to the War Office London on 1 September 1918, she heard on the next day from a general Officer that 'he had an interesting proposal for me: would I like to be head of the Women's Royal Air Force? Since I could imagine no work more worth doing than that of the post I held, I said, "No thank you". He urged the advantages, till at last I asked whether this was by any chance an order. I learnt that it was.'

In the office of the Adjutant-General, she was later asked, 'Well, Mrs Gwynne-Vaughan, have you heard about the Air Force?'

'Yes, sir.'

'Are you pleased?'

'No sir.'

'You surely don't think yourself indispensable to the Corps in France?'

'It hadn't occurred to me to think myself indispensable to the Air Force, sir.'

[She had always been a master of the telling riposte!]

Commandant Dame Helen Charlotte Isa-bella Gwynne-Vaughan 1918-19 (IWM).

Appendix B, Standing Orders to FS Pub 14 (Miss Garfitt).

'The Adjutant-General looked a little startled, but he ended with "God bless you", and I left. I was sick and sorry. . .'

'Next day I was sent to see Major-General Brancker, Master-General of Personnel at the Air Ministry. . . I did not know how fortunate I was in my new chief or in the opportunity that had come to me of seeing the growth of a very wonderful service.'

Her appointment was met with relief on all sides. Her former chief in the WAAC, now retired, Mrs Chalmers Watson, wrote to her, commending the RAF for having 'the horse-sense at last to appoint a worker.' The RAF could not afford a third mistake; its good name, as well as that of the WRAF was at stake. Having chosen her from a number of ladies (few of whom were aware of it) — among whom was the existing head of the WRNS and Mrs Pankhurst, the suffragette — the Air Council was ready to bend over backwards, if necessary, to ensure that this new Commandant's tenure would be a success. Consequently, things that had dragged their feet during the time of Lady Commandant Douglas-Pennant, were done for Commandant Gwynne-Vaughan with almost suspicious smoothness and ease, so that she was later to say, 'I received every possible help, encouragement and backing, with wide powers and considerable freedom of action in all that concerned the women.'

Related to the family of Lord Saltoun, she had enough important connections to impress senior Officers and give weight to her actions. At 39, she was a highly intelligent, clear thinking and articulate woman, quick to grasp essentials and then drive them through with dynamism. An agnostic, with a highly moral

WRAF doing physical training (Miss Garfitt).

outlook and a great sense of duty, she did not suffer fools gladly, yet she had a strong sense of humour and the unusual gift of warmth and real sympathy which won a ready response from all she met. She was skilled in managing men as well as women and her easy relationship with juniors or the young increased with the years. Though devoid of personal pride — later many criticized her for being dowdy — she was shrewd enough to realize where appearance counted. However, as she grew older she became more overbearing and abrupt. Men feared and admired her, but knowing her good intentions and reputation, usually gave way to her demands.

In her first half year she worked at a frantic pace, and nearly all the management difficulties that had so hampered her predecessors were altered. In the September of her appointment she was given the powers of an Air Commodore, and was only responsible to the Master-General of Personnel, with whom she always remained on the most friendly of terms. She interviewed and reposted many of her most promising and troublesome Officers. She got Berridge House opened and equipped. WRAF uniforms were authorized and many of the blue Officers' and khaki airwomen's uniforms started to appear. At the end of the month, she made her first official inspection of the Officers Training Unit and managed to so fire them with enthusiasm and efficiency — she was a superb lecturer and public speaker — that they were all left mentally heartened and smartened.

From that time the RAF became more closely involved with matters WRAF. They were persuaded to take a hand in lectures; their regulations and procedures were, wherever possible, the pattern for the WRAF; WRAF Standing Orders were revised and orders concerning the WRAF started appearing regularly in Air Ministry Orders. Later the Directorate moved into more spacious accommodation in the Hotel Cecil, and administration was streamlined. In December the detested M3 was abolished.

To help with the work, Commandant Gwynne-Vaughan brought with her a number of her former clerks and appointed her sister Mrs Pratt-Barlow, who had her complete confidence, as her deputy and to be in charge of inspections, under the nominal guidance of the Inspector-General RAF. Thereafter, both sisters were constantly on the move making official inspections up and down the country, wherever there was a WRAF contingent, and keeping regular reports on the visits. The pace of everything was speeded up. To Alice Chauncey it was 'as if an electric current had flowed through the force'. Area Superintendents, now appointed, kept constant communication up and down the chain of command.

Sir Sefton Brancker put his feelings into words.

'By the end of the year the WRAF was the best disciplined and best turned-out women's organization in the country. This remarkable achievement was due to the keenness, efficiency and sound administration of Dame Helen Gwynne-Vaughan — it was nothing to do with me, except that I gave her wide powers and all the independence that was possible.'

The next year was to find her consolidating her new force, soon serving overseas in France and then Germany, where they lived up to all she had hoped of them. During this period, drill became mandatory and PT almost so. Training improved, recruiting and clothing issues were rationalized and the WRAF took over their own records.

The Commandant's work was recognized in June 1919 with the award of Dame Commander of the Order of the British Empire (DBE), and then sadly she had to oversee the running down and disbandment of the WRAF, handing over her own office on 4 December 1919, after fifteen months as Director.

During her tenure of office, the honour had fallen to her, last of the First World War Commandants and the first WRAF Director to smooth the path for the WRAF to realize its full potential.

Chapter 7

Alarums And Excursions

'The country owes much today to the foresight of a handful of ex-service women who, without funds and with slender public encouragement, formed themselves into groups for the provision of some elementary training in the duties of Officers.'

Markham Report, 1942

Despite the efforts of Dame Helen Gwynne-Vaughan and others in the Air Ministry and War Office to retain a small permanent women's service after the First World War, the reports had been shelved and the advice ignored. Instead the War Cabinet subscribed to the Ten Year Rule which declared that no war was to be expected in less than ten years. To a people reeling from recent deaths, shortages and economic losses, this theory seemed not only desirable but also eminently sensible. All women in the Army, Navy and Air Force were disbanded and only a small regular force of men remained in the three Services. Life should now return to what it had been before the war!

But it didn't. The trauma of those years had changed circumstances, attitudes and behaviour, sometimes subtly, sometimes violently. There was rising demand for better pay and conditions, particularly among labourers, servants and shop-assistants. The population grew with the marriage-rate. More women sought jobs and new professional opportunities. There was loosening of standards of conventional morality. War had left women more confident, independent and restless, and the older ones had even gained the right to vote. The 'roaring twenties' had emerged!

Nostalgia also played a part. The WRAF Old Comrades Association, planned in 1919 and born in March 1920, grew and flourished, with branches and members appearing all over the country. At the first London Annual Dinner in 1924, Air Vice-Marshal Sir Sefton Brancker quipped, 'I should have liked to address you as Comrades, but I am afraid in these days of being taken for a Bolshevist', for even in this sanctuary of good fellowship the world had a habit of intruding! Ten years later, Dame Helen Gwynne-Vaughan, still its President, was instrumental in introducing a new objective to the Association's rules: 'to encourage preparedness to help the country in time of need'.

There was good reason for the addition. The world was again changing, and not for the better. Employment prospects, so rosy in the 'twenties, had crashed with the Stock Market in the 'thirties, and the Depression brought dole queues, abject penury, unrest and a more sombre attitude.

In Europe, Germany, clawing her way out of a mountain of debt and humiliation, had found a new Reich Chancellor and saviour in Adolf Hitler. By 1934, Hitler, the leader of the National Socialist (Nazi) party, had become Führer, and was so firmly in power that he was able to persuade the German people to sacrifice the present for a glorious future — guns not butter — and German rearmament began. Benito Mussolini, the Fascist dictator of Italy, and future German ally, was doing the same, while Spain was rapidly sliding into civil war. On the other side of the world Japan, continuing its opportunistic conquests in the direction of an enfeebled China, had swallowed Manchuria. Russia still looked for communist revolutions. The United States, under its recently–elected President Franklin D. Roosevelt, withdrew into isolationist policies as it addressed itself to problems at home, while the League of Nations, the only organization capable of orchestrating collective action against war, was destroyed by the jealousies and inactivity of its members.

The chiefs of the British Armed Services, worried about the world situation, had persuaded the Cabinet to rescind the ten year rule as people became alarmed at the growing German threat.

Dame Helen Gwynne-Vaughan had now risen to Professor at Birkbeck College, London University.

'One evening in July 1934, when I was busy with the results of a degree examination, Lady Londonderry telephoned asking me to come and see her on a very urgent matter.'

The idea was that all the women's organizations still functioning should be brought together to form one large organization available for a national emergency under the umbrella of the Women's Legion. Dame Helen came from the WRAF Old Comrades Association, and with her were the VADs, the FANY and the Women's Legion itself.

Several functions were proposed for this (new) Women's Legion, but only two materialized. The first was anti-gas training, the second was the training of Officers. Anti-gas training proved desultory, and despite the keenness of those taking part, when the Home Office decided in 1936 to recognize only those bodies which gave full training in gas precautions, the (new) Women's Legion withdrew, and there, as far as Lady Londonderry was concerned, ended the new Legion. She returned to the former Women's Legion, and the FANYs and VADs returned to their separate status; it seemed that all the organizations were back at what they had been.

They were, but with one notable exception! This was the section dealing with the training of Officers, not surprising with so redoubtable a personage as Dame Helen in charge. She was convinced that beginning and continuing a successful organization mainly depended upon the quality of its Officers, so she therefore

Women of the Emergency Service drilling at the Duke of York's Buildings in October 1938 (Mrs Dacre).

set out to provide, 'trained and experienced Officers of the right type: young, friendly, keen and with a full understanding of the duties which the women under them would have to carry out'.

After the (new) Women's Legion failed, the Officer Training Section remained and in October 1936, it became known as the Emergency Service, a name suggested by Jane Trefusis-Forbes. By 1938 it was recognized by the Army and Air Council, and in January of 1938 the Duchess of Gloucester consented to become its President. Recruiting was done by personal invitation, and the first course started with eighteen students, although over four hundred passed through the school in the four years of its existence.

Veterans and senior cadets, of whom Jane Trefusis-Forbes was the best, gave most of the elementary instruction and trained beginners. The first time Belinda Boyle ever faced a squad for drill, 'it was in the drill hall of 601 Squadron, my squad was so soon out of control that I was forced, as the leading file became entangled in the undercarriage [of a semi-built aircraft], to give the command "Backwards March". They did it —oddly enough — and I even managed to halt them on the right foot!'

For three summers some cadets attended a camp at Abbot's Hill, Hemel Hempstead. Belinda Boyle says of this experience, 'there was the glorious day when an armband was dropped in the rice pudding, and cooked therein. The rice when served, was bright blue, and everyone said, how nice, how clever, etc. There was the great occasion when we slew a rat with a rolling pin among the feet of [those] who had come to inspect.'

Nevertheless everyone took training very seriously.

'The lack of grumbling was surprising. We were more than half frozen, probably badly fed (by me), we worked like navvies and were always short of sleep because of the cold,' and many spent their one holiday in the year in this way.

For the dubious privilege of all this hard work and social ostracism, girls were then expected to pay a fee of 10s a year for membership, a large sum in those days. It is to their credit that they did so, believing that they were doing what they could to help their country, as the situation in Europe became more and more serious.

1936 ushered in the years of disaster. Germany, under Führer Hitler, who in the previous year had introduced conscription, began its relentless march to extend its frontiers, while diplomats and politicans, fearful of war, tried appeals and appeasement, hoping these would work. Italy occupied Abyssinia, and Germany the Rhineland, followed by a Berlin-Rome Axis Treaty and a German-Japanese Pact. Spain broke into hopeless civil war, where future combatants flexed their muscles.

1938 brought the German annexation of Austria and part of Czechoslovakia, and at this point came more negotiations. The British Premier, Mr Chamberlain, told Britain, 'How horrible, fantastic, incredible, it is that we should be digging trenches and trying on gas-masks here, because of a quarrel in a far-away country between people of whom we know nothing.' He returned from Munich with a piece of paper promising 'peace for our time'. He was wrong! At any time, firm action by Britain and France in particular could have stopped Hitler, but the irony was that when they did at last make a stand, Germany did not believe them.

Meanwhile in Britain alarm bells had been sounding, though weakly at first, and service chiefs had been pressing so earnestly for rearmament that the government had already in 1935 approved new defence spending. In 1936, when the Emergency Service really took off, an especially commissioned report on a Women's Reserve in peacetime still came to the conclusion that this was neither desirable nor necessary. Only the Air Ministry disagreed, since it contended that the RAF differed from the other two services, because, in the case of war, it would have to face immediate attack, and an already trained women's organization would be most helpful. In 1937, Cabinet decisions were several times reversed as the world situation fluctuated and politicians changed office. At length in 1938 Hore-Belisha, Secretary of State for War, decided to double the strength of the Territorial Army and on 6 May called a meeting of representatives from the women's organizations interested in working with the military, to consider how they might help both Regular and Territorial Armies.

It was almost a replay of the 1934 New Women's Legion, as once again the ladies from the Women's Legion, the VAD and the FANY, shared the table with the men from the War Office, the Air Ministry and the Territorials. The difference, apart from the Territorials, was that Dame Helen appeared, representing this time, not the WRAF Old Comrades Association, but her Emergency Service.

The outcome of the conference and subsequent meetings was to create an officially recognized Women's Auxiliary Defence Service, or WAD, 'to relieve personnel of the Regular and Territorial Armies and of the RAF, of various non-combatant duties'. However, as nobody wanted to be called a WAD, the name of Auxiliary Territorial Services (ATS) was finally chosen.

It was intended that every county should raise several companies affiliated to the local territorial unit which was to assist in their training but, by agreement with Air Ministry, one company was usually to be a RAF Company, distinguished by a RAF armband. Air Ministry had hoped to include many trades within the ranks of the RAF companies, but because of the hurry it found it easier to enrol the same five trades as the army, though these were all to be seen in one company, unlike the single-trade army companies.

Recruiting for the ATS was not to be limited solely to the ATS. It could also be done on behalf of the ATS by the other three recognized organizations, who in September 1938 had agreed to a statement defining their roles. The FANY — the Women's Transport Service — were to assist the Territorial Association by raising 10 companies of 150 Drivers. The Mechanical Transport Section of the Women's Legion was to raise 23 companies each of about 50 Drivers, to work mainly with the RAF, while the other part recruited staff for Clerical and General Duties with the Territorials. The Emergency Service, shortly to move into the Duke of York's Headquarters, Chelsea, was to continue ATS Officer Training Courses under its Commandant Dame Helen Gwynne-Vaughan and her Chief Instructor Jane Trefusis-Forbes. The whole came under the administration of the War Office.

The Royal Warrant setting up the ATS was signed on 9 September 1938, but the details were still not all settled before the Munich meeting at the end of the month. Its result confirmed people's feeling that war was imminent and women in particular wanted to do something that would help their country if it came. Meanwhile, Civil Defence measures began, and Service chiefs realized that if they did not act promptly, many women suitable for the ATS would be lost to other voluntary bodies. The announcement of the formation of the Auxiliary Territorial Service was therefore brought forward from the intended 1 October to 27 September 1938. The next day, newspapers told women not already engaged in Nursing or other Reserved occupations and between the ages of 18 and 43 (50 if they were ex-service) to apply to the nearest Territorial Headquarters, if they wished to be enrolled.

Keen to join, Monica Dunbar turned up early, just before 11 am at the Oxford Road Headquarters of the Buckinghamshire Territorial Association which opened at 1 pm. To her dismay 'I had the impression that half of Aylesbury had arrived before me, they appeared literally inundated with applicants.' Then followed a series of forms, a Certificate of Health — expensive for those days — and interviews, punctuated by long waits while paperwork shuttled to and fro through the mail.

A campaign accusing the ATS of snobbery started in the Press, protesting against the basis on which commissions were being granted. The counties strained to show that 'their women Officers came from women of small means, gallant women, who did not have servants at home to do their work and travelled many miles weekly to drill at their own expense,' as Elizabeth Dacre of Halton explained, while she fought to increase their 10s annual allowance. Perhaps due to the careful selection process and attendant costs, recruiting in the counties was slow.

Right *Letter to a new ATS applicant, 30 September 1938 (Miss Dunbar).*

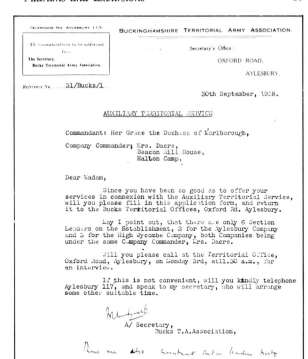

Below *Cartoon* Ellen's own (Mrs Dacre).

The best way to settle the
"SHALL-THE-SNOBS-RUN-THE-W.A.T.S"
question is to put all titled females
into one company with Ellen Wilkinson as
sole private to tell them what to do

Headquarters County of Essex A.T.S.

Chief Commandant.   Territorial Army Association,
Mrs Hughes Reckitt.
                                  Market Road,

R4/807.   Chelmsford.

                February 6th 1939.

Dear Madam,

                I have to acknowledge your National
Service Application Form to join the R.A.F. Auxiliary
Territorial Service.

                I regret to inform you that there is only
one R.A.F. A.T.S. company in Essex, which drills on
Thursday evenings at No 4 Balloon Centre, Chigwell.
                In case it is impossible for you to
reach Chigwell I append herewith a list of all A.T.S.
companies in the county attached to Territorial Units.
These companies undertake exactly the same work (with the
exception of Motor Driving, which section is now full)
as the R.A.F.Company.

                Kindly inform me which company it will
be the most convenient for you to join, and your form will
be sent to the Company Commander concerned, who will
inform you when and where to attend for an interview.

                Yours truly,

                        Eleanor Hughes Reckett

                        Chief Commandant.
                        County of Essex A.T.S.

Company.   Location.   Drill night.

1st Essex. The Drill Hall,Stanwell St.Colchester.   Thursday.
2nd Essex. R.E.Drill Hall,Chestnut Grove,Brentwood. Tuesday.
3rd   "   The Drill Hall, Church Hill,Walthamstow. Friday.
4th   "   Drill Hall,High Street North,East Ham. Wednesday.
5th   "   Drill Hall, East Street, Prittlewell.   Tuesday.
10th   "   R.E.Drill Hall,London Road, Chelmsford. Wednesday.
11th   "   Essex Fortress,Market Road, Chelmsford.
12th   "   "(O.P.U.) Drill Hall,Stanwell St.Colchester. Thursday.
13th   "   Bay Lodge, Stratford.   Friday.
14th   "   "(Clerical) Drill Hall,Gordon Rd. Ilford. Monday.
15th   "   Artillery House, Stratford.   Friday.
40th   "   Drill Hall, Ongar Rd. Brentwood.   Monday.
41st   "   Drill Hall, York Road, Southend.   Thursday.
10th R.A.F.Essex. No4 Balloon Centre Chigwell.   Thursday.

Letter from RAF ATS Company in Essex, February 1939 (Mrs Scandrett).

Any further communication on this
subject should be addressed to
The Commandant,
   School of Instruction,
   Auxiliary Territorial Service,
   Duke of York's Headquarters,
      Chelsea, S.W.3
And the following number quoted:—

SI/A.M./39   24th March, 1939.

SCHOOL OF INSTRUCTION,
AUXILIARY TERRITORIAL SERVICE.

Duke of York's Headquarters,
        Chelsea,
              London, S.W.3.

Sir,

            It is understood that uniform for personnel of R.A.F.
companies of the Auxiliary Territorial Service is now under
consideration, and that the drab authorised for Army
companies may be employed for those who will serve at air
stations on mobilisation.

            Having had the honour to command the women serving
with the R.A.F. during the latter part of the Great War, I
cannot too strongly emphasise the importance of assimilating
the uniform, procedure and organisation of any body of
enrolled women to those of the service to which they are
the summer of/   attached. In September, 1918, the Women's Royal Air Force
                  was the subject of very severe criticism. Air Vice-Marshal
by the end of the Sir Sefton Brancker described it being reorganised "the best
year/   disciplined and best turned out women's organisation in the
                  country." ("Sir Sefton Brancker", by Norman Macmillan,
                  Heineman, 1935, p. 198) The essential factors in this change
                  were Air Ministry Weekly Orders, 1116/18, 1237/18 (para. 16),
                  1254/18, 1496/18, and others of the same kind, whereby the
                  uniform and discipline were approximated to those of the R.A.F.

            Now that blue is universal for the R.A.F. at home,where
women are likely for the most part to serve, it would be a
disaster if they were sent to air stations in the uniform of
another service. It would be better that they should continue
for a time in civilian clothing, with armbands or other badges
allowed, while the authorisation of blue for officers would be
a useful indication of policy. It is realised that there
might be delay, but, to judge from Army experience, the issue
of drab is not likely to be rapid.
                                  under war conditions/
            When men and women are employed together/it is only too
easy for irregularities and consequent scandals to arise and
to be made the most of in the press. One of the best safe-
guards is to enlist the protective instincts of decent men by
making them feel that the women belong to the same organisation. This is most simply and readily done through the uniform
of the service.

            The adoption of blue uniform is therefore urged not
less for the protection of the women than for the encouragement
of their loyalty and enthusiasm.

                        I have the honour to be,
The Under Secretary   Sir,
   of State,   Your obedient Servant,
Air Ministry,

Letter from Dame Helen Gwynne-Vaughan about WAAF uniforms.

London, on the other hand, had been most successful. By the end of October 1938, the Territorial Units had too many ATS Companies affiliated to them and suggested that its London RAF Companies could be affiliated to No 601 Squadron and the Balloon Barrage Squadrons at Kidbrooke. This was agreed and in a later development, Jane Trefusis-Forbes became the first CO of the No 20 RAF (County of London) Company of ATS at Kidbrooke, in addition to her instructor duties at Chelsea.

By December 1938, despite many problems with its own expansion, the RAF was beginning to realize that, if the RAF companies of the ATS were to be useful, they required a different type of training from that afforded by the Army, and the Air Ministry therefore decided to affiliate all its RAF Companies of ATS to Auxiliary Air Force Units.

Dee Ball joined the RAF ATS Company at No 4 Balloon Centre, RAF Chigwell, 'three miles from where I was living. By the time I was enrolled, the section for Drivers was full, only twelve were required. But there were four other trades from which to choose: Cooks, Clerks, Mess Orderlies and Equipment Assistants. I chose the one about which I knew nothing — Equipment Assistant. We trained every Thursday evening until August.'

Dorothy Farr went to Copelaw Street Drill Hall, Glasgow, for training, 'once or twice a week. One Sunday morning, after a lecture by a Flight Sergeant, we were gathered in a group, four abreast, to march through the City of Glasgow. It was raining; we were mostly clad in smart civilian fashion-wear, high heels and all, some with umbrellas — hats were fashionable then. We teetered along the city streets to ribald comments and titters from onlookers.'

In October 1938, the *Daily Express* had sent a reporter down to see the first ATS Officers attending Dame Helen's Officers' School of Instruction. They watched as two drill Sergeants from the Grenadier Guards and two from the Coldstream Guards put the 120 women — 'Britain's blouse and skirt army' — through their paces.

'After an hour of hard drill, the women limped back to their mess-room and collapsed on the chairs. For a week the Sergeants will drill them until they can keep a straight line and take a slow march past. Yesterday the Sergeants, using their brisk barrack voices, screamed: "Eyes right, knees high, head up" and the girls obeyed. They take their orders from 10 am to 5 pm and attend regular Army lectures. One of the Sergeants said: "You don't know the difference between men and women recruits. I've my orders to drill them and they're just as promising as a lot of raw lads from school. I give them the same drill and they're just as bad".'

In this way about 500 ATS were trained.

Later in March, May and June of 1939, Dame Helen introduced three 'special courses for personnel of RAF Companies, outside lecturers being furnished by the Air Ministry and the assistant instructors chosen as far as possible from those who had RAF experience. I think it was to one of them that we owed the dictum, "Always pass the baby up and not down".'

By this time the Air Ministry had decided that RAF ATS Companies should have their records kept by the RAF, and that these companies should concentrate on training their own Officers and NCOs, as they would be the cadre for expansion of the service if war came. As internal training within companies had also become Army policy, Dame Helen decided that the work of the Emergency Service had been pre-empted and in August 1939 it was officially wound up.

Thus 1939 saw the RAF women's service move steadily out of the orbit of the ATS. The principle of a blue uniform was already accepted but still in March 1939, the Director of Equipment was declaring that 'there was not a stitch to be had'. At this point Dame Helen interfered, and suddenly a few uniforms of the desired colour were available by the beginning of July.

In early 1939 the rest of Czechoslovakia fell to Germany — breaking the Munich agreement — and, having secured his rear with a German-Soviet Pact, Hitler prepared to invade Poland. Britain pledged herself to support Polish independence. In June 1939 the *Daily Telegraph* was reporting that approximately two-thirds of the anticipated peacetime numbers of RAF ATS had already enrolled.

'48 RAF companies are now formed — each is attached to a Flying or Balloon Squadron of the Auxiliary Air Force or to a regular RAF station in districts where there is no conveniently situated Auxiliary Air Force Unit. Each Company attached to a Balloon Squadron has an establishment of 72 women, but most Companies attached to Flying Squadrons have establishments of 67 women.'

The difference in numbers was because the Balloon Squadrons were allowed to have five Fabric Workers (a sixth trade) in addition to the usual six Officers, 11 NCOs and 50 'Volunteers' — the name given to ordinary members. Despite the published number of companies being 48, there were in fact, on 18 July 1939, only 47, since although companies ran from 1 to 49, the numbers 18 and 37 were missing. The City of Aberdeen had the honour of being the first company formed and the County of Surrey Company, affiliated to RAF Farnborough, was the last.

Mary Welsh ran a month's camp that year and there she went 'with my faithful hound Axel in attendance. We lived in grand style; I had a tent with a bed and he a basket, propped up on bricks above the torrent streaming across my tent floor. I was relieved beyond measure to find mine was the only tent with running water laid on.'

Early in 1939, the Air Council began to consider the idea of having a woman appointed to the Air Ministry staff to liaise between the RAF companies and Air Ministry, and to advise on various ATS problems. The Treasury suggested hopefully that a lady be chosen 'who would be prepared to serve without remuneration', but it also stipulated that she should not be just a figurehead but a woman who knew her job and would give herself fully to it. After a time it agreed to offer a salary of £800 a year, 'to compensate the lady selected for the income she was surrendering in order to take up the appointment'.

Again Dame Helen was approached with the possibility of offering her the position. Despite her 60 years, Dame Helen was prepared to consider the suggestion, until the likelihood of heading the Army ATS, with less impediments than

Above *Uniforms as seen at the National Defence Rally in Hyde Park on 2 July 1939. They are (left to right) ATS, WRNS, WAAF, London Ambulance Service and Land Army (Mrs Scandrett).*

Below *A WAAF Recall Telegram (Mrs Henderson).*

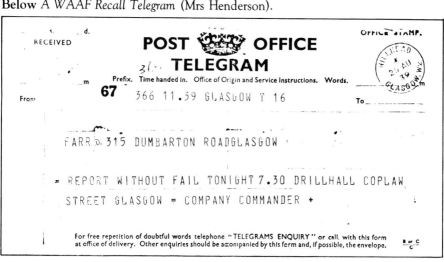

those offered by Air Ministry, proved a greater temptation. Instead she recommended Jane Trefusis-Forbes who on 1 July 1939 became Director, with the rank of Senior Controller. She was the first Director to be appointed in the three women's services. By then, however, she was head of the WAAF, since the growing independence of the RAF companies had moved them so far from the original concept of the Army-aligned ATS, that by Royal Warrant signed on 28 June 1939 they had been reconstituted into 'a separate organization to be designated the Women's Auxiliary Air Force' (WAAF). Even at this late date, nevertheless, the authorities were still repeating 'it will not be practicable to use the WAAF until three or four months after war has broken out'.

In August the companies broke off training for the summer holidays. Rosamunde Morrogh-Stewart, in answer to a rather worried volunteer enquiring about her papers, writes, 'I'm most awfully sorry to have kept them so long — the fact is I have had rather a hectic summer. On 31 August I go up to friends in Scotland for a fortnight.'

Poor woman! She was never to enjoy her Scottish holiday because at the beginning of September 1939, Hitler launched his attack on Poland.

By now, from all sides RAF stations were urging their desperate need for airwomen, as the 'Volunteers' were now to be called. In particular, added to the earlier six trades, they asked for Teleprinter Operators, Telephonists, Plotters and Radar Operators, so at the end of August, Air Ministry agreed to start recruiting these. Meanwhile telegrams, recalling existing WAAF to duty, started to flow out between 25 August to 2 September so that most of the pre-war WAAF was fully mobilized before hostilities commenced. On 3 September, authority for recruiting up to 10,000 WAAF was given and provision for 10,000 more was agreed. Joyce Butterfield was called up on 26 August 1939.

'The telegram just said report to Adastral House by 1.30 pm, with enough clothes for 48 hours plus a blanket. About a dozen of us duly arrived. I was designated as a Teleprinter Operator. It took two days to get things sorted out. We had to make our own sleeping arrangements but be on call for 48 hours. We stayed at hotels nearby, all at our own expense.

'On 30 August, six of us were posted to Worcester with instructions that we did not let the local people know who we were. We still had to pay for our accommodation and food. We eventually arrived at the old workhouse in Worcester, which was still occupied — the inmates were all mentally disturbed! By 2 September they had been moved out and we set to work.

'On September 3rd, we listened to Chamberlain on the radio and knew that this was the real thing.'

The Second World War had begun!

Chapter 8

When The Going Got Tough

'I am speaking to you from the Cabinet Room at 10 Downing Street. This morning the British Ambassador in Berlin handed the German Government a final note stating that unless we heard from them by 11 o'clock that they were prepared at once to withdraw their troops from Poland, a state of war would exist between us. I have to tell you now that no such undertaking has been received and that consequently this country is at war with Germany . . .'

3 September 1939

Hardly had the thin tones of the Prime Minister's voice faded on that sunny Sunday morning, than London air-raid sirens began to wail and men in gas capes, swinging wooden rattles, ran along the streets warning the startled populace to stay indoors. Overhead silver RAF balloons rode skies empty of German bombers. It was a false alarm, but a timely reminder of war.

After that everything went back to near normal. Blackout of streets, shops, transport and homes caused many laughs and accidents, identity cards were issued, and city children evacuated for safety to the country trooped back, gas-masks bumping on bottoms. It all seemed a great game; where was the war?

Only the British Navy in Scapa Flow and the River Plate and the RAF bombing Germany with leaflets saw any action. Britain and France were suspended in a Phoney War, like stillness before storm. Elsewhere, the news absorbed avidly from BBC bulletins was uniformly bleak. Poland fell; Russia and Germany seemed 'agreed' to let Russia start her conquests.

It was fortunate for Britain that by 1939 her shadow factory scheme had gained momentum and heavy industry, including aircraft production, was beginning to expand. Already the secret radar defence network was in being and extending, and 20-year-old youths were in training as a result of the first military conscription of May 1939. Even so, the odds were heavily against Britain with a population of 47½ million pitted against Germany's 75 million. It was clear that woman-power would have to be called on to help with the imbalance.

Up and down the country organizations were besieged by men and women offering themselves for the struggle that lay ahead. WAAF recruiting was handled at Air Ministry, and at Company Headquarters, each of which was allowed to expand by 100 and in mid-September by a further 80 or so. At the beginning of September, a radio request for WAAF volunteers, that had been prepared for an emergency, was broadcast by mistake, and brought out the civil police to control the crowds of eager young women.

'But have you seen them, Madam!' a perspiring policeman warned the Director. 'The queue stretches from Victory House, down Kingsway, through the Aldwych, and along the Strand almost to Whitehall.'

Many unsuccessful applicants travelled half over the country to find a Company with a vacancy on its books.

Before the war the WAAF totalled 1,734. Three short years later it peaked at 181,835. Barred from carrying lethal weapons, girls replaced Officers and airmen in as many tasks on the ground as possible, releasing men for flying and other essential duties. Time proved that girls excelled in work involving delicacy of touch, speed of reaction, patience, intuition and tact. At the beginning, women replaced men in a ratio of three to two, then later one for one in some trades. Limiting factors ranged from physical strength, to retaining basic numbers of airmen. Thus in October 1943 WAAF formed 16 per cent of the total RAF numbers, and 22 per cent of the RAF in Britain. During the six war years, approximately a quarter of a million girls served with the WAAF, and official post–war calculations suggest that without WAAF support, the RAF would have needed about 150,000 extra men.

Volunteers came not only from Britain, but also from the Dominions and the Colonies, which in the earlier days lacked women's forces of their own. Winkie Loughran arrived from Nassau, surviving a hurricane, a submarine and an accident in harbour. The 'Bahamas' flashes on tunic and battledress ensured her a warm welcome everywhere. Another girl had been a dress designer in a New Zealand fashion house, others came from Australia and South Africa, and a large number came from Canada, among whom was Frankie Vachon, a French-Canadian. Then there were Americans like Mary Lee Settle, who braved the U-boats to join the WAAF, far ahead of her own country's engagement in the war. Elaine and Denise Miley travelled from Argentina.

Britain became the refuge for many escaping from a Europe gradually becoming overwhelmed by war. Some formed their own fighting units in exile, others entered the British services. Josette Bens came to join the WAAF from Belgium, which had no women's forces. Kay Moore tells how Ruth, a Czechoslovakian girl, often kept her WAAF hutmates enthralled with stories of how she escaped from her country before the Germans invaded it.

Polish girls, numbering about 1,436, wore different buttons and cap badges and although enrolled and trained as WAAF, were usually posted to Polish Air Force Units. Ida Wyartt helped Polish Mina with her English; Mina had been deported to Russia and 'endured a dreadful journey in a cattle truck. One girl

Bahamas flashes on an airwomen's sleeve
(Mrs Loughran).

Uniform with Norwegian cross
(Mrs Chew).

gave birth and the baby was thrown out.' After an amnesty she had managed to get to Britain.

Jenny Jennings saw numbers tattooed by the Germans on the arms of others and witnessed a touching reunion of a mother and daughter. Eva Mohr escaped from occupied Norway with her two-year-old son and was eventually in charge of the Norwegian WAAF in Great Britain, where it numbered about 50, with about 27 in Canada. Of its members, 'some travelled around the world to join the allied forces. Some crossed the North Sea by fishing boat and motor torpedo boat. Some were involved in the Resistance and had to leave in a hurry. They trained and served at RAF stations, where Norwegian Squadrons were operating.'

In addition recruits came from Holland, France, Greece and later the Middle East and even China.

WAAF formed a cross-section of the population. Pam Barton was the British Ladies' Golf Champion; Joan Hamer enlisted with Sarah Churchill who was found on her hands and knees scrubbing out their bathtub. A millionaire shipping magnate's daughter polished the brown lino of her requisitioned married quarter with a blacklead cloth 'because I honestly thought it gave the floor a pleasant "old-worlde" mottled effect.' An airwoman cook asked permission to keep her two hunters on the station and Janet Rowson joined her mother, a First World War WRAF who died in 1941 at RAF Bridgnorth.

There were many reasons that brought all these girls to enrol — patriotism,

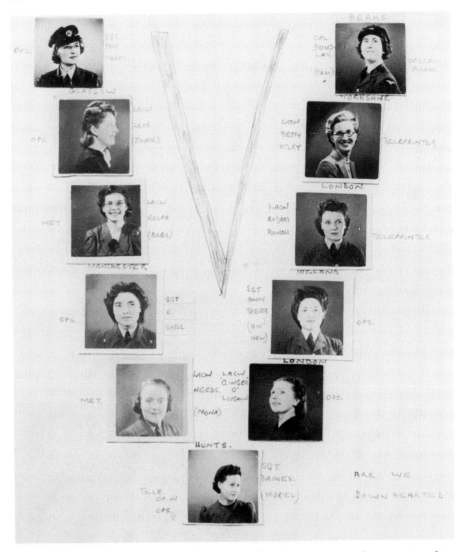

money, freedom, escape from unpleasant jobs, the promise of companionship, revenge on fathers or boy-friends, or for a husband's death. Many chose the air force out of a fascination with flying and a spirit of adventure. Even in 1939, joining the RAF was considered daring!

Early 'joining up' was very much hit and miss. Doris Hacker 'just walked on to the camp and enlisted. I lived at home.' In mid-September, Ailsa Stevenson joined 'in a bleak Glasgow hall. There were two desks. You took turn in the queue. I discovered later that at desk A you could join as a Driver, Mess or Kitchen Clerk. Desk B was for other trades. It was completely fortuitous that I landed at desk A and became a Driver.'

Companies often posted women straight to their stations, where in the general hustle because of the overlap of the departure of the airmen they were to replace, there was rarely time for anyone to teach them their new job. Edda Nuttall recalls applying to the Labour Exchange in late September.

'There was one short interview and that was all. Next came a letter to travel to Hooton Park in the Wirrall and bring warm clothes. I well remember getting off a bus, miles from the station, clutching my suitcase, and walking in the autumn sunshine and feeling wonderful. This was not to last. The RAF was just not ready for us. I don't think they knew what to do with us. We were farmed out to civilian billets and given menial tasks to do — at 18 very disillusioning. Things could only get better, and they did.'

Pat Cox 'had to report to a half-built camp and whatever one's trade we were all put to scrub and clean buildings as the builders completed them. It was absolute chaos, no set hours or routine for several weeks.'

Indeed the RAF was fully occupied with its own expansion, not having calculated for the early appearance of the WAAF and certainly not its rapid growth. It wanted the airwomen to live at home, but in default it adopted all sorts of expedients, lodging them in private homes or boarding houses, or taking over houses, flats and married quarters. Rarely could it spare a station hut, and in the hurry of the moment little accommodation met normal standards.

In her report of April 1940 the Director of the WAAF complained bitterly that airwomen were still being billeted two in a bed at such places as Leighton Buzzard, Norton, Harrogate, Worcester, Locking, Warmwell, Oban and Chatham. By 1941 most airwomen were living on stations, though the Director

Left *WAAF hut-mates from many trades and places* (Mrs Fox).

Right *Consulting orders, October 1939. The two airwomen wear mainly airmen's clothing* (Mrs Miller).

was still complaining about overcrowding, cold, condensation, furnishings, and the lack or inadequacy of recreational or study rooms, drying and ironing rooms and kitchens. Unsatisfactory sanitary arrangements, the later necessity of dispersal — on some stations occasioning a round cycle ride between sleeping, eating and working sites of up to 30 miles a day — all these imposed hardship and discouragement. Warnings that it would be dangerous to allow recruit numbers to outrun accommodation were made time and again, and yet so great was the RAF's need for WAAF that they were just as regularly ignored.

In the first month of recruiting, numbers shot up to 8,000, necessitating a stop on 6 October, until mid-1940, for all except a few special trades. The Companies, whose work had contributed to this rapid growth, were told, 'Now that personnel of the WAAF Companies are serving with RAF Units, the need for Company organisation no longer exists, and the original peace-time Companies will be disbanded.' By March 1940 they had all closed down.

WAAF signed on for four years or the duration of the war. Age limits remained at 18–43, but they were changed in 1941 to 17½–44. In September 1939 girls had little trade and service training. Carol Hastings recalls, 'I picked up what I could on the way, and was forever indebted to a Corporal in the Orderly Room who introduced me to the Air Force Regulations.'

Edda Nuttall was quickly posted to Sealand, 'a proper station, it had planes' and was shown her trade by 'a gem of a Flight Sergeant.' Ailsa Stevenson was not so lucky. 'Instruction was initially by a Drill Sergeant who held us up to ridicule and large numbers departed.' Another Sergeant told his girls, 'All females are bitches.' Sandy Heath remembers an ex-Indian Army adjutant who swore at her in Hindustani. As my mother was an Indian Army "brat", I'd heard it all before and replied in kind. Result — almost terminal shock.'

In the beginning, the airmen with whom they worked tended to regard WAAF as a novelty, treating them sometimes with hostility and more frequently with amusement and leg-pulling, like Edna Jeremiah who was sent to fetch a rubber ladder from the Guardroom. But as time went by and it was found that the girls were staying and prepared to work, they were accepted and often treated as 'one of the boys', particularly in engineering trades, with no privileges, but with fierce protection against outsiders.

WAAF Officers were of very mixed quality. Before the war, 234 had been appointed by Companies, but afterwards they were selected from the ranks by a Travelling Board who studied peace-time members before taking further recommendations. Their selections were destined to become Administrators, ultimately known as WAAF G (General) Officers, concerned with airwomen's welfare. Later Boards picked Officers for special duties, such as those to work on Codes and Cyphers, a branch introduced three days after the outbreak of war. An attempt to appoint suitably-qualified women direct from civilian life did not prove successful and was not repeated.

Clothing was another big problem.

'When I first joined in September 1939 I had no uniform,' says Daisy Hills. 'After two or three weeks I was issued with a RAF blue-belted raincoat and beret with a metal RAF cap badge to pin on it. Also a navy armband with WAAF in red

A group at RAF Duxford in December 1939 before the airwomen's full uniform had arrived (Mrs Nielson).

on it. A few lucky ones had grey lisle stockings and flat, black-laced shoes — not always fitting.'

In many cases girls reported in thin civilian dresses and sandals, expecting to be kitted by the RAF. The WAAF Director had many struggles with the Equipment Directorate, whose move to Harrogate did not make matters any easier. In desperation she resorted to sending out a handful of staff to look for suitable supplies of clothing in London stores. In October, when it became apparent that tunics and skirts would not be available until December at the earliest, she decided to have slacks issued meantime. 'They would at least clothe the airwomen from the waist to the feet and thus avert the very real risk of chills.' Fleecy raincoat linings, gloves and cardigans were also added for the majority. Joyce Pritchard and friends learned that the blue soft-crowned cap with a black patent peak was soon to be issued to airwomen.

'We heard that Moss Bros of London had them, so we sent our size, plus 7/6 and they supplied them to us. On our arrival at our first posting in December 1939, half the camp turned out to see the caps nobody had but us.'

The winter of 1939 was one of the coldest on record. It started early, justifying the Director's pleas for clothing, and lasted late. On at least one station, Thorney Island, where there was ice on the marshes for two months, the CO ordered the girls to have airmen's greatcoats, which the Director managed to have introduced officially for the next winter. To girls working on wet, windy airfields, in the words of Dorothy Kelly, 'our greatcoats were great.'

On Christmas Day 1939, Ailsa Stevenson was one of 'twenty-two cold and miserable ACW2s washing dishes which had been sent from the airmen's mess

WAAF working on a lorry in October 1939. Two are wearing airmen's greatcoats (Mrs Miller).

with a cold helping of turkey and dinner, when about six junior RAF Officers arrived, among them Guy Gibson, asking for a drink. When a super Scots Officer heard that we were from Scotland he got hold of a piper and we had a terrific party doing Scots reels and so on. That evening the Sergeants had arranged a party at the Sergeants' Mess. In half an hour the girls were nearly all incapable due to a mixture of drinks. Greatly daring, I told no less a person that the Station Warrant Officer that I would take the WAAF away if he did not order the men to stop giving the girls alcohol. After all we had come to dance and we couldn't even walk. Soon all was well — on lemonade — and we had the best Christmas ever.' She sums up her first winter at Scampton as, 'Everything was new to us all. Freezing cold. No water or heating for long periods. Cold food. Inadequate clothing, but wonderful people.'

The Nuffield Christmas gift of 82 wirelesses only slightly alleviated the hardship of that first wartime winter when epidemics of flu and German measles swept the camps. WAAF medical care was so stretched that in 1940 women doctors were brought into the RAF Medical Branch to work on stations and in hospitals, where for the most part, although airwomen were their special concern, a woman Medical Officer (MO) treated airmen and women indiscriminately.

The numbers of girls leaving, referred to as wastage, mounted up. In May 1940 they were 27 per cent overall, and in some domestic trades nearly 50 per cent. This caused much official concern, but strangely enough it seemed to work in favour of the service because all the difficulties had formed an unintentional but effective selection process. The WAAF who remained were of a high standard and were welded even more firmly together by common experience and common troubles overcome. When girls left, there was nothing the service could do to stop them, the Judge Advocate General having ruled that WAAF could not be charged with desertion or absence without leave. It was therefore useless to refuse a request for discharge. As airwomen knew what would happen if an airman went absent, it was hardly surprising if they felt that the RAF did not regard an airwoman's contribution of much importance, when they let her go so easily.

Moreover because of the judgement that WAAF Officers were 'not Officers within the meaning of the Air Force Act', they were handicapped when meting out a minor punishment (MP) to an airwoman, whatever her offence, since whether it was carried out or not, depended entirely on her agreement. Punishments jumped from quite mild to Courts Martial, which no one wanted.

By April 1940 improvements slowly began. A programme of building WAAF accommodation started, uniforms had come through, and station establishments had been settled. The next month was also to see the award of the first George Cross to an airwoman. Soon, married WAAF were allowed to serve on the same station as their husbands, providing they were not Officer and airwoman. The Director later said, 'The WAAF was in fact substituting for the RAF. From the outset we had been paid the great compliment of being given the same badges of rank and the same uniform as the RAF. We were serving under the same conditions, with the same equipment, passing through the same tests, being reclassified and remustered in the same way as the ground staff of the RAF. In fact the full foundation of the WAAF as an integral part of the RAF was laid.'

Christmas Dinner 1941 being served by Officers and NCOs. Note the masking-tape crosses on windows against bomb splintering (Mrs Stevenson).

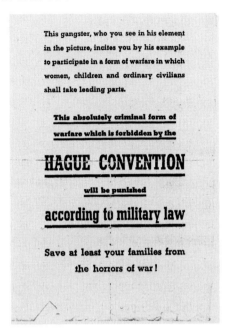

WANTED

FOR INCITEMENT TO
MURDER

This gangster, who you see in his element in the picture, incites you by his example to participate in a form of warfare in which women, children and ordinary civilians shall take leading parts.

This absolutely criminal form of warfare which is forbidden by the

HAGUE CONVENTION

will be punished

according to military law

Save at least your families from the horrors of war!

German leaflet dropped on Britain, after Winston Churchill became Prime Minister (Mrs Scandrett).

Meanwhile, the Phoney War evaporated. Dunkirk was one of a series of catastrophes which engulfed Western Europe. Cecilia Frey recalls, 'Most chilling was listening to the radio newscaster narrating the evacuation and fall of Dunkirk. I remember sitting on a trestle table, and an absolute silence fell over the Orderly Room. Shortly after we were given rifle and hand-gun training and instructed to be on the alert for German parachutists. I remember wandering round Gosport Fort, checking doors and windows in pyjamas, dressing gown and slippers, with a heavy .45, fully loaded, hanging out of each rather flimsy pocket.'

Britain alone remained unconquered. Germany intending invasion, planned to destroy British aircraft and aerodromes together with their operations rooms and radar stations — the eyes of the RAF — staffed largely by airwomen. How would the untried girls entrusted with such vital work react? The RAF held its breath. It was soon reassured as reports poured in from places such as Ventnor radar station, which was so badly bombed on 12 August 1940 that it was off the air for over three days.

Fighter Command signalled, 'The C in C has heard with pride and satisfaction of the manner in which WAAF at Dover, Rye, Pevensey, Ventnor and Dunkirk conducted themselves under fire today. They have abundantly justified his confidence in them.'

Indeed, the coolness and bravery of the WAAF everywhere won the respect of the RAF and the British people, and the Battle of Britain proved the first of Hitler's defeats.

By August 1940, a Substitution Committee was at work considering the introduction of WAAF into more trades, to ease the manpower shortage. As a result girls embarked on more and more technical work, and thus six pre-war trades became 18 in 1940, 54 on the third WAAF anniversary in 1942 and 89 by the end of the war. Similarly Officer branches had grown from one to 22 in 1945.

Demand for WAAF rose dramatically between April 1940 and April 1941 from 150 to 1,000 per week. Consequently, recruiting passed to the RAF with tighter regulations, while the Ministry of Labour checked such matters as national security and reserved occupations. Weekly absorption and require-ment rates fluctuated so widely, however, that a system called Deferred Service was introduced in May 1941, enabling women to be enrolled and then sent home to await their call-up within the next three months. Eventually recruiting was further de-centralized and passed to Combined Recruiting Centres and Sub Depots in towns up and down the country.

Victory House nevertheless remained the WAAF London Recruiting Centre for some time. Mary Bowen spent a good deal of her day there 'trying to get rec-ruits off to the railway station in between air raid warnings'. She had 'countless experiences of falling flat on my face in the street or running along the Strand as

The drive to recruit more WAAF (Mrs Blake).

the German planes swept up the Thames strafing'. From one billet she watched the tragic scene of 'aliens being rounded up at gunpoint from the Ambassadors Hotel'.

Henrietta Barnet arrived on 'the night the House of Commons was hit and much damage done elsewhere. I shall never forget the smell of burning, the noise, the broken glass.' Of the airwomen working on various tasks at Air Ministry she says, 'Never once did they speak of their secret work, seldom were they late for duty, even after a raid. They were known as the Whitehall Warriors.'

The unprecedented growth of the women's services and their involvement in so much secret work finally moved the Government to pass the Defence (Women's Forces) Regulations on 25 April 1941, which changed the status of the ATS and WAAF, who now became Members of the Armed Forces of the Crown. (The WRNS, a much smaller service, preferred no change.) Thus WAAF Officers were officially commissioned and they and airwomen were covered by large parts of the Air Force Act, with its accompanying discipline and regulations. They were no longer civilians in uniform.

By 1941 the war was still going badly. Italy had joined Germany. Greece and Yugoslavia were being subjugated. Bitter battles swung to and fro over North Africa, and Britain's cities were nightly bombed, with London in particular having endured its baptism of fire. Then in the latter half of 1941, the Axis overreached itself. The German attack on Russia and the Japanese attack on the USA at Pearl Harbor brought Britain two formidable allies, whose weight would eventually tell. Stretched into the Far East, Britain endured more heavy losses and reverses, notably in Singapore, but by 1942 she was beginning to take the offensive.

Little wonder therefore that Britain was running short of men in the forces and the industry that supplied them, and began to call up women as she had called up men. On 19 April 1941 came the Registration for Employment Order which required all women of specified ages to register with the Ministry of Labour for work in the factories or the forces. In December came the National Service Act, Number 2, which made virtually all single women and childless widows between 20 and 30 liable for conscription into one of the women's services, subject to certain conditions. This was quickly followed by a Royal Proclamation of 10 January 1942, calling up girls born in 1920 and 1921.

These Acts brought a stream of new recruits hoping to beat their call-up, since once conscripted they lost all choice of what service they were to enter. The first girls conscripted under National Service entered the WAAF on 23 April 1942. Gradually throughout the year women born between 1918 and 1923 were called up until there were 16,246 National Service WAAF.

Nora Plint notes in her diary for 4 December 1942: 'A cold dark winter's morning. The post has come and gone and still no word of the deferment from call-up I had requested. For days I have been waiting and yesterday I told Auntie C that if she saw me not again, she would know I had obeyed the instructions ordering me to report at RAF Innsworth today, together with a railway warrant and the information that it was an offence not to obey the command. I made breakfast, told Father and Colin, and departed for Lime Street Station, not wishing that my vision of a policeman tat-tatting on the door and escorting me away should become a reality.'

Within the WAAF, 1941 brought in the ranks of Leading Aircraft Woman (LACW), Flight Sergeant (Flt Sgt) and Warrant Officer (WO), and 1942 won approval for airwomen to fly while on duty in service aircraft. At work Stella Enfield saw a difference in her second visit to a naval plotting room, where she had first seen 'the U-boats surrounding the Atlantic convoys like a wolf pack picking off stragglers'. By 1943 the Battle of the Atlantic was being won.

Registration of women continued until autumn of 1943 when all without a valid exemption between the ages of 18 and 50 had been registered. Conscription then gradually extended its age groups until late 1944 when it ended — 33,932 girls in total having entered under these terms. Volunteers, of course, often reluctant, continued to be taken at intervals during this time.

The statistics of this new exercise in mobilization and state planning are interesting. Out of a population of 47½ million, 17 million were women over 14 years, among whom 10 million were married. Out of the 17 million, 7 million joined the armed forces, civil defence or industry and in the age group 18-40, nine out of every ten single women went out to work. Unemployment among women, which in 1939 was running at 400,000 and even when registration started still stood at 160,000, disappeared.

In the world at large, 1942 marked a gradual turn of the tide in Russia and North Africa, consolidated in 1943 when the allies began their offensive in Italy. But in mid-1944, Hitler hit England with his new 'wonder weapon' the V-1

An exhibition of a captured V-1 Flying Bomb, November 1944 (Miss Fillery).

SUPREME HEADQUARTERS
ALLIED EXPEDITIONARY FORCE

Soldiers, Sailors and Airmen of the Allied Expeditionary Force!

You are about to embark upon the Great Crusade, toward
which we have striven these many months.　The eyes of
the world are upon you. The hopes and prayers of liberty-
loving people everywhere march with you. In company with
our brave Allies and brothers-in-arms on other Fronts,
you will bring about the destruction of the German war
machine, the elimination of Nazi tyranny over the oppressed
peoples of Europe, and security for ourselves in a free
world.

Your task will not be an easy one. Your enemy is well
trained, well equipped and battle-hardened.　He will
fight savagely.

But this is the year 1944! Much has happened since the
Nazi triumphs of 1940-41. The United Nations have in-
flicted upon the Germans great defeats, in open battle,
man-to-man.　Our air offensive has seriously reduced
their strength in the air and their capacity to wage
war on the ground. Our Home Fronts have given us an
overwhelming superiority in weapons and munitions of
war, and placed at our disposal great reserves of trained
fighting men.　The tide has turned! The free men of the
world are marching together to Victory!

I have full confidence in your courage, devotion to duty
and skill in battle.　We will accept nothing less than
full Victory!

Good Luck!　And let us all beseech the blessing of Almighty God upon this great and noble undertaking.

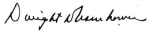

*Leaflet to troops embark-
ing for the D-Day Invasion
of Europe (Mrs Skinner).*

pilotless flying bomb, and later the even more dreaded V–2 rocket. For the service, there was the terrible day when Pip Hugill heard that, 'The WAAF Hostel
for Number 7 Radio School — a large block of flats in South Kensington in
London — had received a direct hit from a V-1, and we had five airwomen dead
and 65 seriously injured. Another four airwomen died in individual incidents.
As adjutant, I had to deal with all the personal effects, including blood-stained
clothing returned in sacks from the mortuary — a sobering experience.'

Gwendoline Ayres describes an attack by a V-1.

'The van is brought to a standstill and we clap on our tin hats. We can hear the
ominous sound of doodle-bugs, and on peering out from the ditch, into which
we have unceremoniously thrown ourselves, we can see the flaming tails of four
flying bombs, as they cleave the darkness in their headlong dash towards their
"military objectives" — innocent civilians in Southern England. It seems
impossible that the flak can miss their target as the shells pour into the bombs.
All at once there is a blinding flash and a terrific roar as one of the bombs
explodes in mid-air. That's one to the guns! The blast causes the van to shudder.
Now the fighters roar overhead in an attempt to cut across the path of the bombs.

Their guns open up and the cannons chatter as they get their prey in their sights. The kites make a run at one of the bombs, pouring shells into it, veering away quickly after each burst in case there is an explosion. The engine of the doodle-bug cuts out, and in its place there is a rushing sound as it makes a headlong dive to earth. We hold our breath till after the explosion, then sigh with relief. The remaining two bombs sail on and can be heard in the distance. A hail of shrapnel clatters onto the roadway.'

1944 also saw the long-awaited D-Day invasion of Europe by the returning allies.

'It is a sobering thought,' Squadron Leader Frank Tilsley admits, 'that for months, hundreds of airwomen walked about this country in possession of Top Secret information for which the enemy would gladly have paid a king's ransom. I remember one very senior Officer complaining humorously that his daughter knew more about the invasion than he did and he couldn't get a word out of her.'

At the time of the Normandy invasion, Doris Quickie was stationed at the RAF Hospital Wroughton.

'All the RAF wounded were ferried to this hospital via Lyneham. As equipment assistants we had to meet each convoy and unload, sort and label the belongings of the wounded. I shall never forget their courage and sheer grit. In spite of pain and some with dreadful injuries, most managed to smile and some even joked. Those wounded men were true heroes. At times we worked through the night until early morning, fortified by frequent mugs of hot tea from the cookhouse staff.'

The disastrous parachute landings at Arnhem shortly followed, relieved too late by the advancing forces. Jeanie Rowley helped prepared the gliders for this mission.

'Ghostly lights in the hangar,
Like clouds passing over the moon.
Three nights we have laboured,
The kites and gliders will be leaving soon
For Arnhem.'

The Normandy invasion, the victorious advance by Russia in the east and the British, American and other allied forces from the south and west, tightened the ring around Germany until it finally broke. In Italy, Mussolini was shot by partisans and Hitler committed suicide in his Berlin bunker.

The atomic bomb finished the struggle with Japan, which signed its unconditional surrender on 2 September 1945, one day before the sixth anniversary of the outbreak of the Second World War.

Chapter 9

The Director's Duties

'(a) To advise the Air Member for Personnel on all questions concerning the training and welfare of the WAAF.
(b) To advise the Air Ministry branches on all questions peculiar to the WAAF.
(c) To act as adviser to the area administrators of the WAAF with whom she may correspond direct, with the object of promoting uniformity of treatment of WAAF problems, particularly in regard to personnel matters.'

AMO N 767 dated 10 August 1939

It was the task of the Director to deal with the day-to-day crises in the WAAF. She had less scope for action than her ATS counterpart and indeed less power than she would have had in the First World War. Her duties were purely advisory and she was not going to be allowed to issue orders or correspond through official channels except through an intermediary. The clock had been put back to the days of Miss Violet Douglas-Pennant. Jane Trefusis-Forbes had three assets, however.

The first was that she was working with men, most of whom had been serving with the WRAF of the First World War and knew their value, so despite the time gap, the WAAF was no stranger to these senior Officers.

The second was her friendship with the vastly-experienced Dame Helen Gwynne-Vaughan. She was later to say, 'Hardly a day passed when Dame Helen and I did not have at least one conversation on the telephone.' Slim, plain but charming, Jane Trefusis-Forbes was 39 years old when she became head of the WAAF in July 1939. Joyce Butterfield was recruited into the WAAF by her that year.

'She was my first WAAF Officer and delighted in riding around on a motor bike and side-car.' Another considered the new Director a 'real wartime lady. She was always neat as a pin, despite her uniform not being new.'

She was the same age as Dame Helen had been when she had taken over the

WRAF in the First World War. With such similar background and problems, she must have valued the help and advice of the older woman and they remained friends until the latter's death. According to Dame Helen, 'We instituted meetings of the three Directors — WRNS, ATS and WAAF —which later were sometimes joined by representatives of the VAD Council. These meetings were informal, being called by each of the Directors in turn. They provided an excellent opportunity for discussion of our common problems, for the pooling of ideas and for agreement not only on the things which were the same in our three services, but of the many that were different.'

The Director's third advantage was in her character and background. Her energy and drive had made her leave school in the First World War to join the transport section of the Women's Volunteer Reserve, although she was bitterly disappointed to find she was under-age for being sent to France. Between the wars, starting with £20, she had built from scratch a large establishment for nursing, boarding and breeding dogs and also training kennelmaids and canine nurses, as a result of which she soon won a reputation as a leading dog expert. To this she added other managerial interests, latterly in Building Trusts.

In 1935, while still working, she had joined the Emergency Service, where Dame Helen quickly identified her talents, making her Senior Cadet and eventually Chief Instructor when the ATS was formed in 1938. At the end of that year Dame Helen tried her out as Company Commander of No 20 RAF Company ATS. In a testimonial written in 1946, Dame Helen recommends 'her energy, enthusiasm and power of leadership. . . She is a good speaker. . . She has tact, vitality and considerable organising power [but] detailed office organisation or the preparation of reports [are not] among her strong points.'

Air Chief Commandant Dame Katherine Jane Trefusis-Forbes, Director 1939-1943 (Mrs Scott).

SERVE IN THE WAAF
WITH THE MEN WHO FLY

The success of Jane Trefusis-Forbes in her first Command led to her appointment as the first Director of the WAAF with the rank of Senior Controller, shortly changed to Air Commandant. She relinquished her business interests to concentrate on her new post, and certainly she needed all her managerial abilities and patience for the task that lay ahead. From the start things were not easy.

'Heads of Departments at the Air Ministry, whom I must consult, were in turn on leave during July and August [1939] and most of the RAF Companies of the ATS had at least partly closed down. It was at once necessary to start records of all Officers and try to discover something of their history and abilities. Then among much else, a training system had to be worked out, enrolment forms and WAAF Regulations discussed and contacts made with Groups and Commands.' Pay also had to be decided, and postings to stations arranged.

Caught by the war, the first official Regulations did not appear until December 1939, although rules appeared in dribs and drabs in Air Ministry letters. The Director worked furiously, but was careful to warn her staff to keep within their limits. The December 1939 Regulations stated 'The Officer in charge of a detachment of the WAAF will be responsible to the Officer Commanding the RAF Unit for the efficiency, discipline, well-being and training (where practicable) of all ranks of the detachment.'

The Director commented, 'If we are going to be responsible for all that, we are more than advisers. . . We have a lot to learn. . . It is wiser to go very slowly and let the power be handed to us on a silver platter than take it as a right.'

Her wisdom was justified when the WAAF became a fully-fledged service of the Crown in 1941, but though her powers were increased in many spheres, from the selection and posting of her Officers to her status as a specialist, so that she now *must* be consulted by the RAF on all questions concerning welfare and administration of the WAAF, she still could not initiate and carry out many matters in her own right, and this position was mirrored by that of her Officers and airwomen throughout the service. Indeed their position was equally nebulous and awkward, answerable to a RAF Officer or NCO for work and a Senior Administrative WAAF Officer for all else, while everyone was under the overall orders of her Officer Commanding. It was therefore not surprising to find that there was a large gap in the way WAAF Officers interpreted their powers and duties on different camps.

By this time, the organisation of the WAAF at the Air Ministry had taken a clearer shape. The Director worked at Adastral House, in the Air Member for Personnel's Department (AMP), assisted by Flight Officer Van Baerle, who had been in charge of a peace-time RAF ATS Company and was a former secretary of the Bishop of Leicester, together with two other Officers, Flight Officer Crowther and Assistant Section Officer Overton. Unofficially, she also trained 112 Officers on 'temporary attachments'. Beneath her in the chain of command were WAAF Officers at Command, Group and Station headquarters. The problem of whether the WAAF was a separate force like the ATS or completely

Left *Poster, Serve in the WAAF with the men who fly* (RAF Museum).

integrated as the RAF seemed to want, was never quite solved, but what was achieved was a compromise between the two. The system was made to work mainly because it received so much intelligent and sympathetic help from all ranks of the RAF.

Meanwhile a large part of Air Commandant Trefusis-Forbes's energies was channelled into solving problems of the growing numbers, trades and substitution ratios of the WAAF. Although she may have sometimes felt that she was working without recognition, the Director must have been somewhat comforted by the message sent to mark the WAAF's third anniversary in June 1942, by her first Air Member for Personnel, Air Chief Marshal Sir Charles Portal, the then Chief of the Air Staff, in which he said, 'We watched with admiration the skill and keenness of your Officers and Airwomen in their work and we are grateful for the increased strength and efficiency which you bring to our common Service. You are making a splendid contribution to our ultimate victory.'

In an hour of levity a little later, possibly when she was recovering from an attack of German measles, or 'Hun Pox' as she quaintly called it, she penned this poem to the same gentleman (although unsigned, it is among her papers and bears the hallmark of her style).

'My dear Sir Charles Portal, do you really think it's fair,
That WAAFs should have no coupons to buy anything to wear?
We know our uniforms are smart — some people say they are 'chic' —,
But wearing them week in, week out, we get a little sick!
And while we're on the subject, I just must call your attention,
To a matter rather delicate — I hardly like to mention —
Now for a shock my dear Sir Charles, I'd like you to prepare:
Have you examined closely, Sir, our service underwear?
They're very thick and ugly, Sir, and honestly they're not
The things to wear, if by mistake, the sun shines and it's hot!
Before I close this note, Sir, I'd be grateful to acquire,
Some information as to handkerchiefs and night attire.
Perhaps you will think these problems out, and let me know by phone.
I have the honour to be, Sir, your obedient Servant . . . Joan.'

The changes and difficulties on stations and at Air Ministry were bound to find their way into the public domain. To some extent this was extenuated because the service was new and conditions were being improved daily, but also because of the outstanding behaviour of WAAF during the Battle of Britain, which won them a special place in public favour. The chief tormentor was the Beaverbrook press, who considered themselves public guardians on the question of morality. The ATS was the main object of attack, but the other women's services were inevitably drawn in, although the WRNS was too small a target for widespread controversy. The *Daily Express* headlined, 'Too many misfits in the ATS and WAAF'. Girls 'temperamentally incapable of settling down to life in ATS or WAAF have cost the country at least £20,000 — the price of four Spitfires.' The *Daily Herald* complained that WAAF had unscreened shower baths in

Three WAAF Billets:

(a) Requisitioned Kyle House, Newton on Ouse (Miss Smith).

(b) Hut at Allerton Park with owner's bed near the doorway (Miss Smith).

(c) Another type of camp hut (Mrs Boot).

one camp and advised 'Cut Red Tape in servicewomen's billeting conditions'.

Growing uneasiness was felt by parents as stories gathered force and volume by repetition. Minor Committees were set up by the Archbishop of Canterbury, The Public Morality Council, and the House of Commons, and despite surprisingly good reports headlined in other papers, rumour rumbled on. At length Parliament grasped the bull by the horns, acting as it did in a similar situation in 1917, and set up a Special Committee to investigate and make recommendations on amenities and welfare conditions in the three women's services. Its report — known as the Markham Report, from the name of its Chairman, Miss Violet Markham, also coincidentally on the 1917 Committee — was made to Parliament and publicly printed in August 1942.

Its investigations were extensive. This extract from the Innsworth Station Diary for 28 April 1942 typifies a station visit.

'Draft 488. Intake 199. Visit of four members of the Women's Services Welfare and Amenities Committee: Sir David Munro, Miss Violet Markham, Mrs A.C.N. Gulland and Mrs J.L. Stocks. After lunch in the Mess, they divided into four parties, and, accompanied by Officers and NCOs representative of each Wing, toured all sections of the Depot, asked questions and spoke to many airwomen and recruits. They then visited the Hospital and returned to the Mess for tea. They seemed almost entirely satisfied with all they saw.'

The Markham Report embodies strikingly sensible views, which, while accepting many accusations, showed how many were irresponsible, unbalanced and even malicious. In its introduction it looked at the recent past.

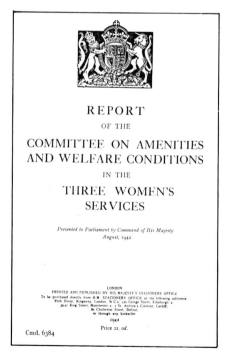

REPORT
OF THE
COMMITTEE ON AMENITIES
AND WELFARE CONDITIONS
IN THE
THREE WOMEN'S
SERVICES

Presented to Parliament by Command of His Majesty
August, 1942

LONDON
PRINTED AND PUBLISHED BY HIS MAJESTY'S STATIONERY OFFICE
To be purchased directly from H.M. STATIONERY OFFICE at the following addresses
York House, Kingsway, London, W.C.2; 120 George Street, Edinburgh 2;
39-41 King Street, Manchester 2; 1 St. Andrew's Crescent, Cardiff;
80 Chichester Street, Belfast;
or through any bookseller
1942
Price 1s. 0d.

Cmd. 6384

Title page of The Markham Report.

'The rapid expansion of the services has been accompanied by a large, if inevitable measure of improvisation. Accommodation, clothing, equipment, had to be supplied under conditions of considerable difficulty. Officers new to their responsibilities had to carry out duties for which they were imperfectly trained. There was for a time discomfort in some units, confusion in others, deficiencies aggravated by very severe weather. Rumours began to circulate. Sometimes they took the form of concrete charges about bad conditions, sometimes of vague accusations about drink and immorality.'

One by one the charges were taken up, examined and where substantiated, recommendations made. The Report scotched entirely the accusations of loose morality.

'Virtue has no gossip value,' as it states dryly. 'With certainty the illegitimate birth rate in the services is lower than the illegitimate birth rate among the comparable civilian population.'

Statistics also showed that the incidence of Venereal Disease was half of that for men and that 'the Members of the Committee have been impressed by the low incidence reported in the Women's Services'.

Since the Report dealt with all the Women's Services, some of its recommendations were unsuitable for the WAAF, but others were taken up and acted upon. Most far reaching, perhaps, was the introduction of postings of WAAF Officers to other Directorates affecting WAAF matters, such as Supply and Organization, Air Force Welfare, Training and the Inspectorate. It also placed a greater emphasis on the length and quality of Officer training — which had been planned in any case, once suitable accommodation and time was available — and it foreshadowed the introduction of a new concept in broadening the minds of airwomen, on which the Director was already working, and which was later to become known as Progressive Training. The Report also led to more decentralization of the work of the Directorate, and an increase in the Councils and Committees meant to improve the WAAF channels of communication and give the Director advice.

The report and its repercussions reverberated in the Air Council and once again a Commandant became the scapegoat for the scrambled start of the women's service. In 1941 Dame Helen Gwynne-Vaughan had been asked to leave her post as Director of the ATS on the grounds of age — she was 62. Now a rift appeared between the WAAF Director Air Commandant Trefusis-Forbes, and the Air Member for Personnel, Sir Bertine Sutton. In the Air Council he fought in support of the WAAF.

'The Committee does not appear to appreciate the fundamental difference between Army and RAF organisations, nor perhaps that certain difficulties in administration are not capable of solution by any service, since they are governed by Cabinet policy.'

In private his willingness to speak on behalf of the Director and her service infuriated her.

'I said I was dead sick of having my views explained by someone else, and that it was high time *I* explained my own views to the Air Council and other people.'

Air Commandant Ruth Mary Eldridge Welsh, Director 1943-46 with Mrs Churchill at a WAAF Fifth Anniversary Exhibition in June 1944 (Mrs Jarvis).

There were also the usual protests that letters and files were not going through the proper channels, or being delayed until no action was possible. There were complaints of discharges, lack of guidance, or any sense of urgency. Many matters were trivial and mere pinpricks, but they added up to a loss of confidence between two people who had to work closely together, if anything was to be achieved. Matters came to a head in two informal meetings on 3 and 4 November 1942, after which although they stayed personally on friendly terms, the Director 'had such a silent war with him that I have contracted Hun Pox. Bless him!'

A way out of the impasse appeared when Canada, which was having difficulties in recruiting its own airwomen, asked for a visit from the Director to mark in October 1943 the first Anniversary of the creation of its Women's Division of the Royal Canadian Air Force. This provided a providential excuse for her to relinquish the Directorship on the grounds that she was being seconded for special duties. It would prevent speculation by press, politicans and even the WAAF themselves, which could shake the confidence of Officers and airwomen in the Director and possibly cause a scandal that would harm the WAAF. Also she would be able to keep her rank and still work for the service. She put forward her ideas on this matter to the Air Member for Personnel. It worked, and in recognition she kept the rank of Air Chief Commandant and remained the senior serving Officer of the service.

Violet Markham, in a letter dated 1 October 1943, commiserates with her.

'I feel nothing but distress personally about this change — it seems so very unnecessary. I think your own behaviour has been *faultless* and I can't say how much I admire it and you. It's an object lesson in perfect dignity and perfect loyalty, and we are all your debtors for it.'

Her east–west tour of Canada telling people about the work of the WAAF was extended to include the United States. In 1944 she became Dame Katherine Trefusis-Forbes (Katherine being her first name), on being awarded the DBE in the New Year's Honours list, and then headed a mission to the Far East to examine the feasibility of employing airwomen there, after which she retired from the WAAF to follow civilian interests. In 1966 she became Lady Watson-Watt, when she married the inventor of radar.

The former Inspector of the WAAF, Lady Mary Welsh, became the next Director of the WAAF on 4 October 1943, and ultimately Air Chief Commandant. She was 47, married to an Air Marshal and had a 17 year old son. She forwarded and extended the work of Dame Katherine in her own particular way. During her tour of duty she turned the new Advisory Council into an instrument of Administration and gradually strengthened the Director's role. She saw the gradual merging of messing and sometimes living accommodation for WAAF and RAF, the further extension of the duties of specialist Officers and NCOs into administration and welfare, and in particular vetted, and then supported, postings of airwomen overseas. Under her, the WAAF settled down and matured.

Dame Mary Welsh, as she became, remained Director through the last war years and during demobilization in the peace that followed. At the end of 1946, she asked to be relieved of her post, and, this granted, she retired. Her rank of Air Chief Commandant was, however, never used again.

To these two Directors, the one who created and the other who strengthened the WAAF by difficult and often seemingly unrewarding work, is owed the continuation of the WRAF today on such secure foundations.

During these years also, the Queen, now the Queen Mother, became Commandant in Chief of the WAAF, and the Duchess of Gloucester began her long and affectionate association with the service. On 25 April 1941, the Duchess was granted a commission into the WAAF, with retrospective seniority to her first appointment as Air Commandant on 23 February 1940. In 1943 she was created Air Chief Commandant and was promoted to Air Marshal on 1 September 1968.

Chapter 10

The Worst And Best Of Days

'Discipline in its true sense is the training of one's mental, moral and physical powers by instruction and exercise.'

NCO Handbook 1942

Because of the hurried beginning of the WAAF and because it was not expected to grow so soon nor so large, the WAAF Depots for Initial Training, turning civilian girls into airwomen in a few weeks, moved from one place to another. Many airwomen then proceeded to other stations for periods ranging from weeks to months to undergo technical training for their trade, usually in company with airmen trainees. Only afterwards were they posted to their first working RAF station.

West Drayton was the first WAAF Depot, but planned as a RAF transit centre it was far from perfect — foggy, liable to flooding on a low lying site, and with spartan accommodation which became increasingly crowded. Nevertheless it was better than a tented camp — an earlier suggestion — and had the feel of a RAF camp from the moment the newcomer entered by the Guardroom. Group Captain Blackburn — bearded to disguise a First World War wound — was Commanding Officer (CO) of the station in which the WAAF formed a separate unit under its own female CO, Squadron Officer McAlery.

Flight Sergeant Farrington became NCO in charge of training. His 'permanent staff had all been given "Sergeant" rank and were referred to as sub-Officers. Most were pre-war volunteers, some were wives of senior RAF Officers, and some even had titles of some sort.'

They were, however, woefully insufficient and inexperienced, the syllabus and lectures still in an experimental state.

During a recruit's fortnight there, she had 14 hours of lectures on RAF organization and administration and 15 on anti-gas measures and station defence. Then in order to prepare her physically for conditions she might have to face on her station and give her a sense of discipline, she spent about 6 hours on physical training and 12 on drill — one of the few subjects on which the staff felt knowledgeable.

Despite the difficulties, health was good — none of the 14,000 women who passed through the Depot was listed as dangerously ill — and enthusiasm triumphed. For Carmel Jackson, 'It was a great start to my service life. I loved the drill and the uniform, accepted the discipline and enjoyed the instruction, though there could have been more.'

Organized games, dances and concerts provided the necessary recreation, which included the station drum and fife band. Janet Rowson was there when it started.

'The WAAF Officer came round the huts and asked if anyone could read music. As I could do so, a fife was thrust into my hand. I put it to my lips and immediately I blew, notes came out. I was in! I promise these were the only sounds that ever issued forth as I proudly paraded up and down the parade ground, appearing to play.'

By May 1940, Mary Bowen notes, 'Over 1,000 girls outnumbered men 30 to 1. Much discussion on what to call female Officers. "Ma'am" finally decided upon.'

Group Captain Gaskell-Blackburn, the CO of WAAF Depots at West Drayton, Harrogate and Bridgnorth, with a WAAF Officer and the WAAF Depot mascot – a bulldog (Mrs France).

Most large stations had a WAAF Band of some kind. They practised in their spare time and were much in demand (Mrs Faw).

WHAT A WAR!

by GILBERT WILKINSON

' Now, girls, o n e, t w o, buckle my shoe; three, four, knock at the door!'

Learning to March, 1942 (Mrs Chadwick).

Local houses were taken over, but by 13 September 1940, when Kay Baker arrived 'apart from PT and a little drill, owing to the Blitz most of our time was spent in air raid shelters. After four days we were moved to Ashville College outside Harrogate.'

This was the first move of the Depot. Initial Training took slightly more than 14 days when Naomi Fillery went to Harrogate in October 1940, the extra being used by medical examinations, issues of uniform — now in supply — and 1250s, the RAF identity card. To her 'the food was excellent and how hungry we were doing all that square bashing' (the ever-present drill).

Snow was early in the winter of 1940. Edna Sutherland 'drilled in the Valley gardens with thick snow on the ground. Uniform had to be worn at all times, except on leave or three day pass. The shoes made very bad blisters on my heels, which excused me from a route march once, but I had to scrub the Mess hall floor instead — it was huge! Most of us were adjusting OK but a few considered deserting and the rumour went around that it was OK providing you sent your uniform back. As I remember, one girl did.'

German bombing was reaching its peak and travel was often difficult. Barbara Kirkham and four companions found the journey to Harrogate quite traumatic.

'As the train arrived in Birmingham, the air raid sirens were wailing and from thereon, all the way to Sheffield, the sound of aircraft could be heard droning overhead. As the train edged towards Sheffield station, a great glow in the sky told us what was happening. The train was blacked out, full of troops, enveloped in a fog of cigarette smoke.' At Sheffield station, which held an unexploded land-mine, 'we were shepherded into a shelter until we had to leave early because of danger. What a sight met our eyes. There were fire hoses criss-crossed all over the place, a nearby hotel had its windows boarded up and smoke was still rising and lingering in a cloud on the morning air. Everything was a shambles. The police suggested we might try to get a bed in the YMCA. When we entered the place, there were firemen everywhere, even standing up straight against the walls, trying to get some sleep.

'We spent three snowy days in Sheffield before we finally managed to contact the WAAF Depot where Wing Commander Gaskell Blackburn, though none of us was absolutely perfect medically, said he would not dream of sending any of us back home after what we had been through.' From that time forward, she found that she was 'kept busy from morning to night with drill, lectures and everything, and didn't have much time to get homesick, especially as it was Christmas and the whole intake was inoculated with Tetanus, TB and other jabs. My fellow trainees were a great bunch and we had many a laugh, sometimes at the expense of the permanent staff, who seemed to take themselves so seriously.'

At the beginning of 1941, courses returned to 14 days to cope with another period of growing demand for WAAF, resulting in intakes of 2,000 girls a week. A Number 2 Depot opened at Innsworth, and Harrogate became Number 1 WAAF Depot. In February 1941, Dorothy Newton spent the first few days 'doing drill in civvies in a park opposite the Grand Hotel [where many of them lodged]. The dining room was pleasant, the beds comfortable, but the ablutions were chaotic.

'After a few lectures we thought we could recognise an Officer until we wrongly saluted a merchant seaman. Some time later we were sent to one of the

WAAF Kitting Up, *1941, a painting by Charles Cundall* (Flt Lt Moore).

PERSONAL ISSUE OF CLOTHING & NECESSARIES		
1 Cape, Ground Sheet	1 pr. Slacks	1 Button Stick
1 Greatcoat	1 pr. Canvas Shoes	1 Identity Disk No. 1
1 Respirator	1 pr. Overboots	1 Identity Disk No. 2
1 Steel Helmet	2 prs. Knickers	1 Kitbag
1 Cap, with Badge	2 prs. Pantees	1 Ration Bag
1 Cap Comforter	2 Vests	1 Anti-Gas Cape
2 Jackets	2 Brassières	3 Eyeshields
2 Skirts	2 Suspender Belts	1 Curtain (anti-gas for Steel Helmet)
3 Shirts	2 Corselettes to women of bust sizes 40, 42 or 44	
6 Collars ; 1 Tie		
1 Cardigan		
1 pr. Gloves	2 Hand Towels	1 Field Dressing
3 prs. Stockings	1 Housewife	2 tins Anti-Gas Ointment
2 prs. Shoes	1 pkt. Sanitary Towels	
1 pr. Laces		1 Hairbrush

Extract from a 1942 list of issue clothing, etc.

colleges at a place called Pannal Ash for further training and lectures, and to decide what trade we wanted.'

But the days at Harrogate were numbered. At the end of May 1941, Number 1 Depot moved lock, stock and barrel to the hutted camp at Bridgnorth, Shropshire.

Betty Snow's travel warrant came by post with instructions to report to Bridgnorth.

'On arrival we were taken to our billets and allocated a bed space. A bed 6 ft by 2½ ft stood before each of us and stacked on top were three square fawn buttoned mattresses known as biscuits [another girl feelingly comments 'and they felt like them too']. These placed end to end on the bed springs were indeed the mattress'.

The trick was to prevent them parting company in the night, usually by wrap-

Left *A member of the permanent staff at RAF Bridgnorth 1941, standing on the drill square in front of the hutted accommodation. The ablution hut is on the rear right (Mrs France).*

Right Cartoon Pay Parade (Mrs Wisby).

ping a sheet around them. There were also two white sheets, supplied to women but not men, and some grey woollen blankets.

'The making of the bed was the first task, with instructions that it would be stacked after use every morning and then made up afresh after the daily inspection [DI].

'The following morning was taken up by interviews to assess one's grade of intelligence. As my turn came, I realized that the next 20 minutes would decide just what I was going to be doing for the duration of hostilities. At this stage, the word "remuster" [changing to another trade] was not part of my normal vocabulary. My turn duly arrived and I sat down confronted by a RAF NCO and a pad of paper and pencil. I was asked if I knew what I wanted to do. Then the time came to put pen to paper and answer an assortment of questions on Arithmetic, General Knowledge and Spelling. It must have been my lucky day for the answers came readily to mind. It was suggested that I be a clerk SD and I was on my way out. Thank heavens that was over.'

When being kitted out she comments on issue underwear, 'which was made to last rather than enhance the female figure, the alternative being that one should wear one's own civilian undies. This was allowed, but it has to be remembered that when we enlisted, our clothing coupons [issued June 1941] were withdrawn. This resulted in our personal wardrobes being depleted very rapidly, so we finally had to resort to them.'

Winnie Smith found in lectures that 'most went in one ear and out of the other. The food was ghastly,' but she vividly remembers the injections. 'I think we were pincushions for them to practise on but not one of us fell by the wayside, unlike the men.' Later on, at pay parade, 'my foot slipped as I made my salute and I ended up at the salute with my chin resting on the paymaster's table. Even the Officer had to smile.'

Sandy Sandeman was a NCO instructor there. A friend later told her that she 'was considered a small holy terror!' and 'the recruits did much dodging around barracks so they wouldn't come under my eye for things like wearing silk stockings, buttons and shoes not shined, etc.'

Bridgnorth as Number 1 Depot closed in September 1942, but Innsworth in Gloucester had a longer life, as Number 2 WAAF Depot, going through three transformations as recruit numbers waxed and waned. It started in January 1941 with the overspill from Harrogate. In mid-1941, intakes rose to 3,000 per week and soon threatened to rise to 4,000 with National Service. Accordingly, in October 1941, Innsworth became a centre only for the few days of reception and kitting. This was then followed by basic training at a third Depot which was set up at Morecambe. In February 1943, as a result of the Markham report, Innsworth returned to reception and training for recruits from the south of England, until August that year when its role with the WAAF passed to Wilmslow.

'In January 1943, at the age of seventeen,
I joined the Women's Air Force — so young and fresh and green.
I did my basic training at Gloucester in the rain,
And found it quite bewildering, with not a little pain.'

So wrote June Jenkins, whose feelings were shared by a fellow recruit Kathleen Myers, who lived locally, and on arrival asked the WAAF orderly who met her, 'Will I get out of camp tonight?'

'Once you are in here, you are in for a week.'

Among the first things to encounter was the medical FFI — free from infection — a check given on arrival at or departure from any RAF station, as well as monthly throughout service life. It was mainly to watch for signs of pregnancy, venereal disease or head lice. Anne Miller describes it as performing 'a quick flash (pants down) for the benefit of the doctor and then the medical orderly went through our hair with a fine toothcomb'.

After this came dinner in a long concrete-floored hut with wooden forms and trestle tables, occupied by die-hards enjoying the plight of the rookies (beginners). Kathleen Myers continues, 'We grab a plate, hold it out to the girl behind the hotplate and get thrown upon it with great vehemence a spoonful of potatoes. We walk a few paces to another WAAF who provides us with cabbage and meat. Another thuds a piece of pudding of unknown variety on the same plate. We retire to a table and declare we'd never eat such terrible food, but by next day we were glad to.'

Kitting usually took place on the same day as arrival. Elsie Goodwin lists all the articles with which she was provided.

'In the Equipment Section or Stores as it was called, you wandered up and down alleyways between counters and racks, collecting items for approximately two hours.'

That night, Anne Miller was shown how to lay everything out on her bed 'in a certain prescribed pattern. By the time an Officer appeared at our hut and inspected our kit, which for the first and last time I had actually laid out in its entirety, it was approaching midnight.' Later, 'inevitable missing items caused

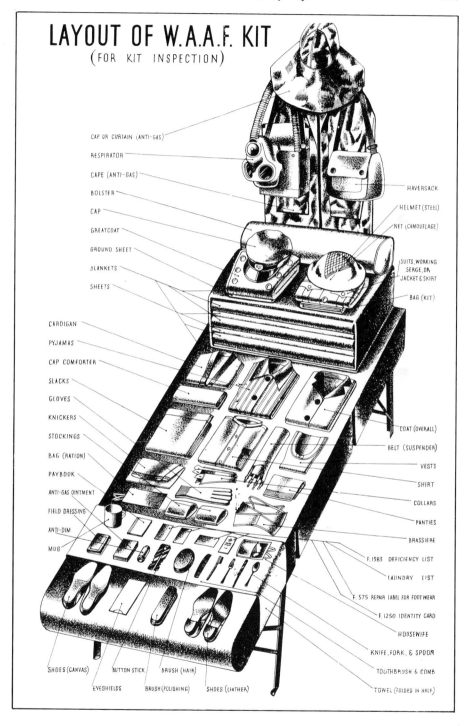

Prescribed layout for service kit, 1944 (Miss Durance).

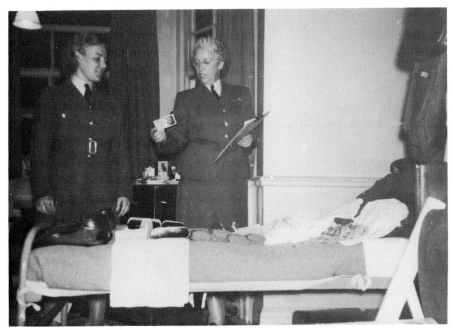

Kit inspections were similar, even in 1956 when this photograph was taken (Miss Whittle).

terrifying repercussions, and fines.'

Summing up the Innsworth of this period, Elsie Harvey thinks, 'We were all, without exception, very thankful to leave Innsworth behind us. The first five days are in my opinion the worst days of a service career.'

It had become, in fact, a very much depersonalized, gigantic conveyor-belt system. Una Styles found it much improved in later 1943, when Innsworth had reverted to reception and training.

'On the whole I enjoyed the experience. The worst discomfort was the weight on one's shoulders of the heavy greatcoats and the hard beds. We ached from these. Then the inoculations added to our pains.'

Anne O'Hara, a National Service Conscript, lists her points for and against.

'Oh those sore feet, aching limbs and tear-stained pillows! Sleeping with windows open in February. Getting used to the tannoy which terrified me at first. Having my hair cut short. Wearing knickers with elastic in the legs. Sewing buttons upside down on my greatcoat and being told in front of the whole parade about it. Shocked to find what powers NCOs and Officers had. Gradually submitting to find I was enjoying it all. Marching in step to the RAF March and loving it. Free laundry. Free hairdressing [or nearly so] — what luxury to have a professional! A doctor when you need him. Free dental care. Beginning to respect NCOs and Officers for the enormous amount of responsibility they had.'

However, back in 1942, having completed her reception stage at Innsworth,

Stella Enfield was ready to be sent for basic training to Number 3 Depot at Morecambe.

'We paraded at 5.30 am. Breakfast of tinned kidneys, a memorably horrid taste. Given two corned beef sandwiches and a bar of chocolate as a packed lunch. The journey took something like 12 hours. By afternoon the sandwiches left were so stale that we opened them up and put chocolate on top. At Morecambe railway station, the landladies came and inspected us — a bit like a slave market. I got a single room in a clean boarding house. The food was terrible — corned beef in different disguises.'

Some were not so lucky. Denise Miley met bed bugs there for the first time in her life, and her billet was hastily changed. Joyce Parsons' billet was very crowded but her landlady 'was a dear. On Sunday, an enormous pot of tea and a huge plate of butties was left at the door and we could stay in bed as long as we liked.'

Anne Miller wrote to her family:

'Morecambe is a typical sort of seaside place with switchbacks and piers and row upon row of boarding houses, where we lodge. An average day consists of 7 am Get up. 7.30 Brekker. 8.30 On parade 10 minutes up the road — march off in your squad (36 girls) to some cinema or hall for a lecture on something or other — gas, pay, leave, kit, behaviour etc. About 10.30 Tea or coffee. More marching and lectures, drilling. 12.30 Dinner at billet. 1.30 Parade, same procedure. PT every other day, more drill, more lectures. 5-ish Dismiss after getting mail. 5.30

'Square-bashing' for a special visitor at Kidbrooke in winter overcoats. Note the belts supporting gas-mask containers and tin helmets (Mrs Hodges).

High tea. Back at our billets. We are free every evening to go to the cinemas, dances etc.'

Helen Shanks found that 'we provided free entertainment on the prom for holidaymakers', while 'square-bashing on the sea-front in winter and gale force winds' is engraved on Joy Silverwood's memory. On Stella Cottman's is 'a sadistic Drill Sergeant (RAF) who marched us to the very brink of steep drops'.

Elsie Goodwin records their gas lectures:

'We had to wear our respirators for 15 minutes after first rubbing the eyepieces with anti-dim solution to prevent them steaming with the heat of our breath. It was almost unbearably funny to see 250 girls all wearing respirators. Every time we breathed there was a sort of snort. We looked and sounded like a roomful of black pigs. We also had to learn to adjust our respirators within five seconds of the gas rattle. When we had practised five or six times our hair looked like washing-up mops.'

Helen Shanks took away a lasting memory of 'an Officer's lecture on the economy use of toilet paper — one piece per sitting, one sitting per day'. Anne Stobbs records 'a completely waterlogged class' sitting down 'for an hour and a half, while a RAF Corporal gave us a gramophone recital of classical music and we sat shivering in pools of water, sneezing our heads off'.

But there were rewards. 'After our Passing Out Parade, our Flight Sergeant said we were the best batch he's had through Morecambe for many a long day.'

The hutted camp at Wilmslow in Cheshire opened for northern recruits in February 1943, and took over for all new entrants in August that year, as numbers started to ease off. Then mainly conscripts, they took time to adjust, but in 1944 they formed such a tiny proportion that conscription ceased, as they were far outnumbered by volunteers.

At Wilmslow, courses lasted about one month — one week on reception, followed by three weeks on training wing. Of this part, Rita Terry, a somewhat reluctant volunteer says, 'We were given the option to return to civvy street

'Oh it's lovely to be beside the seaside'. The pier and kiosk behind the Morecambe promenade form a backdrop to the marching WAAF (Mrs Hierons).

Gas Squad clothed for training without its masks (Mrs Patrick).

about seven to ten days after joining. Quite a number of girls took advantage of this, but much as I would have liked to opt out, I couldn't face the thought of returning home to family and friends feebly saying I didn't like it, which was true, so I was determined to stick it out.'

Pamela Gibbons found the training '... four very long weeks. The accommodation in Nissen huts along with 30 other rookies was something of a shock to the system, having been accustomed to privacy. My mother was a cook, so food fell well short of her standards. Few of us took kindly to discipline, although we were not foolish enough to disobey.'

Yet for Millie Rosenthal, it was 'the first discipline I'd ever received as an only child, and I thoroughly enjoyed it'. Wilmslow continued for the rest of the war and until 1960.

Wartime Moves of WAAF Depots 1939-45

	1939	1940	1941	1942	1943	1944-45
West Drayton	10	9				
Harrogate			No. 1 9	5	South Receiving & Training	
Innsworth			No 2 12	Receiving Only 10	2 8	
Bridgnorth			No 1 8	9		
Morecambe				No 3 Training Only 10	North Receiving & Training 2	All. Receiving & Training
Wilmslow					2 8	

The first course attended by Administrative NCOs to become PTIs at Innsworth (Mrs Heaton).

It is interesting to see that WAAF have always been marked by certain characteristics while in training, be it in basic, trade or other courses. In comparison with their RAF counterparts they were usually more intense and highly-strung. Generally, they were inveterate note-takers, more conscientious, assimilating theory less well than practical work, and prone to worry over progress. Allowing for the disadvantages and limitations of their civil education, when in mixed classes they tended to come in first or last.

Once Initial Training for airwomen was settled, the question of NCO training could be considered. WAAF NCOs had great responsibilities but, except for a few First World War veterans, little experience. Though a short course could not tell them all they needed to know, nor give them all the qualities they required, it. would be, at any rate, a step in the right direction. Naturally stations often tried to provide some training of their own but more was needed. The earliest courses were set up for Administrative NCOs — the Corporals and Sergeants who dealt with the moral and physical needs of their airwomen. Everything from drill and bedchecks to comforting homesick or bereaved airwomen fell into their province. These courses varied in length from two to three weeks and moved, often in tandem with the Recruit Depot, from station to station, although they spent some time at St Athan and Melksham and missed out Morecambe. By 1942, at Innsworth on their fourth move, a further course was introduced for Technical

NCOs, whose duties, for the most part, had formerly been limited only to their place of work. The 1943 reductions in WAAF Administrative staffs made the involvement of these NCOs even more essential, so that their courses were first lengthened to three weeks and then in 1944 combined with those for the Administrative NCOs, on the principle that both kinds of NCO had something to contribute to and teach the other. Hopeful LACWs were also included, and the course then became known as the Junior NCO General Service Training Course. When the war ended, the WAAF NCO Administrative School moved to Stoke Orchard where, except for one course at Digby, it remained until it closed.

The first WAAF Administrative Warrant Officer posts were created in 1941, necessitating a more advanced form of training for Senior NCOs. A special three-weeks course thus began in January 1942, continuing into 1943, which reached down to include Sergeants in all trades. By 1944 the course was at Wilmslow and had become the Senior General Service Training Course, where it met with its Junior partner in what was now part of the WAAF NCO Administrative School.

Organized Officer training was slow to start, and then it was somewhat piecemeal. There were courses for Instructors and Staff Officers, for Codes and Cypher Officers, for Administrative and Non-Administrative Officers, for those already in the service without previous training, for refreshing and updating earlier training (some of these later rejoicing in the letters A, B and C), and last but not least, for an Officer Cadet Training Unit known as OCTU. Until the appearance of the OCTU, Officers were commissioned at the point where the Selection Boards chose them from the airwomen presented. Afterwards, their commissions were only awarded when, and if, they successfully completed their OCTU course. Ailsa Stevenson found the selection process a terrifying ordeal. After interviews with various WAAF Officers, 'You had to have an interview with the CO of your station. Then with the AOC of your Group. I was struck dumb with the AOC. The rings on his sleeve, the medals on his chest, and the twinkle in his eye. [It was the famous 'Bomber' Harris.] Then to Air Ministry. I remember every terrible moment.'

Having wandered between Air Ministry, Reading and Gerrards Cross, the WAAF Officers School, as it had come to be called, came to rest at Bulstrode Park, Gerrards Cross, its CO being the first WAAF Officer to command a station. Under the headline 'Blossoming Out' a newspaper photograph shows some trousered WAAF doing PT among the daffodils with their RAF instructor. The caption reads, 'For two weeks in a country mansion, they undergo a course to fit them to command'.

In July 1941 they took over Loughborough Training College with space enough for not the 100 of Bulstrode but 350, and courses expanded from two to six weeks. They split into many parts and from one the WAAF OCTU emerged in August 1942, alongside the other courses. Unfortunately this stretched the College to its limits, causing part of the overspill OCTU to be housed at Grange-over-Sands.

Finally, at the end of 1942 the WAAF Officers School and the OCTU both

Tea at the Windermere OCTU, 1944 (Mrs Craufurd-Stuart).

moved to Windermere, where they were housed in the Old England and Belsfield Hotels and some huts in the grounds. It was damp but lovely enough to be enjoyed. Joyce Parsons illustrates its informality.

'Whilst at OCTU in Windermere I cleverly twisted my ankle. This meant that I was excused drills and spent many a pleasant hour in a canoe on the lake learning my work.'

The eight-week OCTU remained at Windermere until it closed in March 1945, but the WAAF Officers School had still not finished its wanderings. In August 1944 it settled in Stratford-upon-Avon where Pip Hugill was an instructor.

'Our Mess was in the Falcon Hotel and I lived in the Arden. The airwomen had the Marie Corelli House as their Mess.'

Having no parade ground, the girls drilled in the gardens in front of the theatre, to the great entertainment of the public who had come to see the Shakespeare plays. Nevertheless, most Officers had happy memories of their days there and it was 'the best of all homes' for the School.

However, courses became smaller, the war ended and Stratford closed down in November 1945. One course then moved to Stoke Orchard and eventually, becoming too small, finished in March 1946.

This poem, although written of Bridgnorth in 1942, well evokes the spirit of these training days.

'Wooden huts in rows so tidy,
Homesick thoughts beneath the hills,
Narrow iron beds we hide in,
Bright the lino polished floors.

Stifled yawns at morning lecture,
Rubber stench at gas-mask drill,
Whispered jokes and pangs of hunger
Long the queue for Dining Hall.

Eager march to stores for fitting
Uniforms we proudly don,
Underwear for Active Service?
Vanity and frills begone!

Shoes and buttons, badges shining,
Floor and metal polish smell,
Tannoy's interrupting whining,
"Attention, all WAAF Personnel!"

All too soon the time for leaving
Hills and huts and shining floor.
Kit inspected; pay paraded;
Final march to Guardroom door.

Filled with bright anticipation,
All aglow with shining brass,
Pray salute us, proudly passing,
Aircraft Women, Second Class!'

Kathleen Chamant

Chapter 11

Petticoats In The RAF

November 25 1943, the diary of ACW1 Joan Hamer, fabric worker, Pembroke Dock.

'Up late again. Friends threaten to pull biscuits from under me. Quick wash and dress. Ablutions very primitive — only cold water. Never unknot tie, slip loop over head and pull up. Whizzed downhill to main camp on bike — no lights. Never made breakfast yet.

'Inspection parade this morning — some bigwig with scrambled egg [gold leaves for Group Captains and above] on cap. Found I was the only WAAF wearing trousers. Brass hat looked puzzled but said nothing — WAAF Sgt Mac did afterwards. Worked down the "dope" shop today. My turn to collect big jug of milk from cookhouse. Got chit from Sgt "Blondie" — poor lad, we lead him a dog's life! Cookhouse staff always object to parting with milk, but we have to take it as fumes from the dope get on the chest. Fingers still sore from screwing fabric to elevator frame.

'Went across to NAAFI for tea and wads [buns]. Why does NAAFI tea always have that peculiar taste? Called in Parachute Section on way back. Love to watch them packing the chutes — don't think I'd like to do it though.

'Managed to get across to bath hut. Water hot for a change. Mice been at my soap again — have to move it from that cupboard. Why are there never any bath or basin plugs? What do people do with them?

'Sunderland back from mission — flew low dipping over camp. Must have seen a U boat in the Bay of Biscay. Looked through window. Saw lads winching a Sunderland up the slipway — another job for us later in the week when the fitters and riggers have stripped it. One of the girls in workshops got a machine needle right through her finger, stitching heavy canvas. Poor lass passed out when it was removed.

'Liver on menu for tea — ugh, don't like it. Called in Sally Ann [Salvation Army canteen] on way to billet — hymn-singing along with a cup of tea — but at least they make better tea than NAAFI.

'Bull night tonight [domestic night]. Not allowed out — officially. Clean around bedspace, and so on. Someone's lit stove — thank goodness. It gets very cold on this site. What a bind [nuisance] having to stay in. Finished chores — feeling rather hungry. Wonder if I should try climbing wall to go to pub down the road for sandwiches? Better not. Landlord not too keen on WAAF. Ah well! Bed made, might as well get in — at least it will be warmer. Goodness, these beds are hard, will I ever get used to them? Pillows are a dead loss too — straw filled — must bring cushion back next time I go on leave. Someone's lent me a good book, so I'll read till lights out. Must try and make it to breakfast tomorrow!'

This was the typical, unremarkable day of an average WAAF. As Aggie Bolton points out, 'From films and novels one would think that the only airwomen around were clerk SDs [plotters and operations room staff] or to provide a bit of slap and tickle for the pilots. All honour to clerk SDs of course, but there were dozens of other trades. As for pilots, I don't think the average WAAF ever spoke to one. Some girls were in for years and never saw a plane. We did occasionally get asked for a date by aircrew, but we hardly ever accepted. There were too many snags, it had to be hole and corner stuff, and male ground crew were upset and could be offensive about it. We shared work, mess and NAAFI with them and preferred to be on good terms.'

A normal day began with reveille at 6.30 am, with breaks for drill or parades, lunch and high tea, work usually lasting from about 8.30 am until 5.30 pm. A supper of cocoa and sometimes sandwiches or biscuits preceded bed at 10.30 pm. Airwomen generally had 2 late passes a week, which could be spent off camp until a minute before midnight, 24 hours off per week, 48 hours per month and 7 days' leave every 3 months with 4 free railway warrants a year. Unfortunately the standard 48 hour working week frequently became 60 hours or more, particularly for domestic staff like Cooks. Watchkeeping duties, involving shift work and awkward timings, occupied 18 per cent of the WAAF.

Though accommodation varied, huts on camp, whether of timber, concrete or corrugated metal, were best remembered, and a hot bath and keeping warm were the chief preoccupations. In the long cold winter of 1943-44, it was Queenie Lee's task '. . . to stand in the freezing snow and issue each hut-orderly

Aerial view of part of a typical RAF station (Mrs Lambert).

airwoman one lump of coal and half a bucket of coke to last an evening. We all went to the local woods to collect firewood. One airwoman acquired a pickaxe and dug up a disused cinder path which burned beautifully.'

Daphne Smith 'can still remember climbing the high wire fence of the coal compound to get extra coal, while my mates kept watch, nearly getting caught'. Paddy Martin and the girls of her hut found it a struggle with only one stove. It was 'a choice of fuel for the stove or heating the bath water. Most opted for the luxury of a hot bath.' Lavender Benthall found a way round part of the problem by 'taking my hot water-bottle to the pictures and getting it filled at the YMCA on Cardiff station to bring it back to my icy bed. Next morning I used to wash in the luke-warm contents.'

Above *NAAFI van* (Mrs Mathews).

Left *September 1941 at Brampton. Another hazard was water shortage. In the background is a bowser bringing in the strictly ration-ed water* (Mrs Dexter).

Above right *Laundry Day in a WAAF hut* (Mrs Douglas).

There were from 12 to 30 beds in a room, arranged along the two sides, alternately head to foot, to prevent the spread of infections and with a bed space of 1½ ft to 2 ft between. After 1943, there were often two-layered bunks. The Director felt that the furnishing scale should approximate as near to the RAF's as possible, which in bedrooms usually consisted of a small shelf above the bed and a few pegs for uniform. An orange-box as a bedside table was a prized possession, as was a chair.

Underground air-raid shelters were usually nearby but if all else failed in an air-raid, there were always the beds, as Hazel Goodeve found.

'Our Sergeant shouted to us to get under our beds with our tin hats on. I was scared, until I saw my friend Edna had not been able to get under her bed, so her bottom was sticking out with her tin hat perched on top.'

Daphne Smith and the girls 'at Great Dunmow had a plague of rats as big as cats. They took over our Nissen huts and we had to keep the lights on all night in the hope of scaring them off. A question was raised by one of our girls' fathers, an MP, and the rat-catcher was called in.'

But there were compensations, as Joan Pearce describes.

'A hut could be very cosy on a winter's evening, with the coke stove glowing in the centre and girls sitting chattering, mending stockings [and "our dainty winter woollies"], polishing buttons, shoes and other things. Especially if the majority got on well with each other. There could be friction of course, but my main recollection is of comradeship.'

Members of a good hut would make up the bed of someone arriving late from leave, and have a hot cup of cocoa waiting on the stove.

Moves from one hut to another, or one kind of accommodation to another, on the same camp, happened regularly, often to the bewilderment of members who had been away for more than a day and had to trek around the camp in the dark to find their new home. Joan Martin records a pleasant surprise.

'When we moved into barrack blocks it was just like moving into Buckingham Palace. Now we had nice cosy buildings, where we didn't have to use our gas capes tucked over our blankets to insulate the warmth, and the mice must have missed their game of running up and down our clothes hanging on the walls.'

Kay Stewart was in a pre-war Married Quarter.

'I shared a room with one or two other girls. The bath was in the kitchen and the copper had to be lit to get hot water. We all congregated there after work. It was warm, full of laughter and chatter, with one girl in the bath, another ironing, another washing clothes or hair.'

Understandably, older women found the almost non-existent privacy very trying.

Airwomen found many uses for metal helmets. One was for protecting hair under the shower in the ablutions, where handbasins, toilets, showers and baths (water depth was limited to the four to five-inch line painted inside) were sometimes together and sometimes separated and scattered, for hygiene and safety reasons, a good distance away from the huts. Chemical toilets or 'inconveniences' were not pleasant, though kept scrupulously clean by the daily rosta of duties [fatigues]. Joyce Fletcher explains.

'The RAF aircrafthands who had to take the lorry around RAF and WAAF sites to empty the Elsan toilet pans were known as the Lollipop men and their lorry "The Joy Wagon".'

'Cleanliness is next to Godliness, but it sure has its problems in winter,' remarks Doreen Compton, thinking of the long cold walk to the bath hut, of which Wendy Wenman tells a good story.

'One night after we came off watch at midnight, a small timid WAAF left our hut to go to the ablutions. Within minutes she was back, pale and trembling. "It's Rosata!" she gasped [the ghostly nun of the Priory], "she's in the ablutions." As she entered, she had seen a cubicle door shut noiselessly, carefully. There was no

Inside an ablutions hut, with curtained 'loos' (Miss Hodges).

sound, only a watching feeling. She went outside, then taking a grip of her courage, returned inside only to see a different door slide to, and still no sound or sign of movement. Doubting whether any self-respecting ghost would go in there, a friend and I went to investigate. As we reached the ablutions we almost collided with an aircrafthand, who disappeared into the night, grumbling, "What's the matter with all you women tonight? I've been trying to empty these ruddy buckets without embarrassing you for over an hour!" '

By now the girls were getting more difficult to embarrass. Joanna Markham details the unorthodox uses for another necessary item.

'I am sure that Lord Nuffield, the great benefactor of the WAAF, had no conception of the uses that were found for his free issue of sanitary towels. We cleaned our shoes and buttons with them. Paper tissue interiors were opened up and used as hankies. The cotton-wool type removed make-up and similar uses. The gauze casing was used for straining coffee grounds. Those with loops were wonderful for wearing across your eyes when trying to sleep after night duty; the loops fitted neatly over the ears.'

Accommodation costs for airwomen and Officers on camp and in lodgings were covered by a system of RAF allowances which made them, in effect, free. Food on camp was also free, but the WAAF only received four-fifths of the men's rations, for was it not known that women's appetites were smaller than men's? As eating in a mixed Mess became more general, this inequality was hardly noticed, because rations of men and women were pooled, and they were in any case equalized in 1944, but it showed in leave ration-money, and for Officers in lodgings. There is little doubt, however, that the services generally had more and better food than the heavily rationed civilians, though its quality varied according to the cooks, and grumbling about food is an occupational privilege of the services. Doris Quickie tells of 'Tea with a strange indefinable flavour which came from an urn previously used for onion soup', and Nancy Cox describes an incident during a meal, when 'The Duty Officer, as usual, asked, "Any complaints?" One airman stood up and said that he could not cut his fish. When the Officer investigated, it was discovered that the dish-cloth had fallen into the batter and been fried.' What grated most on WAAF sensibilities was washing their irons [cutlery] and mugs — labelled and kept by each personally — in a greasy trough of almost cold water after the meal.

Notwithstanding, days filled with hard work and exercise made everyone hungry. Pat Martin voiced a typical reaction.

'The food is good, you'll all agree. We clear up every plate,
And the consequence is, the poor old WAAF are rapidly gaining weight,
Our shirts no longer fit our frames, our collars do not meet,
And all's the fault of the Air Force cooks, who give us too much to eat.'

Uniform had to be bought by the WAAF Officers, partly funded with a grant which rose quickly from £15 to £30, and eventually to £55, as girls, commissioned from the ranks and having to live on their pay, could not afford it. For airwomen, their service clothes were free. Many remarked the delight on the faces of some girls receiving their first service issues, who had never owned so many lovely new clothes in their lives before. Uniform was a great leveller, and

Food, 1941 (Mrs Mitchell).

The Gainsborough Studio Wedding Dress (Mrs Martin).

was also worn all the time, except on leave, even to dances! With clothes rationing outside and no clothing coupons, threadbare items had to be replaced by the service. Elsie Goodwin describes what happened.

'Exchange Clothing Parade was held once a month to replace worn-out clothing with new. Queues of girls would form with items over their arms. Each article had to be freshly laundered and darned or mended respectably. The Officer would take the article in both hands and tug it. Only if the material around the mend split would she allow a replacement. It was humiliating to have to wear stockings with huge darns at heel and knee, but so long as they hadn't laddered, they would not be exchanged — so we used to make them ladder! The airmen of course were allowed to hand in unmended kit. Darns and patches were considered outside their métier.'

Among the items which stayed permanently with an airwoman throughout her service career were, beside her helmet, her tubular kit bag, her two fireproof identity discs — worn around the neck at all times — and her gas mask. As handbags had not yet made their appearance, and the pockets of the best tunic were not supposed to be filled, Dorothy Newton explains how airwomen solved this problem.

'The respirator box was used for carrying all the bits and pieces an airwoman needed when going on duty — money, make-up, hankies, comb and one or two other odds and ends — it was a wonder we had room for the gas mask, not to mention our protective eye-shields as well.'

As the majority of WAAF were young women, of less than 25 years of age, marriages were not infrequent, and though the girls were very proud of their uniform, they still relished special clothes for their wedding. Helen Warden, a plotter in the Operations Room, tells of what happened to her.

'One duty all being quiet, I had some lace spread over the ops table, cutting out a pair of cami-knickers for my trousseau, when in walked the Wing Commander in charge. I was lucky. He just smiled.'

Events turned out well for Peggy Sheppard, too.

'Mrs Roosevelt had sent six wedding dresses from America to be worn by service brides, and I was to borrow one. When the wedding date was changed because of postings, I could not have it. My WAAF Officer then arranged for me to borrow a wedding dress from Gainsborough Film Studios, so I went to choose one. I felt like a film star for one day.'

But on stations, particularly where there was flying, the girls worked under the shadow of tragedy. As Daphne Smith relates, 'I remember hearing the bombers leave and counting them coming in over the field early next day. Sometimes we lost a lot of friends and you would see WAAF red-eyed from weeping for one special boy. A terrible loss of human life, but you had to carry on with what had to be done.'

Joan Hamer, visiting the RAF Chapel on the camp to pay her respects to the three New Zealand crew of a crashed aircraft, saw and smelled the coffins of the

An exchange clothing parade as seen in a camp concert (Mrs Wing).

burned airmen, a memory which still brings tears to her eyes. Jeanie Rowley one day had 'an eerie sensation in our crew-room of hearing a voice saying, "Help me". I hunted round but there was no one there. Two days later, an Albemarle crashed on the crew-room killing six people, one a close friend.'

The airwomen faced tragedy and danger with equal bravery, not thinking that in time of war, it was out of the ordinary. Joy Forbes-Ashby was on one of the extra duties that fell to all WAAF, 'Firewatching. Kicked firebombs off the roof of the Ops building one night when things got hectic. Swore at the Group Captain and Wingco when they showed a bright light coming up on the roof where I was doing my stuff. Didn't suspect that Brass [Senior Officers] would be so dumb, but hid behind a chimney anyway.'

Accidents to airmen and airwomen at work were also not uncommon, despite all the rules on safety. Betty Duncan and her friend were listed seriously ill in hospital after being caught by a stray bullet as they crossed the parade ground at Middle Wallop, although fortunately both eventually recovered. At least one WAAF Mechanic, Margaret Horton, took an unexpected ride on the tail of an unsuspecting Spitfire and survived.

There were also the minor tragedies peculiar to women, though fortunately as the Markham report had indicated, unmarried pregnancies in the services were fewer than outside. Barbara Kirkham, as a NCO, gives a balanced opinion.

'The airwomen were in a very vulnerable position, young, away from home probably for the first time, with the kind of freedom they had never known before, faced with a bunch of happy-go-lucky daredevils, living for today and hang tomorrow. There were bound to be some calamities and some with tragic sequels. In those far off days, society was far from permissive.'

For the girl it was a terrible disgrace, from which she might never recover. Fortunately the WAAF were so carefully chaperoned 'that there was little opportunity for mischief'. Barbara Foad, who as an Officer dealt with many sad cases, found that, 'One thing that emerged overwhelmingly in my experience was that it was invariably the girl who was a quiet and law-abiding character who fell victim to pregnancy, through sheer ignorance of sexual matters. I remember sitting up half the night with a girl who was having hysterics because the boy who had escorted her back from the camp dance had kissed her with his mouth open and she was firmly convinced she was now pregnant, as her grandmother had told her that this was what caused it.'

She also makes some very caustic comments on the reactions of many girls' parents who had to be contacted as soon as pregnancy was confirmed. The Service tried to be considerate and arranged for a girl to be looked after by a welfare society if not by the parents, but the girl had to leave the service, and her rapid exit was sometimes unintentionally insensitive. There were, of course, married women in the service who went out when pregnant, and there were quite a few who already had children when they joined. This was accepted providing they made suitable provision beforehand. Mrs Esdale-Pearson had a four-year-old daughter in a nearby boarding school.

'During the holidays I used to have her near the camp and she was allowed to come into the camp, with the exception of the dining hall. The other girls were

A small theatre in Station Sick quarters (Mrs Winstone).

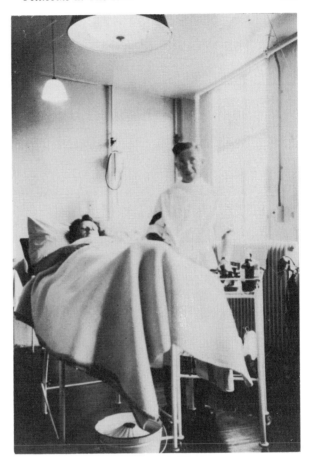

all wonderful with her.'

The services had an enviably good health record. Apart from regular medical inspections (FFIs), mass radiography and free dental care, there were WAAF wards, first in WAAF accommodation and later in RAF Station Sick Quarters (SSQ) or Sick Bays. Serious cases were sent to RAF Hospitals or civilian ones in emergencies. Sheila Woolaston had her own explanation for the good health of WAAF.

'One did not report sick unless one was desperate. One had to report at 7.30 am with small kit and sit on a form, back to the wall, for two or more hours, waiting for the MO. I usually cured myself with aspirin, hot water bottle and bed. Funnily enough, I had better health than ever before. Was it significant that the reporting sick ordeal kept one fit?'

But there were always exceptions. According to Joan Oliver, 'When I was at Hurn, I had suspected appendicitis. So I cycled to Bournemouth hospital for my medical, and then cycled all the way back to tell my NCO that I had to go back next day for an operation.'

Several Convalescent Depots were opened for airwomen, particularly for

those in jobs where a rest, away from it all, might prevent them becoming ill. Daisy Wragg at Elton Hall, near Peterborough, was impressed by 'a great basin full of fresh honey on the table at breakfast, and beautiful grounds to walk in.'

WAAF G Officers — the 'Queen Bees' — and Administrative NCOs were in charge of airwomen's welfare as well as the inevitable drill sessions and parades, such as those for morning colour-hoisting, important visitors, recruiting drives, Wings for Victory Weeks and events to encourage the sale of National Savings Stamps. Their work also included the Programme of Progressive Training, introduced enthusiastically in 1942 by the Director and pursued with a marked lack of enthusiasm by the airwomen. Arthur Bryant, the historian, praised it as an all-round scheme of education for citizenship, ranging from drill, PT and leadership, to handicrafts, civics and current affairs. It was the Director's belief that all had some particular knowledge that they could impart to their fellows, thus becoming more valuable in their own and others' eyes. It did give a spur to service education which, though available, was little used by most.

Once a week was a day for bundles, when items like towels and sheets, labelled like all personal items, were collected for the camp laundry — most girls preferred a Chinese laundry for their collars.

There were black days, too, when someone was put on a charge and had to attend an Orderly Room, usually for a petty offence with a minor punishment, such as being confined to camp, extra duties, loss of pay, leave or admonition. Occasionally there were some unusual cases. Mac MacPhee '. . . accepted a lift by plane to Debden and back, with a Sergeant Pilot needing experience. On our return we got lost and landed in a ploughed field. We were arrested by the Home Guard and finally returned to Martlesham. The CO was furious — signals flying all over the place. He ordered me to be put under arrest. I told him that in that case I would have to have an escort. So he finally decided to forget the whole thing. I think the pilot received some further directional training before going into action with his fighter squadron.'

Frankie Vachon's charge sheet must have raised an eyebrow or two. She was '... reported for cycling on camp in uniform with a jackdaw on my head. I thought it most unfair, but having explained to my CO that the bird wasn't mine and that I had several times brushed it off my head only to have it return to its perch, my case was dismissed.'

Cups were offered for hockey, netball, tennis, table-tennis and, with small success, cricket, but PT and Sport was only liked by the few who were good at them. The RAF insisted on regular participation as part of healthy exercise, but many were the ploys, like hiding in swimming cubicles or reporting sick, to avoid them. Women over 35 were eventually exempt PT, and eurhythmics were often substituted, considered more gentle for women. But alas, even camouflaging PT as Health and Beauty Classes, did not find much favour, except that airwomen generally agreed that it was harder to dodge than to do it. Joan Young recalls, 'We did our PT opposite the Royal Albert Hall and played rounders in Hyde Park with American GIs as spectators.' Winkie Loughran enjoyed sport.

'At Islay, Inner Hebrides, we requested hockey sticks from PSI. In my second-ever game I found myself playing against a huge RAF man — an Irish International hockey player. He was very encouraging and helped to improve my game. At Walmer, Kent, we had the use of the Municipal Tennis Courts only a hundred yards from our civvy billets.'

Above left *Savings Week Parade at Chichester Cathedral* (Mrs Scandrett).

Dress: The torture of a Chinese laundered collar.

Right *Cartoon* (Mrs Sturgeon).

Above *Airmen built this tennis court between air raids at RAF Exminster. Tea after tennis was a great treat: 1942* (Mrs Panton).

Below *Competition for Miss Wyton – the smartest WAAF on station* (Mrs Williamson).

Above right *1940 Pantomime at RAF Felixstowe* (Mrs Jacobs).

Ivy Smith's endeavours won unexpected rewards: 'I was a member of the station netball team one summer. We won three inter-station games without playing, but we enjoyed the meal that was laid on each time!'; and Jean Nabb has an amusing story to tell of how she, a learner, after being entertained by the Guinness team and politely drinking their beer, was so relaxed in the shooting match that followed that she went on to hit the bull every time, to the utter disbelief of all present. 'I never shot again.' Josie Underwood comments that on most camps, sports facilities were excellent. Stella Enfield, however, remarks on the exceptions and adds, 'There were no NAAFI facilities on the small radar sites, and no entertainments or medical facilities. We saw an occasional travelling film show. *China Seas* with Clark Gable was one such. The film broke regularly with resulting catcalls and cheers.'

On larger camps the activities for girls were many and varied, if they had enough energy after work was finished. For Joan Hamer, 'One of the airmen was trying to teach me to drive. I had one or two lessons and thought I was not doing too badly until one day, when I was practising on the runway, I looked up and saw a plane which was coming in to land on the runway that crossed ours. I shut my eyes, my instructor swore and grabbed the wheel, and that was the end of that. I still can't drive.'

Hazel Goodeve 'was at RAF Knightcott, with the RAF Regiment, when an appeal went out for dancing girls to take part in a panto put on by Tony Hancock. Only four of us survived the training and we must have been a scream in silver lamé tops and skirts, the boys singing 1,2,3,4, in time to our steps. Tony Hancock, in army boots and tu-tu, was wonderful.'

There were also station gardening competitions, dramas, bands, handicrafts

Above *Exhibition of RAF and WAAF handwork at RAF Lyneham, 1944* (Mrs Calvert).

Below *WAAF dancing for POW funds at RAF Cardington* (Mrs Cutting).

Arriving for a discussion group on post-war housing by the usual method of transport, in July 1943 (Mrs Ragg).

exhibitions, church fellowships, choirs, lectures, dances, concerts and visits from the Entertainments National Service Association (ENSA). Thus many saw Gracie Fields, the Crazy Gang, Vera Lynn and a host of other famous stars, who gave their time to entertaining the troops. In August 1944, 11 girls went to entertain the RAF in France, and then the United Kingdom, as Ralph Reader's 'WAAF Gang Show'. Among them was an airwoman Medical Assistant, Amy Humphries, who used to enliven her hut in the dark at nights with her piano accordion. Kathleen Cooper remembers another special occasion.

'Northolt in its heyday was a Polish Fighter Station. One day we volunteered somewhat nervously to take part in some Polish dancing — nervously because we had met few Poles and were a little frightened of those we saw. Our teacher, a lady-like man, was given to much handclapping and head clutching. Costumes and — with difficulty — boots, were hired from theatrical agencies — the boots, red leather and knee-high nearly caused the mental collapse of our instructor, but we liked them. When we discovered, all too soon after trying on our glorious costumes, that we were to be presented to the Grosvenor House Officers' Sunday Club in London, we nearly collapsed. "Oh no. You are sweet, sweet! You must go" wailed our instructor, when we tried to back out. So it was to a very varied company of all nationalities that we flew out in our colourful finery into the ballroom. Later we were besieged by a rich assortment of men eager to foxtrot us around the floor. "Hey," cried an American, "can you speak any English?" Alas we quelled the temptation to pretend.'

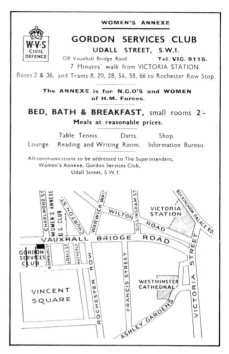

Catholic Women's League Canteen in   Gordon Services Club leaflet (Mrs Gold-
Gloucester (Mrs Jones).   smith).

In partnership with the RAF, the Padres of different religious denominations also looked after the spiritual needs of the airwomen. Church parades soon became a regular feature, and girls took part in the choirs and Young Women's Christian Association (YWCA) activities, where many appreciated the relaxed informality of these gatherings. Chaplains also ran weekend Moral Leadership Courses to which many airwomen went, though criticisms varied from their being left-wing to excellent.

Associations, Clubs and Voluntary Societies provided welfare and assistance of all kinds to the girls in blue. They manned leave centres, hostels and canteens, provided recreation facilities or invited girls into their homes. Airwomen in camps near London could often get free, or at least reduced-price, seats for the best theatres or cinemas there.

On most stations the girls, far outnumbered by the men, voted their social life 'terrific', and being young they far preferred dancing to any other occupation. They were usually well provided for on and off station, transport being laid on if it was to a local army camp or with the Americans. Kay Stewart found that, 'The Americans invited the WAAF at Upavon to dances every week. On arrival we would be presented with a little gift such as perfume, a flower buttonhole, etc. Dancing to the Big Bands was exhilarating. Lots of silk stockings in spotlight dances to be won. Food in plenty, including doughnuts and coke during the interval. At the finish we were allowed five minutes to say goodnight to our boy friend of the evening before our service transport drove us away. These dances were much missed after mid-'44, when most Americans left for the second front.'

The WAAF worked and played hard, and if they seemed to live with a peculiar intensity and in a heightened emotional atmosphere during the war it was perhaps because life was so precarious, and they knew time was short. Bedrock was the companionship of those around them, and thus many girls consider those to have been the happiest years of their lives.

In common with many other WAAF, Jean Nabb feels that it is now time to reappraise their achievements.

'We had to make adjustments to an entirely new set of circumstances. Coming from all walks of life, with large gaps in educational and social backgrounds, we were all thrown in together. Few today realise what types of work we did, the conditions in which some of us lived, and appreciate the life of a wartime servicewoman. We had to conform to the same rigid discipline and regulations as the men. We drilled, marched and stood for equally long periods. We worked side by side with our male counterparts, or in many cases worked alone. We shared the same dangers and hazards, during air raids and heavy bombing. We showed the same courage and resourcefulness. Yet some of my happiest days were spent in the least glamorous work and the hardest physically. We were there within our own right, as a uniformed force with over 100 trades and skills —not as lesser paid assistants doing unskilled work.

'That is why I feel strongly that WAAF serving during the war have never been given the accolades they deserved.'

Chapter 12

A Woman's Work

'They also serve who only stand and wait.'

Milton

Non-technical trades were the earliest undertaken by the WAAF. They were graded and paid lower than Technical trades but in time, as their range and variety extended, some girls moved up and could even be found among the top groups.

One of the original and most popular trades was the Mechanical Transport (MT) Driver, where the vehicles included trucks, salvage waggons, crew coaches, de-icers, ambulances, tractors for bombing up aircraft or pulling petrol bowsers to planes, tenders for laying flare-paths, mortuary vans, waste disposal lorries and staff cars. At first girls were not supposed to drive anything over 15 cwt, but this was shortly raised to 30 and probably much exceeded. Of these girls, Daphne Sumner says 'I used to think they did a wonderful job. Our Group was spread about from Acklington near Newcastle down to Coltishall in Norfolk. They were out in all weathers, finding their way without signposts.'

She could have added, with headlights heavily masked, only a little cross of light rendering them visible, and always the constant reminder 'stop wasting petrol'. Quite rightly she feels that 'as a job, it was no sinecure'.

Betty Curtis, a conscript, wanted to do something exciting such as driving. At her enlistment interview she was asked, 'Can you drive?' 'No!' 'Can you ride a bike?' 'Yes.' 'You'll do.' Later, when asked about medical arrangements on her station, she replied, 'Very good. I drove the ambulance.'

In the beginning there was no training; afterwards there was a course of about seven weeks with a high failure rate. For Rose Jenkins:

'The work was hard, the hours long;
Weeton guarded its reputation —
Fools and WAAF were not suffered there;
We had to prove our dedication.
We took our place beside the men,
To none was there shown any favour.

In '43 I took my test,
And success was sweet to savour.'

On some stations to which she was posted, she found difficulty with the dazzling lights on the airfield — 'Were they perimeter, vehicles or kites?' She felt the kick of the steel starting handle which she had to 'swing' on the lorries, and most of all she endured the strain of what sometimes was 24 hours on duty at a stretch, followed by a day off and so on, continuously, until she had been known to sleep 16 hours non-stop, when off duty — this was quite common at busy times on stations! But it was all repaid by 'the comradeship which was terrific' and she felt privileged that on one of her postings she served with 617 Dambuster Squadron.

Another MT Driver, Dorothy Buxton 'went out with airmen to pick up bodies (or parts) after aircraft crashes'. One operations night, when numerous crews landed at Thornaby, because their airfields were fog bound, instead of keeping them waiting for their beds by ferrying them a few at a time, she drove slowly with headlights on to show them the way, and 'surrounded by airmen carrying their flying kit, I did the job in five minutes.'

Cartoon, 2MT Driver (Mirror Group Newspapers).

" 17194328, *LACW Snook, Bessie, Driver M.T., Group V, and one passenger . . .*"

On a similar occasion, Mary Hewitt was caught by enemy raiders 'following our aircraft home and bombing the runway. I had an incendiary land on the canvas top of the standard van I was driving. The Armoury Sergeant I was taking to the Flight Office punched it upwards and off on to the grass, kneeling on the passenger seat and yelling "Keep going, Mary. Keep going!" ' At another time Monica Dunbar — whose tan leather gauntlet-gloves indicated that she and all Drivers were members of this special élite, very much a law unto themselves — drove a passenger suffering a fit to the nearest hospital.

'A woman doctor and nurse hurried ahead of me, flung open the doors and then sprang back like a couple of scalded cats, exclaiming "It's a man".'

It turned out that this was a Maternity Hospital, the General Hospital being around the corner.

Not many WAAF took over the responsible duties of MT Officer but Section Officer Craufurd-Stuart did just that, having started as a Driver, experience which stood her in good stead, as can be seen from a day in her diary for September 1944 at Church Lawford.

'Consulted WO and Flt re servicing of vehicles. Agreed to use the small bay. Two Drivers volunteered to man it 100 per cent, in lieu of driving. Checked progress on inventory. Call from Wingco of Flying Training — snow plough to be available within the week! Flt and Drivers rummaged, found, cleaned and reassembled both machines. First plough wouldn't fit (30 cwt). I noticed it was crooked and in it slipped. My stock soared. Call from CO. What have I done? "Grass round-about a muddy mess. Your Drivers!" Consult Flt. "Not us — the

Dental caravan and its driver (Mrs Cozens).

Liberty Coach." I will go and look later. It was, thank goodness!'

An even more unusual job fell to Miriam Cozens as an out-station Dental Caravan Driver, for all of which equipment she had to sign! Her usual complement was one Officer, one Dental Orderly and herself — 'Driver, tea-maker and scrounger'. One camp where she was sent was so 'hush-hush' that she had only a grid reference. Even the local police had no idea where it was, there being 'no RAF or camp in these parts', but a young AC2 eventually found them and led them a hair-raising ride to the station.

'It was fascinating, being covered entirely with netting on which had been planted small evergreens and other vegetation, also a cottage with out-houses made of plywood — all on top.'

No wonder she couldn't find it!

'We worked all hours. At times it was very hard work, sometimes very amusing and at others too sad to be remembered.'

A further trade introduced pre-war was that for Cooks, from whom the strongest impression gained is that of overwork, endured for the most part with good humour.

On early stations there were often many kitchens separately serving RAF Officers, WAAF Officers, RAF SNCOs, WAAF SNCOs and airmen and airwomen. Staff and war shortages, however, soon brought about a merging of WAAF dining facilities with those of the equivalent RAF, made official in 1943, but in some stations already existing in 1939. The first WAAF Cooks were experienced in civil life and usually only served WAAF Messes, but in February 1940 when recruiting was urgently reintroduced for them, training courses began, first at Halton, then at Melksham and the RAF School of Cookery, after which they worked with the RAF or where directed. At Melksham, Grace Strawley learned, 'very basic food preparation, even how food is developed from seed. We were taught how to cut up a side of beef [bone a side of bacon], and also to cook in a field kitchen out in the open spaces'.

The biggest difficulty at first was learning how to cook for large numbers. Quantities were often in tons and gallons. One of Edna Plavsic's tasks after breakfast, she recalls, 'was scrubbing out each eighty-gallon boiler', used for porridge, soup, vegetables, gravy, tea (served in bucketfuls) and kidneys for breakfast. The only way was by propping a small ladder up one side, being careful that all taps were turned off. At another time, while in training, she asked for a whisk to make batter.

'It was for a thousand pieces of fish. The Corporal's face was a picture. "Call yourself a Cook, Miss. You're a bloody mistake, that's what you are," and my hands were pushed up to the elbows into a big galvanized bucket and I just had to swish around. It turned out better than I thought!'

When Dorothea Barrie joined the WAAF, her thirteen-year-old brother said, 'Tell her she has joined the wrong side. It's the Germans we want to kill, not our boys!' She found that they were 'very short-staffed in the Cookhouse. We were three on a shift cooking for 1,000 men. We worked very hard.' Her diary for 24 December 1944 reads:

'I started work at 4.30 am cooking the porridge in a large boiler, which was coal-fired. Also helped with rest of breakfast. Then went to help serving the airmen in the servery. I continued cooking lunch, working 'til 2 pm. As it was Xmas Eve and we were short-staffed I stayed on to help prepare the turkeys and Xmas puddings for the next day. I finished at 7 pm to wash and change. Met six friends at 7.30 and we walked the three miles to Tetbury singing carols.'

Work was usually organized in three shifts, 'starting about 4.30 am one day then the following day from 8 am until 7 pm (when we did the cleaning and preparation of vegetables)'. One girl stood for 17 hours, when short of staff, just taking eyes out of the potatoes, of which they used about a ton a day in large kitchens. The night shift was from 7 pm till 4.30 am, and on more difficult camps there were sometimes only two shifts of 12 hours each, and fewer staff. In later years, Italian prisoners of war were brought in to do the heavier work, when available. By 1945 airwomen were about 61 per cent of the total Cooks in the RAF.

A Cook's work was not confined to food preparation and cleaning. On flying stations, sandwiches had to be prepared for night-guard patrols, postings and pilots on operations, and packed in big cardboard boxes, with the extra allowance of fruit and chocolate counted out and later signed for by the recipient. Hay boxes were made up for those requiring hot meals away from camp.

WAAF received a half pint of fresh milk a day, otherwise most milk was condensed. Fresh eggs were a rarity which came only about once a week, so dried egg powder was used in their place. Jam and margarine (called cart-grease) came in 7 lb tins, bread was sliced by machine, often by a defaulter. Sausages were much

Cooks under training (Mrs Scott).

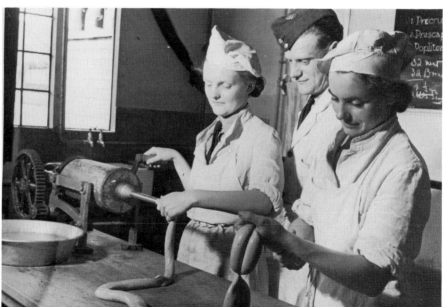

used — although Rustie Attridge could never face them after she saw some airmen and airwomen in the kitchen using them as a skipping rope one night! The cold meat standby was corned beef or spam, while Fridays brought fish cakes or fish and chips. On the whole as Dorothea Barrie felt, 'although many complained about the food, it was quite good, but the presentation was poor'. As the service misquote from Goldsmith ran, 'God sent the food but the Devil sent the Cooks'.

While they worked, there was special clothing for Cooks — extra socks, blue overalls, wrap-over aprons, one waterproof for washing-up — as well as the white caps and overalls of their trade. Nancy Bennett is still amused that they had to wear leather clogs with wooden soles for kitchen work, which used to clack on the stone floors, which were often wet. Indeed the kitchens must have been noisy places with the hissing of steam from the boilers, the clatter of plates and utensils, the banging of pots and the voices of the staff. In such a humid atmosphere too, creatures like cockroaches and earwigs proliferated, despite regular purges.

At Locking, Grace Faw remembers that, 'The lorries bringing supplies were mostly driven by WAAF and we Cooks and Butchers (C&Bs) were responsible for unloading them, as there were few men available. As a rule we ate our meals in a place at the end of the kitchen-storage area — and there was plenty.

'We had a Flight Sergeant who was Welsh. When he would arrive, he usually had a broad smile and would look at me and say, "Sing, Taffy, Sing." He would start us off and it wouldn't be long until we had a chorus going. There was a lot of camaraderie and we had a lot of help from the trainees.'

A few were fortunate enough to go on longer courses in London, some with a French Chef, but these were usually destined to be SNCOs or Catering Officers of whom by 1943 there were 252. Some like Betty Hyde were promoted from LACW, although already fully qualified in a Domestic Science College. She supervised meals for 4,000 at St Eval. Ingeborg Parker-Smith — also qualified — was one of the first Direct Entries as a Catering Officer in 1942. Like many others she served as Hospital Caterer — the RAF was first to introduce this as a specialized service — which she found fascinating.

'Apart from catering for the usual type of hospital patient, one had to cater for severe burn cases, plastic surgery cases and much tuberculosis. It was essential to serve up individual and very attractive meals in these distressing cases to assist recovery. Also there were many special diets such as diabetic.'

Another trade brought in before the war and very much undermanned and overworked was that of Kitchen or Mess Orderly, later classified as Aircrafthand and the duties widened to General Duties. Because those in this trade did unskilled work, often completely unsuitable for women, they tended to be given the heaviest jobs, particularly as the shortage of men increased. Perhaps those working in kitchens were the luckiest. Hazel Biggs says that she became a 'spud basher' after seeing a recruiting film for waitresses to look after bomber crews, 'but all I saw was peeling spuds, slicing bread and washing up, and I never did get to wait on those bomber crews, though I suppose we did our bit and helped out.' Waitresses brought into Messes quite early on replaced civilians rather than airmen, and suffered the same shortages as Cooks.

The RAF was hesitant about introducing WAAF as Batwomen into Officers' Messes, mainly because their work was so personal. In a special Air Ministry Order (AMO) of 1941 when Batwomen were about to be introduced, it saw fit to remind Officers that they 'should comport themselves with due regard to the presence of women'. Batwomen looked after the occupants of several rooms, prepared their uniforms, cleaned their rooms, set their fires, gave morning calls and cups of tea and did the beds. Sally Cornwall, looking back, thinks, 'We didn't seem to have more than five or six rooms to clean, nor did we seem to have the same Officers for very long. I still remember how my heart used to sink when I saw the door and door frame of a room joined together with string and sealing-wax [done when a man was reported killed] and I was still able to see in my mind's eye the photos and personal things inside.

One airwoman while batting had a shock one dawn when collecting shoes to clean, when she discovered a shoe with a leg attached outside one Officer's room — it turned out to be an artificial leg! Another time going to clean a bath, she found that the elderly occupant had died while bathing, and yet again going to make a bed, she found the Officer had shot himself 'and made quite a mess'. But most agree that they found 'their' Officers very good to them.

Different again was the work of WAAF connected with Balloons. These silver 'blimps' had been used to deter attacks by enemy planes as far back as the First World War, and a vast barrage was already flying above London and certain other areas at the start of the Second World War when Balloon Command had come into being.

In 1940 Nancy Scamp joined the WAAF and became a Fabric Worker, as she could use a sewing machine and tie a reef knot. Her work was mainly on the repair of the fabric of barrage balloons. Then 'in April 1941 we were asked if any of us were interested in volunteering for an experiment to see if WAAF could work on Balloon sites'. Air Marshal Gossage doubted the ability of women to stand up to the physical hardships required of operational RAF crews, nevertheless from 300 volunteers, 247 WAAF passed the medical tests to begin training. All the girls had to be physically robust and able to lift heavy test-weights; they were dubbed 'Young Amazons'.

'In May 1941, off went several of us, who had been together since joining up, to No 1 Balloon Training Unit at Cardington. We did a course of about ten weeks, learning how to splice rope and wire, inflate balloons with hydrogen, drive winches which operate the winding gear to put the balloon up or down and learn the theory of it all. We ended with a week at the old aerodrome by the mooring mast for the R101 Airship, doing the work we might expect on the sites. Needless to say we were quite successful.'

In 1918 it had required 53 men to manage a balloon. By 1942 it took seven airmen and two NCOs. Different numbers were tried with airwomen but it was finally settled that an all-woman balloon crew needed 12 airwomen and two NCOs, a large substitution but necessary because of the heavy nature of the work. Jean Nabb was one of a crew of airwomen who went to take over a site in Glasgow.

'We found ourselves in a built-up tenement and warehouse area, outside a high wall with a large wooden sliding door in the centre. This couldn't be a balloon site! There wasn't room to swing a cat around! We entered a very small area indeed, covered in cinders, with "Bertha" bedded to our left and occupying a large part of the site. We couldn't fly from here, I thought. About seven airmen with kit bags came towards us, laughing. "All yours, girls," they said. "Don't look so worried. Bertha can't fly. Too dangerous. Too many large buildings and steeples too close." On site there were two huts, one with bunk beds, and a small brick and stone building for ablutions, with a stone slab running around three walls at waist height, holding round enamel bowls for water. It had open slits for windows, no glass, and a cold water tap. Hot water was obtained by heating it in an old oil drum, if the fuel had been delivered and the fire would light.'

Such was a typical Balloon Site.

While working in the South during late 1941, Irene Wright remembers an unpleasant experience.

'As Winch driver on Balloons, the really bad raids on London left one wondering if we would live through the next day. One night during a very heavy raid, I hurled myself into the cab, listening to my Flight Sergeant bellowing orders through his megaphone, but there was so much noise going on that I never heard his "stop winch". There was a terrific jolt. "What's happened?" I said. "Oh nothing dear," he roared. "You've just lost the bloody Balloon." That ended after many sleepless nights with me appearing before a Court Martial, absolutely petrified. Anyway I was absolved with a finding of "Mechanical Deficiency". Phew!'

Girls working on the balloon winch in RAF battledress, trousers and boots (Mrs Watson).

Jean Nabb notes a typical day in her diary for January 1943. By this time 1029 Balloon sites were being run by all airwomen crews, who then formed 47 per cent of the total personnel in Balloon Command.

'Thank goodness the girls on cooking this week can cook. Enjoyed breakfast [girls of the crew in pairs took it in turn to do the domestic chores]. Bertha on close haul. Audrey and I are on the Winch. We will also be on Guard duties 2-4 pm and 8-10 pm. Sergeant said if no emergencies and weather OK, someone could have the evening off. We had to cut the cards again. Bertha had to be bedded down for topping up. Back to close haul. She's running nicely into the wind.

'We were given truncheons (quite a size these — handy weapons) and torches, from girls on guard duties.

'Wind becomes stronger. Cooks had a bind. Rations not arrived from HQ.

'Someone at the gate. WAAF Officer. No identification. We refused admittance.

'Make-shift tea. No rations.

'Sergeant called. Wanted to know names of Guards on duty at 3 pm. Girls laugh. Say we'll be for it. Instead we were praised for sticking our ground. Weather changed. High wind. Rain. Bertha yawing over. Caught by sudden high wind. All called out of bed. No time to change. Headquarters forecasts gale force winds. Bertha a raging monster, smashing tail guy against the perimeter fence. Lined up for a tug o'war. What a struggle! Had to keep trying, when she didn't pull against us. Heaved Bertha finally into the wind. I didn't hear the command to let go, as I was on the end of the rope. It rushed through my hands. Not burned, but red and sore. All we need now is an air raid! (We had one, early in the morning.)'

For such exposed, exceptionally heavy, outdoor work, the Balloon Operators were given men's rations of food and special clothing, which Eileen Dean describes as, 'battledress top and trousers in rough serge, seamen's pullovers, stockings and sou'westers, plus grey woollen pants to the knees and men's hob-nailed, real clog boots. It so turned out that I never felt so warm and comfortable.'

The deployed Balloons were a success, as Jeanie Gallimore indicates.

'In 1944 near Bristol we were strafed by the guns of an aircraft flying low over our Balloon site. Dodging a hail of bullets, we released the balloon from the tail guy and I let it go to "shine". As the aircraft came round for a second attack, it hit the balloon cable and crashed. It took six hours to retrieve our cable which had cut off all the electricity for miles around.'

However, it was dangerous work, and airwomen were badly burned or killed while on duty. But the war gradually moved into a different phase and the advent of D-Day and flying bombs required mobile units with greater physical strength, whom the RAF could also send overseas. Additionally, too many women were in hospital with ruptured stomachs. The WAAF trade was slowed down and in 1944 finally became obsolete.

Ivy King, a Balloon Rigger, mainly concerned with rope rigging and splicing,

Right A WAAF Balloon Section working alongside the Tower of London (Mrs Dacre).

Below A week's menu for balloon girls in August 1940 (Mrs Choppen).

MENU.   Aug 1940.

	Sunday	Monday	Tuesday	Wednesday	Thursday	Friday	Saturday
Supper	Cheese, Pickles, Cocoa	Cheese, Cocoa	Meat Paste, Cocoa	Cheese, Pickles, Cocoa	Meat Paste, Cocoa	Baked Beans, Cocoa	Cheese, Cocoa
Tea	Corn Beef, Lettuce, Sauce, Jam, Apple.	Eggs & Chips, Lemon Curd	Salmon, Beetroot, Jam, Orange	Corn Beef, Mashed Potato, Jam, Plums.	Cold Meat, Pickles, Jam, Apple.	Herring in Tomato Sauce, Lettuce, Lemon Curd.	Potato Salad, Jam, Slab Cake
Dinner	Roast Beef, Cabbage, Roast Potatoes, Yorkshire Pudding, Figs & Custard	Cottage Pie, Potatoes, Marrow, Stewed Fruit & Custard	Steak, Roast Potatoes, Beans, Plum & Apple pie	Brown Stew, Cabbage, Baked beans, Boiled Jam Pudding, Jam Syrup	Liver, Sausage, Fried Onion, Cabbage, New Potatoes, Baked Apple & Custard	Lamb, Mint Sauce, Peas, Roast Potatoes, Rice Pudding & Raisins	Beef, Carrots, Potatoes, Boiled Jam Roll, Jam Syrup
Breakfast	Egg, Bacon, Porridge, Tea or Coffee, Marmalade	Bacon, Chips, Cereal, Marmalade	Baked Beans on Fried Bread, Porridge, Marmalade	Sausage & Mash, Cereal, Marmalade	Fried Fish, Tomato Sauce, Porridge, Marmalade	Bacon & Kidney, Cereal, Marmalade	Egg, Fried Bread, Cereal.

found, 'In 1944 during the preparations for D-Day, I was stationed at RAF Titchfield, which was a hive of activity. We were on parade for work at 7.30 am and worked till 5.30 pm servicing the large Barrage Balloons and the smaller ones. The whole station was packed with RAF and the field full of tents. For extra entertainment the station cinema was opened in one of the Balloon Repair hangars. After a while I became involved. I enjoyed it. Eventually I was transferred to work full-time as cine projectionist with the films, going to Aldershot in the side-car of a motor bike to fetch them. I have never been so cold. On Christmas Day 1944, I spliced a few feet from a Balloon Training film on to the start of the programme, for fun. The Duty Officer was not amused!'

When in 1945, Balloon Command was finally disbanded, its work finished, the King in his farewell message gave a special word of praise to its air-women.

'They have shown a great devotion to duty and have made an outstanding contribution.'

And so the list of non-mechanical trades can go on with so many stories to tell. There was the large group of medical specializations, from the Dental Orderly, who showed no emotion when her surgery was strafed and then screamed when a mouse ran under her feet, to the Nursing Orderly who hid the oranges and lemons a severely injured patient was bringing home for the children of his village; from the Radiographer who saw so many cases of tuberculosis, to the Masseuse who helped ease the pain of injured airmen; from the Chiropodist

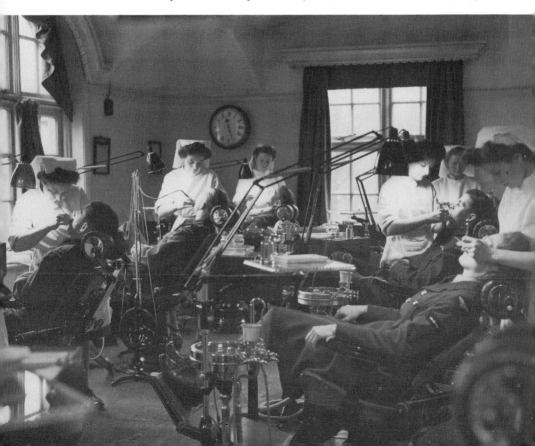

A nurse catching up with paperwork in Station Sick Quarters (Mrs Harmer).

dealing with so many malformed feet from ill-fitting youthful shoes and high heels to the Laboratory and Operating Room Assistant, the qualified Dispenser and the Orthopist who checked pilots' vision, particularly for night flying, despite the officially sanctioned myth that carrots enabled them to 'home' in the dark! Among the last came the Psychological and Psychiatrist's Assistant helping in the selection and assessment of aircrew, and the Dental Hygienist who lectured her patients with all the fervour of a missionary on the keeping of healthy teeth.

Left *Dental Hygienists being trained, 1943* (Mrs Southey).

Right *Photographer carrying rolls of aerial photographs, 1943* (Mrs Griffin).

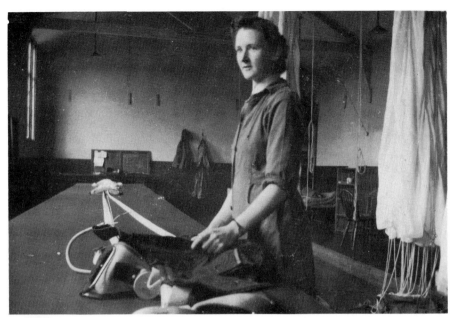

Above *Tailoresses in the Tailor's Shop doing alterations. Note the Flt Sgt's jacket on the ironing board (Mrs Evans).*

Above left *Airwoman in dungarees at the long table used in packing parachutes at Newton Aerodrome, 1942. Note the stretched harness and hanging unpacked parachutes (Mrs Haughton).*

Left *A pilot holding a weather balloon with Meteorological Officers and airwomen outside the Met Office (Miss Park).*

Right *Stores work was much the same, whether in the '40s or '70s (Mrs Scott).*

WAAF Pay and Trade Groups in 1942 — AMP 130, 6th Edition.

DAILY RATES OF PAY OF AIRWOMEN OF THE WOMEN'S AUXILIARY AIR FORCE.

Rank	Group I s. d.	Group II s. d.	Group III s. d.	Group IV s. d.	Group V‡ s. d.	Group M s. d.
Aircraftwoman, 2nd Class	2 6	2 4	2 0†	2 2	1 4	1 4
Over 1 year	—	—	—	—	1 10	2 0
Over 2 years	—	—	—	—	2 0	2 2
Aircraftwoman, 1st Class	3 0	—	2 8	2 8	2 4	2 6
Leading Aircraftwoman	3 8	3 4	3 8	3 0	2 8	2 10
Leading Aircraftwoman, over 3 years	4 0	3 8	3 8	3 4	—	3 2
Corporal	5 0	4 4	3 4	3 8	3 0	3 6
Corporal, over 3 years	—	—	—	—	—	4 0
Corporal, over 4 years	5 4	4 8	3 8	4 0	3 4	—
Sergeant	6 4	5 8	4 4	4 8	4 0	4 8
Sergeant, over 3 years	—	—	—	—	—	5 4
Sergeant, over 4 years	6 8	6 0	4 8	5 0	4 4	—
Flight Sergeant	7 8	6 8	5 4	5 8	5 2	6 4
Flight Sergeant, over 3 years	—	—	—	—	—	7 0
Flight Sergeant, over 4 years	8 0	7 0	5 8	6 0	5 4	—
Warrant Officer	9 4	8 4	7 8	7 8	·7 8	9 0
Warrant Officer, over 5 years	11 0	10 0	9 0	9 4	9 0	—

In addition to the above rates, airwomen will receive war pay at the rate of 8d. a day, and a post-war credit of 4d. will accrue for each day of paid service.

† Recruits accepted as fully qualified in cookery will be entered as Aircraftwoman 2nd Class in Group III, i.e. will receive pay at the rate of 2/- a day.
‡ Under certain conditions duty pay is issuable to parachute packers, telephone operators and W.A.A.F. police and driver's bonus of 2d. a day to M.T. drivers.

The trades for which candidates may be accepted are as follows (the trades are placed in the groups indicated for purposes of pay (*see* para. 8)):—

Group I	Group II	Group III	Group IV	Group V	Group M
R.D.F. mechanic. Wireless mechanic.	Acetylene welder. Armourer (guns). Balloon operator. Electrician, grade II. Flight mechanic (air frame). Flight mechanic (engine).	Cook. Fabric worker, Aero. Fabric worker, rigger, Balloon. Hairdresser. Parachute repairer. Shoe repairer. Tailor.	Administrative. Charging board operator. Clerk, equipment accounting. Clerk, general duties. Clerk, Pay accounting. Clerk, personnel selection.	Aircrafthand general duties. Armament assistant. Balloon parachute hand. Batwoman. Bomb plotter. Cine projectionist. Drogue packer and repairer. M.T. driver. Maintenance assistant	Chiropodist. Dental clerk orderly. Dispenser. Laboratory assistant. Masseuse. Nursing orderly. Operating room assistant. Optician orderly. Radiographer.
	Instrument mechanic. Instrument repairer, grade II. Meteorologist. M.T. mechanic. Photographer. *R.D.F. operator. Sparking plug tester. Wireless operator. W.T. (Slip Reader operator).		Clerk, special duties. Clerk, special duties (watch keeper.) Equipment assistant. *R.D.F. operator. R.T. operator. Teleprinter operator. Tracer.	Mess steward. Orderly Parachute packer Telephonist. Waitress. Workshop hand. W.A.A.F. police.	

* Group II after 6 months' efficient service.

Outside the medical group there were so many different trades. A few will have to stand for the many. Pre-war the Equipment trade brought in girls who were soon to deal in stores of everything from clothes to aircraft parts. One airwoman saw many of her friends killed and a girl's hair set alight when a Lancaster crashed on the roof of her section. Clerks General Duties were another early trade with typing, postal, map store and technical duties, where many handled secret material about operations big and small yet stayed silent. Costs and accounting for all items came into the field of Clerk Accounts, Equipment Accounts and Provisioning Clerks, while some helped in Selection of Personnel for ground and flying duties. Then there were Photographers dealing with aerial photographs and the cameras carried by aircraft on mission; Cartographers and Tracers produced maps in exquisite up-to-date detail; Model Makers made miniature dioramas and scale models; Parachute Packers were airwomen on whose skill the baling-out pilot's life depended; Meteorologists from whose accuracy an operation might be a success or a failure; and the WAAF Police who aimed at preventing trouble before it happened and whose work was mainly outside station boundaries. There were Tailoresses and Shoe Repairers, Hairdressers and Carpenters, Physical Training Instructors and a trade of Pigeon Keeper that was never filled.

Officers started their war in Administration, but they later appeared in a number of the airwomen's trades. A few with specialist qualifications, such as those in the Medical field and Meteorology, came in direct from civilian life, but after the war began, with a few exceptions, Officers were commissioned from the ranks of the airwomen. Unfortunately, many airwomen who had won their way up to Flight Sergeant and Warrant Officer, refused to be commissioned because of the drop in pay and higher expenses at the lowest Officer rank of Assistant Section Officer (ASO). This was apart from the loss of friends and the companionship that they had so long enjoyed.

In fact pay was always a sore point. Whereas in the First World War it was considered generous, it was far from that in the Second. Despite their free keep — food, accommodation, clothes and dental plus medical care — most airwomen complained that they were out of pocket long before their pay day. 'Never had so many waited so long for so little'. Perhaps that was the reason that pay was fortnightly rather than weekly!

Trades were divided into five groups, with the 'M' medical group eventually added. Group I tradesmen, who were deemed to do the most skilled and difficult work, were paid most, but pay increased with rank and length of service, from the lowest ACW2 to the highest Warrant Officer. Airwomen began the war in the bottom three groups and in only six trades, and ended in all the groups, with nearly as many trades as airmen. Officers too, whose work was divided into Branches, started with one Branch and ended in the majority.

Nevertheless, the main disability endured by all wartime WAAF was that their pay was always two-thirds of their equivalent rank in the RAF — itself not overpaid — including the extra daily war pay of 4d as against the RAF 6d. In all the services, women were ultimately eligible for allowances and pensions for dependants, for war disablement pensions for themselvs and for two-thirds of men's gratuities at the end of the war.

Women had long endured this discrimination, though never inured to it, but since there was a war on, they grumbled and then let it pass. There is little doubt that such treatment fuelled the civilian equal pay lobby after the war.

Chapter 13

Mechanics Are Not Unfeminine

'As an Engineering Officer was heard to say, "It isn't a woman's work and not all can take it, but if you get a good Flight Mechanic, she is usually Bloody Good!" '

Jeanie Rowley

In spite of their achievements in the First World War, the idea of women doing skilled technical work was still so strange to the population of the Second World War that as late as 1943 a government-produced booklet designed to dispel the myth had to start with a chapter entitled, *Is Mechanical Work Unfeminine?* Nonetheless, the man-shortages of 1940 hurried on the introduction of women into further fields, both non-technical and technical, including simpler, hived-off, ancillary elements from certain skilled trades.

The only vacancy available was for a Charging Board Operator (CBO) when Phyllis Butcher volunteered, after her fiancé was killed on Operations. Of her trade she said, 'I had never heard of it, nor had anyone else. They used to say to me "Are you going to be a Cook and Butcher?". It was a dirty, horrible job, acid on your clothes and fingers, gloves meant for men always too big, but it was most rewarding too.' She might have added that work on the huge, lead batteries and accumulators was also heavy.

Another job allied to the Electrical trade was the Sparking Plug Tester (SPT). After training at Melksham, Trixie Irving worked in the Plug Bay, attached to the Station Workshops at Leuchars, where the aircraft of Coastal Command flew on convoy duties. At first 'the men would rather we made tea', but the initial newness gone, they soon accepted the airwomen and Trixie was very proud to feel that she was really helping in the war effort. In her work, 'After an aircraft engine change, when the sparking plugs came out of the aircraft, they had to be washed and cleaned in high octane petrol. Then they had to be checked for faults and the electrode at the end of the plug had to be reset to 12-15,000th of an inch, so that the spark would cross the gap and so ignite the engine.'

She was much envied by the other WAAF when a few trades like hers, and MT and Parachute Packers, were issued in 1942 with battledress, and how proud she was to wear trousers!

'On the first day wherever we went, we were followed by wolf whistles from the men. I must admit I did feel a bit special then.'

A little later, despite the misgivings of many at the Commands, it was decided to try airwomen out in what became known as the 'Experimental Trades'. There were quite a number, all in the higher paid Group II but entry was closed for all except a few carefully selected airwomen. One of these was Isobel Money, who was sent from her Balloon Centre at Kirkintilloch to RAF Heathfield.

'The staff at the Electrical Section was amazed — landed with six WAAF under training (U/T) Electricians. Unheard of! We caused quite a sensation. During our stay, it was decided to set up a 1st Entry WAAF Electricians. We were posted to RAF Melksham to do a condensed course of nine months — two or three years normally. It was pretty hard going and a high standard set. Out of 40, 22 of us reached the West Drayton Board and 16 of us passed with flying colours, myself included, and got our LACW. The work involved general electrical maintenance on aircraft, rewiring, battery maintenance, terminals, stripping and reassembling generators and motors, instrument checks on all electrical parts and signing Form 700 accepting responsibility for work done. I found it most interesting. At first there were comments about women doing men's work, but realising that we could do the job as well as they, the airmen soon absorbed us

An electrician working on a Harvard, wearing battle-dress-top, trousers and gloves against the cold (Mrs Moore).

Left *Flight Mechanics on a course, checking valve timings, 1943* (Mrs Govier).

Below right *Flight Mechanics (Airframes) with their pilot and his Mustang, 1944* (Mrs Griffin).

into the routine and on the whole treated us with respect and co-operation.'

Another experimental group was that of Armourers who, together with Armament Assistants and Bomb Plotters, worked with aircraft, machine-gun units, Air Gunnery and Bombing Schools. One of this rare breed was Iris Mason, who helped to train 200 or more airmen every fortnight on a machine-gun firing course.

'Three of us worked alone in a large Nissen hut stacked with about a million rounds of .303 bullets and 20 mm shells. We had 12 machine-guns and one Hispano gun. All the ammo we used was rusty, for practice purposes, but of course live. We had incendiary, armour piercing, tracer and plain ball ammo. Our job was to break it down in belts of roughly one hundred and put a tracer in that had been dipped in special inks and oils, then rebelt to 1,000 with a tracer every so far. We could never push the tracer back so we knocked them back with a piece of wood — very foolish and dangerous. We also timed bursts of gunfire with a stop watch and marked the target when it was dropped from the aircraft. We were highly respected by all staff, and army officers used to visit us and shake us by the hand.'

Despite this 'macho' image, they were still very human, as Jean Yates, an

Armament Assistant, was to find at the time airwomen were warned against the special danger of landings of enemy parachutists, when she, like all others, had to take her share as Duty Airwoman.

'Living in a Nissen hut in an orchard, I had to wake the Cooks up at 4.30 am. I had left the Guardroom with my torch when I came up against something wet and cold. It moved . . . I ran back to the Corporal in the Guardroom. We found that someone had left the gate open to the farm and all the cows had come in during the night.'

By 1942 the experimental trades were agreed to have been a success, and they were opened up in time to absorb many redundant airwomen from earlier ancillary trades, together with Balloon Operators — all peculiarly well fitted to embark on these new, more skilled occupations. After leaving Balloon Command Elspeth McKinlay became a Flight Mechanic (Engines), and her first station trained glider pilots and had Whitley bombers which towed the gliders. Here she was told — and she wasn't sure if this was a joke — 'if we dropped a spanner in the Rolls-Royce v-shaped cylinders, we would be shot'. Her diary entry for 12 July 1943 gives a good idea of a typical working day:

'Did a Daily Inspection (DI) on my allocated Oxford aircraft. Found the air-cooled engine had some blown gaskets and low oil-pressure. Put it right. The aircraft had to be tested later for night flying. The Airframe Mechanic and I went up with the pilot. First he feathered one propeller, restarted it, then the other, then both together. You could see the props just turning slowly and the nose going down in an alarming way, so I was very relieved to see him pushing the throttle forward again and the props becoming invisible.'

At another station Margaret Jones de-iced the propeller with her bare hands. She was a rarity, a girl with a mechanical background.

Jeanie Gallimore remembers remustering from Balloons and becoming a Flight Mechanic (Airframes) when she wrote this poem.

'Sitting on a hangar floor
Covered in oil and grease,
No time at all to sit and stare,
No time for a bit of peace.

We who help to keep them up
And bring them back again —　·
The back room "shower", the ground crews —
We are never mentioned by name.

The heroes are the air crews
And we don't grudge them that —
But don't the ones that do the work
Deserve a pat on the back?'

'At St Athan we commenced a six-month course which covered everything from rope/wire splicing to carpentry and metal lathe work. It was super! We had marvellous instructors and I took to it like a duck to water. We trained on all kinds of aircraft. On station, one girl to four men and a Corporal was the ratio to a crew. We did exactly the same work, and no one covered for us except the Corporal and woe betide if there was anything amiss after he checked. Being women we made sure there wasn't!'

One memorable day, a new NCO in charge of Servicing was posted in from the Sudan.

'He was amazed on walking into the hangar to find "Women" working on major servicing, and me, in particular, inside the nacelle of an undercarriage, with the wheels, legs and other parts strewn on the floor beneath me. He peered up and asked rather condescendingly, "Do you know what you are doing up there?" He was confronted by an irate WAAF clad in a boiler suit and covered in oil and grease, who said, "Who do you think you are talking to?" and, "Yes, I do know what I am doing up there". After this episode he sought me out to pick fault with everything I did, till one day he tore the patches off the inspection panels that I had painstakingly sewn and doped, saying that they were not tight enough. I told him that the dope was not dry, threw the brush at him and told him to do it himself. Now this was not the way to talk to one's boss and the warning came! I was on a charge, closely followed by "Will you come out for a drink tonight?" I paid him back by marrying him.'

Another Balloon recruit was Frankie Cousins who went to be an Instrument Repairer. 'We did our usual inspection of the kites, checking instruments, gunsights, gyro, oxygen bottles and so on.' On an air test, she sat at the controls of a Wellington bomber and 'flew it over Oxford for a couple of minutes and was scared stiff'.

The RAF sent Doris Hall to a London Technical College, on the first course in electrical and mechanical engineering on which women were allowed. But, the men met them with such absolute disgust, refusing to take them seriously, that she changed her trade. On one station her WAAF camp was situated away from the main station, and, perhaps appropriately, next to the closed order of a Nunnery.

'I could not resist looking over the wall. It seemed strange to see the beautiful gardens, the nuns deep in meditation and a Lancaster bomber roaring over them very low. None of them even looked up.'

Gradually the number of technical trades increased, although some were either so skilled or unusual that very few airwomen were attracted into them. There was no shortage of volunteers for MT Mechanic, but in July 1943 there were still only 11 Acetylene Welders and, as a Link Trainer Instructor, Edda Berry was the only one at the end of the war. With four others she was billeted in an hotel room when she trained in London, and had to walk everywhere because of her low pay, but it was 'great fun'.

'The Link Trainer looked like a bubble car with a hood, perched on four large bellows. It was decided that we should have battledress, as WAAF skirts were too tight for climbing into it. After learning to operate the machine, we needed to understand how the Approach Systems worked [her station operated the Lorenz Beam Approach].

'My first station, Netheravon, in its Fleet Air Arm name of HMS *Daedalus* was reported sunk (so he said) by 'Lord Haw-Haw'. My second station was Little Rissington. There my fellow instructors were mostly very helpful, though a few of the pupils gave me a bad time and a few even worse, but they were the excep-

MT *Driver and Mechanic working on a camouflaged van* (Mrs Fielder).

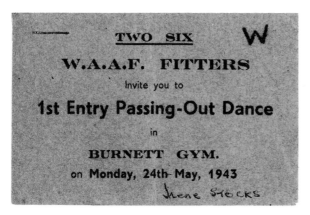

1st Entry WAAF Fitters Passing Out Dance (Mrs Fairlie).

tion. An understanding boss or fellow instructor usually came to my rescue. I was never made to deal with objectors and on the other hand some quite senior flying instructors came for me to supervise their obligatory regular work-out. My demob assessment read "Good at handling men!" '

Helen Shanks moved up from Flight Mechanic to one of that little band of Group I trades as an Engine Fitter, and some of her oily rags from work helped to light the ugly black stoves of the huts at night. At Dumfries on 17 April 1944 she notes:

'Still waiting for a new engine to come into the hangar. Ran up the last kite and then went on test flight over the Solway. "Bloody dull trip" the pilot called it. I enjoyed it thoroughly.'

There were also Group I Airframe Fitters, Instrument Repairers and Electricians all at a highly skilled technical level. Representatives of the Signals trade were to be found in these higher groups too (see Chapter 14).

The most widespread and usually least secret of these trades was Telephone Operator. These were among the first technically skilled airwomen to be recruited by the RAF when the war broke out, forming part of the normal working force of most camps and replacing men on a one for one basis. They were shift workers doing eight to twelve hour shifts, and sometimes, when short-handed, 24 hours on and 24 hours off. Despite being a popular trade, it was sometimes short of airwomen, as switchboards on many stations were totally run by WAAF. Most entered the service already trained but Bobby Sadler's RAF training was by the civilian GPO at Newcastle-upon-Tyne.

'On camp, if lucky, I worked on large switchboards with other girls, but I have worked on aerodromes on the outskirts of fields, alone in tiny bomb-proof exchanges. We had special gas clothing issued with microphones in the gas masks, but the gloves were so awkward that we couldn't pick up the plugs on the switchboard. Behind us was a big axe in a glass case to smash the switchboard to little bits if the enemy took the aerodrome. As we were all small slips of girls, we couldn't even lift the axe, let alone do the rest.'

But Telephonists could rise to great heroism when the need arose. Pat Harris recalls that she and the girls on her switchboard stayed at their posts 'when the roof of the telephone exchange was set on fire by incendiary bombs during the

Liverpool blitz', and airwomen at Biggin Hill received awards after similar incidents.

Thus WAAF showed that they were just as involved in the war as the men, if only as ground support. Even so, some WAAF did fly. A small group of women, having learned to fly before the war, and seeing the desperate shortage of trained pilots, wanted to put their forbidden talents to some use. Headed by Miss Pauline Gower they became part of a women's section within a civil organization known as the Air Transport Auxiliary (ATA), formed in 1939 by men — experienced pilots but ineligible for the RAF — who with a similar organization in the USA, did second-line duties, ferrying aircraft from aircraft factories to air-fields and fulfilling other minor transport roles. Amy Johnson was one of their

Two ATA members in their flying suits (Miss Horsburgh).

Some WAAF who joined the ATA, proudly wearing their wings (Miss Horsburgh).

women members who died on a ferrying mission. WAAF who wanted to join the ATA had to be granted a temporary release from their service to do so, but by 1943 the source of trained pilots was dwindling to such an extent that the RAF took the unprecedented step of calling for WAAF volunteers to be trained for the ATA. The response was overwhelming. An Intelligence Officer at Air Ministry, Peggy Eveleigh, 'applied, together with about 1,400 WAAF, for flying training in the Air Transport Auxiliary, it being decided to give some 30 WAAF a chance of this. I was one of the lucky ones accepted and my first day at the ATA training school was the most exciting of my life — only beaten when I flew my first Spitfire in September 1944 — two of us were qualified on this and other fighter aircraft. We were given temporary release from the WAAF to become pilots and deliver aircraft all over England in 1944 and 1945.'

It was dangerous work, however. Frances Horsburgh, a Canadian, who to the horror of her parents had left her home in the USA to come to England to join the WAAF, was another of this little group. She recalls, 'Two of the girls training as Ferry Pilots were in accidents which almost cost their lives. One flew into the sea in a Barracuda, in dense fog. It was a miracle that she got out of the aircraft and that a fishing boat was nearby. The other girl was doing low flying with an instructor and they flew into electricity wires. He never flew again but she finished the course.'

They did sterling work with women of many nationalities. They wore a dark blue uniform with gold badges and wings based on the RAF pattern, and received ATA pilots' pay. At the end of 1945 they were disbanded, but in St Paul's Cathedral there is a memorial to them, engraved with these words:

'Remember then that also we in a moon's course are history.'

Chapter 14

Can Women Keep Secrets?

'I held my tongue and spake nothing: I kept silence, yea, even from good words; but it was pain and grief to me.'

Psalms

The public knew little about the work of WAAF in the Signals and Intelligence groups because the women involved, aware that men's lives depended on their secrecy, did not speak. For this reason, they have not gained the credit they deserved. Among the earliest trades recruited into the wartime WAAF were Special Duties Clerks — Plotters and Radar Operators. Indeed, radar was one of the great success stories of the war, and it might be said that it saved us in the Battle of Britain.

Some of the basic principles of radar go as far back as the Englishman Maxwell in the 1870s and the German Hertz in the 1880s, but it was Robert Watson-Watt who developed it in the 1930s, to the point that by early 1939 there were 20 stations operating radio direction finding (RDF as it was then called) in an unbroken chain along the south and east coasts of Britain, and from 1940, the west coast was covered. After some details of the system were made public in 1941, it became known as Radiolocation, the term 'radar' being coined in 1942 by the American Navy from the phrase 'radio detection and ranging'. Its function was as an early warning system, enabling Britain to use her very few available fighter aircraft at the outbreak of war to the best and most economical advantage; they only had to take off when notified of the approach of hostile aircraft, rather than maintaining costly, continuous patrols.

It was of course top secret, though at least one WAAF was shaken when told by a villager, 'Oh you'm down at that site in Farmer Giles's field'; and there it was, two Bedford trucks full of equipment, where the farmer's calves stood around licking the axle-grease off the wheels.

Sometimes the Operators worked in huts or caravans, on other sites in massive concrete underground structures, depending on the type and period of the radar. Here with the RAF they strained their eyes on a flickering cathode ray

Left *Model of a Radar Aerial Tower, 1939-45* (Miss Jackson).

Below *A Home Chain (CH) Radar receiver room, 1940* (RSRE Malvern).

Below right *Bawdsey Manor in RAF Bawdsey, Suffolk, used for WAAF accommodation and offices* (Mrs Clayton).

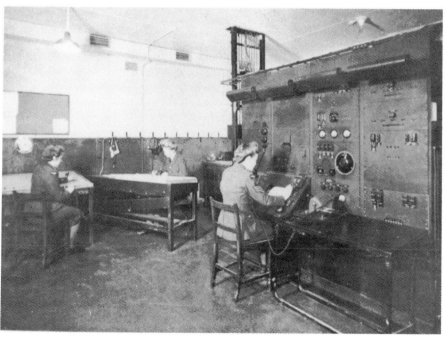

tube (CRT) like a television screen, tracking aircraft round the clock. They were divided into four watches if they were lucky, three if not, working an average 56 hour week, and usually short of sleep because of the erratic hours. Thus, though the work was fascinating and the girls were proud to do it, working conditions often left much to be desired.

There were four main types of defensive radar in the first wartime years. Bawdsey Research Station was the earliest of the line of home chain installations, known as CH, which used a high beam from 360 ft radio masts. Next came CHL, the home chain created to spot low-flying aircraft, then later CHEL was introduced with even shorter wavelengths to catch really low flying aircraft. Finally GCI or ground-controlled interception guided British planes fitted with radar screens into position to attack enemy raiders As radar became more sophisticated, it evolved electronic navigation and bombing aids like Gee and Oboe, and also RCM or radar counter measures which among other things could jam or misdirect enemy aircraft.

In all these operations WAAF played their part. Pearl Gannon worked 'in a small caravan situated within 50 miles of the coast. The aerial which was large and square was attached to one of the caravans and manually pedalled from the inside. On one particular day objects were sighted coming up the estuary — enough to induce an invasion alert. The women took control of the radar while the men manned the guns outside. I was sent to the aerial caravan to pedal. RT silence was maintained by every one as they listened for any hint of German voices. I pedalled on. Meanwhile a fault had been discovered in the control sets and we had gone off the air. Later I discovered that I had been pedalling for two

Above *Windswept type of landscape familiar to Radar and Wireless Operators, Swanage 1941* (Mrs Clayton).

Below *Controller and two Radar Operators at RAF Northstead in 1945* (Mrs Webb).

hours and no one had remembered to stop me. The invasion turned out to be balloons that had broken free and were gently floating inland.'

Airwomen displayed great courage and presence of mind during air-raids where the radar aerials made their installations an easily recognized target, so that several stations received direct hits and heavy casualties. There were other less obvious hazards, too. Owing to the isolated and exposed positions of many sites, more than one girl was nearly blown off the edge of a cliff, or like Joyce Taylor, had to fight to turn the cheese-shaped aerial of CHL manually in the strong winds of Scotland. Sometimes aerials crashed through the roof of cabins creating havoc and worse, rendering them non-operational.

The shortage of skilled men caused the RAF to employ more and more WAAF as Operators, until by 1944 most Operators were female. The few men left in such posts as Technical Officers, Mechanics and Senior Controllers, worked in a predominantly female atmosphere.

Because of these same shortages, it was decided to find out if WAAF Radar Operators could be trained as Radar Mechanics, or Radio Operator Mechanics as they were then known. In common with many others, Cyril Ludlow, at one time their Training Officer, 'was very dubious of course, but I found they were surprisingly good at learning and for some strange reason it always seemed to be the most glamorous girls who volunteered'.

This extract from the 1941 diary of Jean Mackenzie, with its typical RAF understatement, gives a lively picture of her training.

'*17 Oct* The ASO sent for Sybil and me to tell us that we had both been posted to Yatesbury for a Radio Mechanic's course. We were so upset to leave our beloved Rye and "A" Watch.

24 Oct Yatesbury is as grim as ever. Apparently we are here for a six-weeks experimental course and if we pass we shall get our "props" and be entitled to put ROM after our names, plus extra pay.

29 Oct Second day of course. Sybil and I wiring up circuits in the lab was a sight to behold. Neither of us has a clue and we get fits of giggles which infuriates the Flight Sergeant.

30 Oct Spent the afternoon in the Lab blowing fuses and learning the intricacies of the Avometer. Awful Gas Drill in the middle. Spent the evening trying to work out decimals and fractions. Wish I hadn't been quite so hopeless at maths in school.

10 Nov Amazing. We have all passed. I think Flt was as shaken as we were. The first hurdle over.

10 Dec Having all managed somehow to survive and pass the ROM Course, we rush to the notice-board to find out our postings. I should have known it. I am posted to RAF Stenigot and Sybil to RAF Poling.'

Despite her initial reservations Jean went on to get her Corporal tapes, and the experiment with Radar Mechanics was a success. Wherever possible, girls replaced men on a one to one basis.

Each home RAF Command dealt with similar work and aircraft on stations dotted all over the British Isles. Thus, during the Battle of Britain, the Operations Room in Fighter Command Headquarters at Bentley Priory, Stanmore, dis-

"Can't 'elp about your operations. I've got to do my spring cleaning."

In Memoriam to a Radar Mechanics Course, drawn by their instructor, Harry Sutcliffe (Mrs Morrison).

Cartoon (Mrs Durance).

played the whole map of Britain, showing details of the incoming hostile aircraft and the Fighter Squadrons from north to south available to combat them. Information came to them from many sources, and in particular from the Filter Room, which was the clearing house and correction centre for all the data from radar stations, movements and intelligence information. This was then broken up and relayed down the line to Group and Sector Operations Rooms dealing with their own geographical portions of the map. In these so-called 'Ops Rooms' the Plotters worked with their long croupier-like rakes around a large table, while in the gallery above them sat RAF Controllers, deciding on action, according to what they already knew from intelligence sources, heard from sightings of the Royal Observer Corps or saw on the table before them.

Plotters could laugh at themselves, as in this poem by Flt Lt Tapsell.

'This is a story, sad but true,
About an Ops Room plotting crew,
Which, although not highly paid
Tried quite hard to plot a raid,
But the plots got in a mess
And had the damsels in distress.
Firstly, with a hurried glance,
They chose the wrong square over France,
And when the Hun got near to Dover,
Someone knocked the raid plaque over!

This put them in an awful fix
And Angels 'nine' went back to 'six'.
Then came an awful rending noise,
Which shocked the girls but pleased the boys,
Because you see, a WAAF had got'er
Skirt caught on the teleplotter.
And in the midst of all the babel,
Controller shrieked "Can't see the table ..." '

Of course the reality was that they were very good at their job and worked so fast that men were taken off the plotting tables because they could not keep up when it got busy. In fact, there were two kinds of Plotter, Filter and Operations. Filter Plotters were in direct contact with Radar Operators, and found the position, height, direction and number of aircraft, either friendly or hostile. The filtered information of all aircraft over the sea was then passed to the Operations Plotters, who were chosen for speed and unflappability.

In her diary for June 1944, Violet Walker gives a vivid picture of a Filter Plotter's work.

'Going on duty, night shift, 10 pm–8 am at the underground centre 80 ft

A painting of the activity in Kenley Operations Room, 1943. Exhibited in the Royal Academy, 1944 (Miss L Buchan, WAAF artist).

down. Taking a good deep breath of fresh air, down in lift, past Teleprinters floor, Ops floor, to Filter floor. Sgt tells us which of the three tables we shall serve, Observer Corps, Fighter or Filter (the largest), or to act as "teller" from Filter to Ops, or later on new Peartree screen, or to operate the Tote. On Filter table — busy night, big raid. Went over to macroscopic plotting. Could hardly keep up. Just watch the clock, change your colours and listen closely to your radar station at the end of your line.'

At first, Group Captain Bouchier resented the appearance of girls on the Fighter Station he commanded because he did not think they would cope during raids. Later he put his conversion on record.

'During the daylight mass-bombings of August and September last year, in a flimsy building on the aerodrome, I saw my WAAF Plotters with their earphones pressed to their ears — to keep out the inferno of noise from the torrent of bombs that were bursting all around. Steady and calm at their posts plotting, not a murmur or movement came from a single one, though the whole building was

Information sources of Fighter Command Operations Rooms

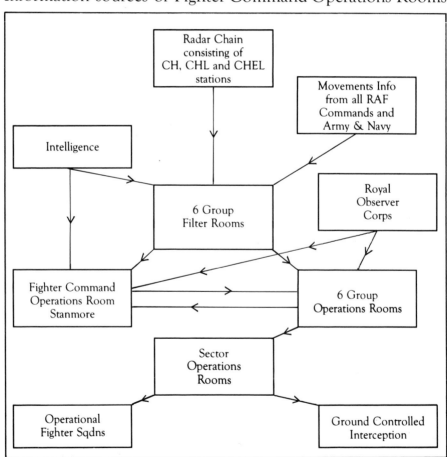

rocking and each knew that she and the building might at any moment be airborne.'

The work of Special Duties Clerks was a resounding success and by September 1942 they numbered about 6,228. This obviously paved the way for the introduction of WAAF Officers into Intelligence and Operations posts, where they became Operations and Filter Officers in charge of Filter Rooms, Movements Liaison Officers, Air Raid Warnings Officers and so on, many going even further to great things including Scientific Observers. They were very special girls of highly individual and intelligent minds, living at a very intense rate with little time to relax and unwind.

Eileen Younghusband moved from Plotter to Filter Officer. Her work consisted of 'sorting the plotters' information very swiftly for aircraft identification and for "telling" to the Operations Room. Dedication during duties was phenomenal. I feel that the work done by the Filter room has never been properly told, especially in relation to plotting Mayday-type BIF tracks, the "Diver, Diver" warnings and the Big Ben alarm, plus the subsequent "killing" of all V-2 launch lorries against military targets — thanks to WAAF Radar Operators and Army sound detectors in Belgium.'

In October 1941, Sergeant Watchkeeper posts were also created, to enable WAAF Sergeants to take over some of the work of RAF Operations and Intelligence Officers.

Teleprinter Operators were another early trade in Signals, who manned a vital, interference-free network from station to station throughout the RAF. Joyce Caldwell remembers with amusement 'our intake were the first WAAF to invade the all-male sanctum of Cranwell for No 1 Teleprinter Course'.

By attaining 'the speed of 60 words a minute on the old black GPO three-bank machines' Gladys Warnes became a LACW. 'Then I was sent to Air Ministry Whitehall for training to read and use the Murray Code.' For this she used a perforating machine, punching various combinations of five holes forming one letter.

'We had to read it at a rate of at least five words per minute and type accurately without any erasures. We also used the teleprinter switchboard, where we typed instead of spoke and we typed codes and cyphers in four-figure or five-letter codes. Each service had one main Central Board in case of damage. There were also Morse Slip Readers, who fed and typed out messages in plain language.'

Because of its variety, Irene Knowles, who had a bad stammer, was recommended to it by a kindly RAF Officer. 'I loved everything about the job and miraculously my stammer got less and less. My family couldn't believe it.' The only reason that the RAF finally decided not to make all Teleprinter Operators women was that some men had to remain for overseas requirements. Even so many posts were entirely WAAF.

The pitch and clarity of women's voices was their great asset as Radio Telephone Operators as they passed information to pilots in Flying Control rooms, in Forward Relay cabins sometimes a hundred miles from base and on Homer Relays helping crippled aircraft steer a course for home. Again they were manned in watches day and night. They spoke briefly, using code, and had to

Left *On Flying Control Duty, 1942* (Mrs Hills).

Right *A Wireless Mechanic looks out of an Airspeed Oxford cockpit, where she has been testing the R/T equipment with which the pilot communicates with the ground, 1944* (Mrs Higginson).

contend with weak reception and enemy interference. All had to be alert, fast and accurate. A typical duty day is described by Doris McCreight.

'I reported for duty in the Control Tower just before dark. Before me was the expanse of the airfield with Lancaster bombers ready for take off on another bombing raid over the Ruhr valley. Behind me was the blackboard listing crews and aircraft identification with estimated time for take off and return. There was radio telephone (R/T) silence before take off and we would watch them go off in rotation. I used two microphones, one for long range and one for local frequency. The first aircraft over the coast on its way home would call up and, as they all progressed into local frequency, I would land them from orders given by the Control Officer, priority being given to those with injured aboard. Ambulances stood by and crews would land and be debriefed. There were always those who did not return and I would spend the rest of the night listening out for a mayday call. When all hope was gone, it was sad to see the blackboard wiped clean.'

Wireless Mechanics were in the top group for pay and skill. Their work was chiefly on maintenance of signals and aircraft wireless equipment. On one occasion, at her pilot training station, Vera Collins was called out to a plane where the inter-com had gone out of order (US). Knowing the usual trouble, she equipped herself with spare plug-in sockets, so that she was able to report the job finished to the disbelieving pilot, before he had finished his walk back to the crewroom. 'I felt I had struck a blow for women mechanics.'

Nevertheless the responsibility of being Duty Wireless Mechanic for the first time was enough to unnerve any airwoman. A fault on the airfield field telephone occurred during Doris Brewster's first duty.

'Gathering only a few tools and hurrying into the November night air, clad in

battledress, I felt like a doctor summoned to an urgent case.'

She then spent hours trying to trace wires over the airfield, assisted by a helpful Sergeant, after which, while warming herself at the Duty Beacon van, she was asked if she could help with the mechanism of the Beacon which had gone out of gear.

'Eventually with the aid of my nail file, the red winking eye once again gave out its position to overhead traffic.'

WAAF Wireless Operators were first employed on 'listening' stations, where information was collected and recorded from foreign transmissions. These so-called Y stations could be a bit scary as Gwendoline Cocks was to find.

'Wireless cabins were always situated in the middle of a field, well away from the other buildings. One night while on watch (we were not supposed to work singly), I heard someone coughing outside. I was scared as the door had no lock, though we used to put a broomstick through the handles of the double doors. However, this night all was well, as the coughing was followed by "Baa, Baa". There were sheep in the field!'

The work could sometimes develop unforeseen dangers. For Winkie Loughran, 'There was trouble with the wireless set. Our Wireless Operator could hear nothing, sending or receiving, except howls and grinding sounds. Our Wireless Mechanics had left for Burma, so a Radar Mechanic pitched in to help me find the cause. We climbed the roof of the Ops block and found nothing, then we tried the alternative — a very high pylon. The RAF driver had to hold the ladder for me as I was too light to hold it for him. It was blowing a gale and I hardly expected to make it, with my small size and weight, but I clung on for dear life up that ladder. The trouble was there all right — wires rubbing against the pylon itself. We managed to free it and so resumed contact with the world.'

Wireless Operator 'listening in'. Note the 'sparks' badge. March 1945 (Mrs Bowyer).

Post-Operational interrogation of the crew of a Bomber Squadron at RAF Lindholme, 1942 (Mrs Collin-Smith).

Broadcasting from the Mobile Operations Room at Udine, Italy, to DAF and the 8th Army, 1945 (Miss George).

Once she was also instrumental in catching a German spy on her radio's secret frequency.

WAAF Signals Officers were slower to be introduced but by early 1943, there were 180 posts for them. Dorothy Henderson was one of the first and remembers it was not all plain sailing.

'Initially a Code and Cypher Officer, I heard that some women would be seconded and specially trained as Signals Officers and I applied. We were given a relatively short training course, including working in the underground network beneath Whitehall, where on a cream door marked puckishly WC, a room awaited Winston Churchill, should the need arise. Later came a further nine months' training.

'I recall, the first time after I was posted as a Technical Signals Officer, picking up my phone to answer "Signals Officer here" and hearing the amused comment in the background the other end, "There's a little WAAF here calling herself a Signals Officer!" Then to me, "You mean a Code and Cypher Officer, don't you dear?" I said, "No, I meant Signals Officer". "Oh God", said my caller. "Women Signals Officers." I later had splendid support and loyalty from male SNCOs. It was they who had found the idea hardest to accept at the beginning.'

Gradually the idea of using WAAF Officers to brief and interrogate air crews and act as Intelligence Officers was also tried out and found effective. This poem gives a good picture of some of their work.

'I am the Station Intelligence Officer
Stuffed full of secret matter
Which I digest with interest
And reproduce as patter.
I have all Jerry's searchlights taped,
I plot all dummies he has faked,
I pierce with eyes of practised cunning
His camouflage, by merely running
Casually through photographs.
I say "Here's heavy, there's light flak"
I tell you, "Here they'll mark your track"
And mention "Here you'll find I think,
A rescue raft. It's in the drink. . ."
I know his factories, towns and dromes
And every blessed craft he owns . . .
So you can take from off your faces,
Those cynic grins, for now you know
Why I am called the SIO.'

WAAF, in fact, were employed in many different kinds of Intelligence work. Yvonne George found herself on one extraordinary assignment — for once not at all secret!

'I was posted, as the only female member of the Desert Air Force (DAF) to broadcast messages to the army and RAF boys at the front from a mobile broadcasting truck with the British Forces Station for the Eighth Army and Desert Air

Force in Italy. I suppose it was the original British Forces Favourites Programme.'

Of her work in another intelligence department, Sergeant Nancy Gibson says, 'I was posted to a branch of the Secret Service known as MI9 which dealt with escapes and evasions of British and Allied personnel from enemy occupied territory. It was an inter-service organization with headquarters at Beaconsfield. I was billeted with a Staff Sergeant, who worked with MI19 and dealt mainly with interrogation of captured enemy prisoners. One of my first tasks was to type a list of Officers shot on recapture, after a mass escape from Stalag Luft III at Sagan. It upset me dreadfully.

'My Wingco on occasions visited the Awards Bureaux in Paris, Brussels and the Hague. These were set up mainly to give some rewards and reimbursements to those who had sheltered evaders at great risk to themselves.'

Intelligence WAAF were expected to cope with all varieties of work, but theirs was not the only highly secret work. WAAF were also employed in what came to be known in 1941 as the Central Interpretation Unit (CIU) at Medmenham, where aerial photographs were expertly examined for information by teams of Photographic Interpreters. Here Constance Babington-Smith will ever be associated with the discovery of the V-1 flying bomb sites, enabling bombers to attack the silos and thus delay these horrors by nearly six months. It was about this time that Jean MacKenzie found herself on special work.

'When the V–1 and V–2 sites were discovered some of us were chosen to man special 24 hour cameras — Oswald and Willie. We were taught to develop the films which were sent daily by despatch rider to London for detailed scrutiny.'

The results were, actually, rushed to Nuneham Park, Medmenham's satellite. Medmenham itself divided its work into three phases, around which gathered many functions. Margaret Moy dealt with an important bit of equipment.

'W Section was where maps were made from stereographic photographs, using the highly secret "Wild" machine. This was a very skilled job done by a team of Ordnance Survey men, so the two other WAAF Officers and I had to help with the back-up work required in a busy office, one on each shift. There was no recognizable sleep pattern and it played havoc with my digestive system. I was helping to draw maps of the mountains of North Africa, ready for the landings and then the German marshalling yards, where the mass of railway lines used to dance before my eyes.'

Liz Campbell quotes an In Memoriam to Z Section there — 'Overworked in War, May it rest in Peace:

'Weep O stranger, when you see,
This grave of a mighty section,
But deem it not impiety
To dread a resurrection!'

Because they were both in the business of gathering intelligence, there was a constant interchange of information between Medmenham and Bletchley Park, known as Station X, the home of codes and cyphers. Here, together with its knowledge of the German Enigma machine, Bletchley Park, unknown to its enemies, could read most of their most secret codes and break their cyphers. Those who worked there, among whom were WAAF, were described as the 'Geese that laid the golden eggs but never cackled' by Winston Churchill. The information thus gleaned was called Ultra, and the source sometimes referred to as Uncle Harry or in the RAF as Fred. The Y interception of wireless messages and signals traffic overheard and logged at the many listening stations was therefore essential to their work.

Because she hoped to get to an operational station, Peggy Smith remustered to a Teleprinter Operator, but she was disgusted to find that 'instead I landed up at Bletchley Park which was more like working in a factory. We did shifts, and there were no windows in the huts we worked in. Only when there was a lot of traffic was there any excitement, because we knew there must be something important happening.'

The following dedication to Bletchley Park was contributed by Peggy Edmed and Nan Lamb:

'I think that I shall never see,
A sight so curious as B P.
This place called up at war's behest
And peopled with the queerly dressed,
Yet what we did we could not say
Nor ever shall till judgement day.

The Air Force types who never fly,
Soldiers who never do or die,
Land-lubber sailors, beards complete,
Long-haired civilians, slim, effete.
Why we were there, we never knew,
And if we told, it wasn't true.

For five long years our war was there
Subject to local scorn and stare.
We came on foot, by coach or train,
The dull, the brilliantly insane.
What were we for? Where shall we be,
When peace at last demobs BP?

And when I die, think only this of me
I served my country at BP.
And should you ask, "What did you do
For Britain's sake in World War Two?"
God only knows and he won't tell
For after all, BP was Hell.'

In London, King Charles Street, Whitehall, was the hub of much Signals traffic. Early in 1940, before Dunkirk, Joyce Grose, a telephonist, remembers being interviewed for a highly secret post there.

'This was to work on the new Green Line switchboard that operated for the VIPs. We worked long and unusual hours, but enjoyed it.'

Of course men and women of different trades and ranks, service and civilian, worked in Whitehall. During the 1940 winter blitz, underground staff could sometimes hardly breathe when the dust, caused by falling bombs, came through the air ducts.

In 1942, the Cabinet Office and Chiefs of Staff decided that a cypher office should be set up by the RAF, to co-ordinate all signals formerly handled by each separate service, including messages from the Prime Minister. It was to be composed of WAAF Codes and Cypher Officers, who were to be entrusted with the work from start to finish. They were therefore carefully selected not only for their technical knowledge and ability but also for their secretarial skills and, of course, their discretion.

This Air Ministry Special Signals Office as it was first called — later renamed The Cabinet Office Cypher Office by the request of the Cabinet Office — was headed by Squadron Officer Joan Williams.

'I was at that time in charge of the Air Ministry Cypher Office and was asked to begin the new office. At the start it consisted of eight Officers but the establishment increased with the volume of work to 48 by the end of the war, when a few airwomen had been added to type the non-secret messages.'

That their work was appreciated can be seen from this letter by General Jacob, written on 13 April 1943.

Right *Cartoon poster:* Careless Talk Costs Lives (Author's collection).

Below *A spot of quick sightseeing before starting work in the Marrakesh Cypher Offices (Lady Llewellyn).*

'I have only just been reminded that today is the first birthday of the AMSSO. How time flies! And yet we have now got so accustomed to the speed, efficiency and adaptability of your staff, that it is hard to realize that it was only a year ago that you came on the scene to put an end to our troubles. Anyway I would like to thank you all for the really excellent work you have done for the Cabinet Office and to wish you very many happy returns of the day.'

At the time of Churchill's illness in the Middle East, Joan Williams took some Cypher Officers to help in North Africa.

'We flew out in a party to Casablanca. Four went on to Tunis to work for the Prime Minister at Carthage, until he was well enough to fly to Marrakesh, where I had already set up the cypher office in the Lodge of the Taylor Villa where Churchill was to recuperate. We were there for three weeks.'

Jean Rose was one of the lucky ones in Marrakesh, where they wore civilian clothes and were dubbed entomologists. 'In addition to working very hard, we had a fantastic time', but the accent was on intense hard work, not least for those left behind in London to receive the messages. The party ended their return journey home on board the *King George V* when, at the Saturday night dinner, the toast 'To Wives and Sweethearts' was moved and seconded, for the first time in naval history, by women — a WREN and a WAAF — who also added 'To Husbands and Boyfriends'.

Joan Williams also took some Officers to Quebec for the 1944 Conference. Nor was this the end of their travels, as a few helped at the Conferences of Yalta and Potsdam, and on the Cripps mission to India.

Recognition for these girls, coping with work almost too much to be borne yet borne with pride, included among other awards, an OBE for its head. Their office originally underground in Air Ministry, was later moved to the ground floor at Storey's Gate next to Churchill's Map Room.

Thus in this and many other tasks, Officers and airwomen of the Second World War acquitted themselves with more than honour in the dangerous and secret work with which such a large number of WAAF had been entrusted. As Joan McGlashan emphasized about her days as a Plotter, 'Having signed the Official Secrets Act, not even my parents ever knew anything about my work.'

Chapter 15

It's A Long Way To Go

'We the globe can compass soon
Swifter than the wandering moon.'

Shakespeare

Airwomen did not leave the United Kingdom until mid-1944, with by far the largest number sailing for Egypt, followed, after D-Day, by the Far East and Europe. Thus WAAF were to be found, together with the other services, scattered over approximately 29 countries, from the icy arctic to the tropics. In hotter climates, lacking suitable clothing, they went into the army summer uniform of khaki drill (KD) like the men, the colour and weight much disliked by the women — but necessary because of home wartime shortages. Many Officers and all airwomen were volunteers, their destinations secret. Nevertheless they all appreciated the opportunity to travel.

However, the first WAAF to leave Britain were a few Code and Cypher Officers, sent to New York in 1940, before the United States entered the war. After a while their numbers increased by a steady flow into 1941, when they joined the RAF Delegation in Washington, whose Cypher Section became busier and larger with America's involvement in the war. 1943 saw the gradual appearance of a small number of Officers from five other branches, totals peaking to over 80 persons. A few were loaned for a short time to the Australian Mission, Washington, and in 1944, three went to Melbourne, Australia, to work on the UK Army and RAF Liaison staff for Australia and New Zealand. In late 1945, they were joined by two airwomen — a much envied posting. Some Officers also worked in Canada and on loan to the Royal Canadian Air Force, while others were scattered thinly over numerous other bases on the eastern and western seaboard of America, with members of the other services.

At the RAF Delegation in Washington, Frankie Tudor, a 'Cypherine', remembers it was 'hard work and play'. While there she met Nurse Sommers who had escaped by submarine from Batan, Madam Chiang Kai-Shek, and an American Colonel who had rescued twelve airmen off an ice floe in Greenland.

Above *Cartoon*, Why me? (Mrs Sturgeon).

Above *WAAF Officers in front of some anthills near Darwin, Australia* (Mrs Lumsden).

Below *Funeral of two WAAF Officers in Washington* (Mrs Tudor).

Off to work in RAF Gander (Miss Dawson).

Her saddest memories were attending the funerals of other WAAF — two whom she knew were killed when coming off duty. On two days in 1944 she records doing 5,800 groups of outgoing and 6,800 incoming cypher messages on the typex machine. Little wonder therefore, that she was delighted to be sent to Nassau for five months during her two years tour, in line with the wisely developed practice of sending WAAF to quieter out-stations to ease the strain of the Codes and Cypher work at the Delegation.

In 1943, Frankie Tudor 'caught the 4 pm bomber which flew us to the Bahamas' where she rhapsodizes over 'our most wonderful little house here. The lawn runs down to a private beach and the sea. Everyone lives upstairs because of the sandflies and mosquitoes. Fortunately we think the hurricanes have passed.'

Betty Taylor did not enjoy her posting to Elizabeth City, North Carolina, USA, as 'the Americans in the south couldn't understand women in the services. To them we were just comforts for the troops.' There it was also 'terribly humid and the mosquitoes were enormous'. She did, however, enjoy her posting to Gander in Newfoundland, where she was allowed to do two tours, as she found the work so interesting, despite the cold. 'We often had to walk or ski to work because of drifting snow.'

One event of her stay there is recorded by Heather Dawson.

'In 1944-45, the RAF, USAAF and the Russians were ferrying new aircraft from Canada and the USA across the Atlantic via Gander. A Russian Colonel was based there and lived at our CO's house. The CO improved his English and taught him card games, at which the Colonel soon beat everyone in sight. He had an angelic baby face, which belied an extremely tough character. We found that

Trying on oxygen masks (which pepped us up no end) in a Hudson, en route from Montreal to San Diego (Miss Dawson).

dancing with him was like being clamped to a brick wall. One day after the snow had closed the airfield for a week, the Colonel ordered his crews to take off at once. One refused to leave his girl-friend, so a crewman knocked him out and his unconscious body was flung on board.'

A varied selection of tours fell to Dorothy Marsh.

'After a successful interview at Air Ministry I was posted to Dorval, Montreal. Later I was posted to Elizabeth City, North Carolina, where the Catalina flying boats were being ferried out to Murmansk by Russian pilots. Then a posting in June 1944 to Goose Bay, Labrador. More planes going to Russia, this time Mosquitoes.' [Then back to Dorval and the UK.] 'Not bad for a farmer's daughter!'

There were other stations too, including, for a short time, Trinidad, as well as Bermuda, where Betty Taylor once saw a German submarine in the clear water, as her Catalina flew overhead.

Code and Cypher Officers were also the first WAAF to be posted to the Middle East. Here previous cypher traffic had been handled by civilian women, mostly Officers' wives, but as the British and German offensives in North Africa built up, these were not enough, and thus 30 WAAF Officers arrived in Cairo in September 1941, after a long and difficult sea journey via Freetown and Lagos. Their work was to include training more locally-commissioned Cypher Officers.

Although a hotel was booked while they did a fortnight's familiarization course on Middle East Signals procedure, afterwards, while some were posted to units like Alexandria, Jerusalem and Ismailia, those based in Cairo were reduced to trudging around the city from pension to pension in their off-duty periods to find a lodging within their means, a risky contingency in every sense. In addition, Cairo was at bursting point and there was the threat of the Germans taking over. Ida Davis helped to make WAAF evacuation plans, since none were sure if they were covered by the Geneva Convention if captured. 'We had to have escorts going on duty, as the Egyptians were spitting at us and throwing stones.'

By the end of 1942 the UK WAAF Officers contingent had grown to around 200 and most working in the RAF HQ ME had moved to a new purpose-built centre (much disliked by those who had finally found comfortable flats and houses in Cairo). Penny Henderson describes it thus.

'Telecommunications Middle East (TME) lay beyond Heliopolis and in the desert. Here we lived and worked in fairly basic conditions — no adequate cooling system, long concrete blocks where we slept and a vast underground signals and cypher centre where hundreds of messages poured in day and night.

'On 30 October 1942, I came up from "the Hole" after late evening watch. A brilliant moon was lighting up the desert and all was peaceful. But from the coded messages we had been dealing with, we knew that this was not to last. It was hard to imagine that the most enormous bombardment was about to begin not many miles away. I will never forget that sobering and awesome moment, waiting for all hell to be let loose at El Alamein.'

In 1943, the RAF decided to employ locally-recruited girls as airwomen in the Middle East. Kenya and Palestine were to be training centres, but recruiting was slow, although actively publicized in Kenya, Cyprus, Egypt and Palestine. The Jewish Agency produced the largest numbers, many being recent refugees. For the RAF, this was taking a risk, since even then the political situation in Palestine was delicate, as the Jews only hated the Germans a degree or so more than they hated the British, whose peace-keeping mandate alienated both Arab and Jew.

Pamela Barringer, eventually to become CO of the Palestine Training Depot, notes in her diary for 1943:

'May 24   Advanced party arrive Lydda, 7 am.
June 14   Rest of WAAF Officers and NCOs from UK arrive.
June 22   New intake arrives — 4 from Haifa, 21 Tel Aviv and 21 Jerusalem.
June 28   WAAF Birthday Parade through the streets of Jerusalem. Tea at YMCA.
Oct 27   Visit AHQ Levant in Jerusalem. Get authority for battledress.
Nov 13   Move to Ramleh.
Dec 24   Airwomen have 48 hrs leave. After duty went to Bethlehem for carols.
Jan 3 1944 New course arrives. First commissioned Palestinians.'

As an instructor at the Depot, Pip Hugill remarks on the mixture of races represented there.

'I know it was quite usual for me to lecture on say Badges of Rank, to a class of about 25, split into three or four groups, each with its own interpreters in attendance. The fluent English speakers would cluster around me, drinking in the "straight from the horse's mouth" version, while others would be receiving

Number 1 Entry of Palestinian Recruits at Lydda (Mr Leftly).

heaven alone knows what, in French/Greek/German and Arabic!'

The resulting airwomen varied in quality but were frequently highly emotional. Edward Stott, a test pilot at Aboukir, Egypt, tells of an incident when one of these girls pulled a forbidden knob in the cockpit of a Hurricane, ejecting a Very light. She promptly fainted and her colleagues fainted in sympathy. In all, 19 were laid out in rows before medical assistance arrived.

Around 750 local service girls joined the WAAF before airwomen from the UK were sent to the Middle East. In March 1944, our first volunteers set sail for Egypt, and while on some of the ships airwomen were bored with virtually nothing to do, on others they worked very hard. Space was usually at a premium, with many other troops aboard, but the girls travelled in reasonable comfort, thanks to tri-service conditions agreed in January 1944.

Everyone was struck by the lights, after blacked-out Britain. Cairo 'was just like fairyland' says Sergeant Moores. All airwomen spent a few days at a temporary Personnel Transit Centre before proceeding to their new unit. It was under canvas and presented a fire hazard in Barbara Kirkham's estimation, who then goes on to describe her Cairo posting.

'There were at my arrival two WAAF billets. Zamalek I housed the Palestinian airwomen and about five minutes walk away, right on the side of the Nile, was Zamalek II, our accommodation. Ours was a block of flats on the tip of Gezira Island. Alongside the water itself was a boat repair and building yard and we could hear the men chanting as they went about their work. Eventually we moved to Zamalek III, on the opposite side of the road to Queen Nazli's Palace. We often saw the King's motorcade pass through the city.

'Our Admin Staff were great, but they would insist on us getting out of bed to

Left *Poster recruiting for the WAAF in the Middle East* (RAF Museum).

Above *Zamalek II* (Sgt Kirkham).   **Above** *Christmas menu, 1944* (Mrs Ford).

Below *Bedtime on the balcony of Zamalek II in issue pyjamas with a background of a Cairo minaret* (Mrs Grogan).

take part in PT sessions before the sun was too high.'

In fact, most felt that, perhaps owing to the mellowing sunshine, discipline was far more relaxed in Egypt.

On the more remote stations airmen working on difficult jobs, in a land of scruffy dress, sweat and bad language, resisted the posting in of WAAF. But more than one Orderly Officer inspecting meals after the first airwomen appeared in a dining hall, could barely disguise his amusement at his suddenly polite and smartly turned out company.

At El Gedida, where Maureen Kiddy was stationed, 'We were in tents on the edge of the desert, each tent having three steps down on to a concrete floor, with a brick wall about two to three feet high over which went the canvas. We were three to a tent. I remember being on my own one night, the other two being on leave, when a sand storm blew up. We kept to the concrete paths in the hope that sand fleas wouldn't jump into our socks. We had no chores to speak of, as these were done by Arabs. There were plenty of leisure and sports activities, clubs and a very good social life — if one could keep awake — the heat made one very sleepy.'

There was of course the other side of the coin, as Enid Palmer points out, 'bugs, fleas, dysentery and dirt everywhere'. Gippy tummy was endemic, with occasional diphtheria, while sand in your shoes, your soup and your sheets was more than a joke.

Compensations were leave in all sorts of exotic places, formerly an impossible dream to most girls. So they visited the Pyramids, Luxor, the Valley of the Kings, the Sinai Desert, biblical locations in Palestine, Lebanon, Syria and Petra, where

Carving her name on top of the pyramid (Mrs Grogan).

being stoned by Arabs and Jews alike was only one of the necessary hazards of such adventures. In 1945 there were nearly 3,500 airwomen working in the Middle East which by then included Cyprus, Syria, Aden and Iraq.

An extract from Betty Ward's Journal for 1944 captures the typical reactions of a LACW to an overseas posting.

'12 *October*   From 11 days' embarkation leave, reported to West Kirby.

13 *October*   Lecture from Padre, FFI, X-rays, visit to the chiropodist, followed by a thorough going over by the MO. That's my spiritual and earthly care.

14 *October*   Kitting out very exciting until we get khaki stockings. So far we have been issued with 13 pairs of knickers (blue, khaki and white). With my leather-sided issue sunspecs and my topi there'll be no chance of sunstroke for me.

16 *October*   More lectures. A Group Officer on morals — "In case of pregnancy WAAF will be returned home immediately". Avoiding the difficulty of carrying full kit, plus a baby in arms? Injections and inoculations — yellow fever and typhus quite the worst.

17 *October*   Films on security, fleas, lice, mosquitoes. What have I volunteered for? Shipping parade. Yesterday's newspapers have already told the world that we have departed for India. Premature what?

18 *October*   Glasgow. We board the Cameronian. Quarters good, about 14 bunks in our cabin, with showers and toilets almost opposite. Water on half-hour night and morning. It's going to be fast in, fast out.

24 *October*   After five days of sickness I've almost found my legs. The weather is getting warmer and the convoy seems almost white against the blue, blue sea. After blackout everyone is below decks. There seems no air. How do the men survive? [About 3,000 of them.] Compared to their quarters below, our 'A' deck cabins seem like the Ritz. We have shows etc and help the men sew the flashes on their KD.

25 *October*   Passed Gibraltar and we've entered a land of flying fish and leaping porpoises with sunsets turning the land to purple and the sea bright red.

26 *October*   Off Algiers. WAAF allotted space to sleep in turns on top deck at night. Morning comes not one minute too soon. I ache all over. We discover that we have been gently rained on by soot from the funnel.

29 *October*   Engines stop. "Complete silence will be maintained at all times". Submarines! No one dares to speak. We lie rigid in our bunks. After an eternity the engines start up again. Ah well! I am going to live to fight another day.

1 *November*   Enter Port Said. Egyptian children dive for pennies and ask for snow (silver) pennies. Dirty children in even dirtier clothes fight on the quayside over fish. Our ship takes on water, fruit and supplies, plus three gallons of castor oil (for us dysentery wallahs). The

Right *Yellow Fever Innoc-
ulation Certificate, 1944
(Mrs Kirkham).*

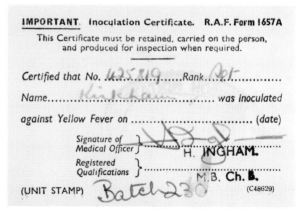

IMPORTANT. Inoculation Certificate. R.A.F. Form 1657A

This Certificate must be retained, carried on the person,
and produced for inspection when required.

Certified that No. ....Rank..............

Name... was inoculated

against Yellow Fever on .... (date)

Signature of   ⎱
Medical Officer ⎰ ....
                     H. INGHAM.

Registered   ⎱
Qualifications ⎰ ....
                    M.B. Ch. B.

(UNIT STAMP)   Batch 230   (C48629)

Right *Goodbye* (Mrs
Plummer).

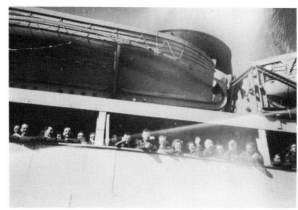

Below *Deck Hockey with
the WRNS on a troopship,
1945* (Mrs Lumsden).

	decks are all lit up again at night and we have a dance.
2 November	We start down the canal. I see my first camel — strange it's almost white. The natives in their long white nightshirts cheer and shout. Alongside we see toll houses, wreckages of subs and ships, and a pocket-handful of little tents in an oasis of emerald green against a background of sandhills.
5 November	We watch the dolphins jumping the waves and locusts skimming the water.
8 November	Arrive Aden. A Talk. Could Aden be Eden? The ship takes on water. We have another wonderful sunset with the sea the palest of blues, white clouds turning salmon pink to red with the sea reflecting the red against a background of purple hills. Such rich exotic colours!
9 November	Leave Aden. Now designated our own deck area, duly roped off and segregated from the men — the heat is obviously expected to affect them. The Indian Ocean is like a millpond, plenty of flying fishes but no sight of land. We just wilt in the heat. The KD issued to us is anything but cool.
14 November	Approaching India. Sandy beaches and tall palm trees can be seen in the distance. We arrive in Bombay Harbour.
16 November	What a train. Slatted seats. Grilled windows to keep out monkeys and mosquitoes. During the night the train stops — on fire. And again!

Left *Through her airman interpreter, a Corporal checks the Christmas 1944 mail times with an Indian* (Mrs Pearson).

Above right *View of the Viceroy's Palace from an office window in New Delhi* (Mrs Wing).

17 November Food on the train is good. Not much in the way of scenery. Most seems desert. Railway stations teeming with a mass of milling people.

18 November Arrive in New Delhi, safe and sound. Yes it's been worth it!'

Betty Wing, from a later draft, remembers the camp for which they were bound.

'We arrived at New Delhi Racecourse Camp. Half was used for our accommodation and the other for horse racing. It was strange to see station and civilian sports in progress at one time.

'Billets were long concrete buildings, cool but sparsely furnished. Each bed space held two charpoys (beds) and one almara (wardrobe). We were encouraged to keep all clothes, other than top clothes, in a tin trunk to ensure their freedom from white ants. Mosquito nets were compulsory.

'We were met by a friendly bunch of girls, but one thing that did strike us as strange was the pallor of their complexions. [The enervating Delhi climate sapped the girls' health.] Because of this all WAAF personnel are to be sent to the hill station at Lower Topa for three weeks' leave at regular intervals. The climate there resembles an English summer.'

In Delhi the temperature could sometimes soar above 115°F against which fans and wet bamboo screens did little to cool the working WAAF, although quarters were cleaned and tended by native servants. The monsoon was a blessing, and so were the baths and swimming pools. Topis were rarely worn. One girl chuckled over her hat collection of flat cap, forage cap, tin helmet, burma bush-hat, topi and later RAF beret, which made her feel like Winston Churchill.

Near the camp was the Viceroy's Palace, occupied by Lord Wavell, who occasionally issued much sought-after invitations to garden parties in the grounds. Margaret Holmes was fortunate enough to be entertained to dinner with 'lavish table appointments and a meal taken off gold plates. Special permis-

sion was given to wear civilian dress.'

WAAF could also be found in Bombay, and a few out-stations, leave centres and hospitals. Delhi was now headquarters of the British Air Force South East Asia (BAFSEA), as the Air Command Headquarters had moved to Ceylon, and in early 1945 small drafts of airwomen journeyed there by sea and air. At the beginning, their accommodation was bamboo huts and they remarked on there being no shortage of fruit, tea and sugar.

Nevertheless, it was a difficult posting for some. In Kogalla, Ceylon, Nancy Barnett's unit was, '. . . in a jungle clearing, with Catalina flying boats that swept the Indian Ocean for Japanese ships, planes and U-boats. Three of us kept the teleprinter system working between us, night and day. There was little but heat and work, away from civilization. Poisonous snakes, and lots of creepy crawlies left the surrounding jungle to visit us. The hut roofs blew off in a monsoon. Off duty, in our hut we were always in the nude. The heat was appalling.'

By now the efforts of the allies were shifting towards the war with Japan. In Ceylon other WAAF sections opened including one at Trincomalee to help in the assault on Rangoon. Plans were also in hand for the Headquarters ACSEA and its WAAF personnel to move to Singapore as soon as Malaya was safe, a move which it completed in mid December 1945. WAAF also appeared in Hong Kong in February 1946. But political problems in India were to change the Far Eastern picture, once the war was over.

Algiers, although in Africa, was the Headquarters of the Mediterranean Air Command, and WAAF Cypher Officers had been there from 1943, moving with the war to Tunis. Airwomen were sent there in 1945, much against the wishes of the Director, but in the event, they only stayed for six months. Vicki Slack was one of those '. . . posted to Algiers and billeted in the Hotel Oasis on the edge of the Casbah. There were signs on all the roads leading to it, saying it was "Out of bounds". I did do an official tour and found it very unnerving, I wasn't very keen on Algiers at all. The crippled people and disease were horrific. Ramadan was difficult too. Our hotel was in a square with a mosque on one side and stalls all round outside the walls. They were lit by yellow lamps and the smell and noise were awful.' But to be quite fair, for others, 'the sunlight and the scent of orange trees seemed like heaven'.

There were also a few WAAF in battle-scarred Malta and on the Rock of Gibraltar — a different Command — with upwards of 200 in Italy, where WAAF Officers from Tunis had followed the war, and been joined, when conditions were better, by airwomen.

In the summer of 1945, Henrietta Barnet, a later Director, was posted to Caserta, Italy to be responsible for airwomen employed in Italy and Algiers. Here she visited Vienna to explore the possibility of sending airwomen there.

'There was no heating, little lighting, the shops were empty and the streets devoid of any Austrian man or boy, all having been sent to Siberia. Russians patrolled the streets and the Austrian women lived in constant fear. A little later a few airwomen were posted in. They were employed in the Schönbrunn Palace where our headquarters was situated and once again proved their worth.'

Airwomen — Flying Nursing Orderlies — were the first WAAF to arrive in Europe after the D-Day landings, and within two-and-a-half months afterwards, the best ever contingent of WAAF Officers and airwomen were under canvas in Normandy. They worked with the Allied Expeditionary Force and the 2nd Tactical Air Force, following their various units in increasing numbers through France

Above left *Trying to keep cool in Kogalla* (Mrs Worrall).

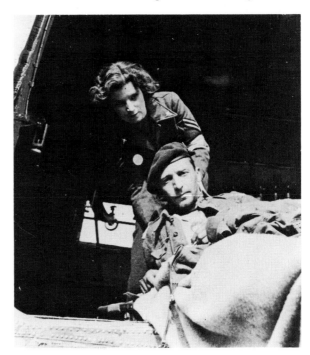

Right *One of the first Flying Nursing Orderlies in France with a casualty on D-Day + 7* (Mrs Budd).

and Belgium into Germany, where they eventually became part of the British Air Forces of Occupation. By late 1945, they numbered well over a thousand.

In Belgium, Dorothy Scholefield found, 'Our only hardship was cold showers in most places and cold water in Brussels. There, we were living in a large barracks and were taken to work in a RAF transport lorry to offices situated in the city centre. The most frightening events were dodging into doorways to avoid the V–2s.'

A scattering of airwomen served in Holland, Norway and Denmark after the end of the war, as did a few Officers who also worked for a short time in Sweden, Greece and even Moscow, with RAF exhibitions. In view of the incredible list of countries to which wartime women in the RAF travelled in the course of duty, it is surprising to find that less than 9,000 left the UK, about 4.5 per cent of the total in the service. Certainly this was never from any lack of volunteers, but rather it arose from the caution of the authorities to maintain the safety of 'their girls'. In an open letter from Egypt, Helen Fernandez countered envious criticisms.

'Airwomen are in the WAAF to replace men and that is what they have done at home and what they are doing overseas. We did not know what or where we were coming to — security saw to that. When we first came out here we worked alongside men, now many of us are on our own — the men have returned to the UK and we are here to carry on. Are we to blame if there is sunshine here and we enjoy it; that there are luxuries here which we greatly appreciate after having been without them for so long; that on our off-duty hours there are social amenities which we take advantage of?'

Even with a disastrous war, the spirit of adventure was alive and kicking!

........and apart from the heat and the flies, it's just like home!

A letter with tropical hazards (Mrs Sturgeon).

Chapter 16

None But The Brave

'As soon as we beat England, we shall make an end of you Englishmen once and for all. Able-bodied men and women will be exported as slaves to the Continent. The old and weak will be exterminated. All men remaining in Britain as slaves will be sterilised; a million or two of the young women of the Nordic type will be segregated in a number of stud farms where, with the assistance of picked German sires, during a period of 10 or 12 years, they will produce annually a series of Nordic infants to be brought up in every way as Germans. These infants will form the future population of Britain ... Thus in a generation or two, the British will disappear.'

Walter Darre, German Minister of Agriculture, April 1942

Today such threats sound melodramatic and ridiculous, but they were chillingly real at a time when Hitler was attempting to wipe out such races as Jews in gas chambers and labour camps all over Europe. Little wonder that British civil and service resistance, from men and women, was almost total, and inspired enormous feats of quiet heroism and startling bravery. Among these must be recorded the women of the WAAF, who did countless deeds of courage, the majority never told or rewarded. Girls were too pragmatic. To them unusual days called for unusual actions and they did their best because there was nothing else to do. The Log Book of No 14 Balloon Centre, Cardiff, for 3 March 1941 gives an Incident Report, typical of its kind, made by ACW1 Upton.

'Returning from an evening class at the Technical College, we got on to a tramcar and went upstairs laughing and cracking jokes as usual. We knew that an alert had been sounded. Suddenly the tramcar stopped and the driver and conductor vanished as hundreds of incendiary bombs fell around us. Thinking that at any moment one would fall through the roof of the tramcar, we managed to get down the stairs and into the road. Fires were starting everywhere. Rushing to one and then another, we threw sand over them and succeeded in putting them out.

Suddenly a voice shouted "Bomb on the roof!" A warden pointed to a house and Corporal Griffiths rushed over to it and knocked at the door. The occupant opened it, not knowing what had happened and when we told her she looked stunned. We rushed upstairs looking in one room and then another until we found one from which smoke was coming from under the door. We tried to open the door but a thick carpet hampered our entrance. When we eventually succeeded in opening it, what a sight met our eyes. The smoke was so thick, it almost blinded us. Corporal Griffiths handed me a handkerchief, which I tied around her face. The two sons of the house appeared and gave us all the assistance they could (By the way, they were both very handsome). After a struggle to extinguish the bomb, we succeeded in getting the fire under control. The owner of the house thanked us with tears in her eyes (maybe it was the smoke) and we went on our way.'

An incident at Horsham-St-Faith in the summer of 1942 will always be remembered by Section Officer Hodges.

'The duty driver for the firetender that night was a small, blonde, coal-miner's daughter, ACW Williams. Incendiary bombs were being rained down on top of the bomb dump, too high up, out of reach of the shovels and fire extinguishers of the RAF Duty Firemen, so that it seemed that the whole dump, several thousand pounds weight of bombs would explode at any moment. "Oh come on, do something," shouted Williams, and grabbing one of the special long-handled shovels, she scrambled up to the top of the stacked five-hundred pounders and, as fast as the incendiaries came, she whisked them, still flaming, down to the ground for the men to extinguish as they landed. The German aircraft continued circling around low and coming again and again with incendiaries.

'When one of the men passed out, Williams jumped down off the dump between attacks to give him first-aid but couldn't bring him round. So she drove the fire engine carefully over him, with its wheels on either side to give him cover. Then back up to the top of the bomb dump again to cope with more incendiaries. One of the firemen said, "She looked like a proper little fairy up there dancing among the flames." Later she explained logically, "Well. They couldn't reach up there to put them out, could they?" '

For more than four years the Dover area faced the bombardment of German long range guns from occupied France. Working in exposed buildings on the edge of the Channel cliffs, over 200 airwomen of all trades, but particularly radar, continued their work throughout that period and none asked for transfer away despite the casualties, fatal and otherwise. A Radar Operator there, Josephine Mawle, describes another kind of courage.

'Shelling was fairly regular especially on moonless nights, and particularly after D-Day and before Calais fell. On camp one shell went through the NAAFI and exploded in the shelter used by most of the WAAF. Three girls were killed and several injured. I was in another shelter, but as duty First Aid Orderly, I had to go in and do what I could to help the Medical Orderlies.'

Being in vulnerable locations, WAAF died, both at home and abroad, many graves being cared for by the Commonwealth War Graves Commission. Official 1946 figures record that during the war 187 WAAF were killed on duty, 4 were missing (later found to have been killed in German Concentration Camps), 420 were injured and 277 died from natural causes — though it is to be wondered how far such illnesses as tuberculosis, pneumonia, rupture, stomach ulcer, meningitis and breakdown, could be attributed to prolonged stress, hard living and working wartime conditions Servicewomen still with us today suffer from the effects of those war years, and in the WAAF Rolls of Honour, no sacrifice should be forgotten.

Some courage was of such a remarkable kind that it did not go unrewarded. The first WAAF award went to Corporal Joan Pearson, a Sick Quarters Attendant, for her actions on 31 May 1940. In her account she describes waking at 01:00 hrs on hearing an aircraft crashing near the WAAF quarters at Detling in Kent. She ran to help.

'A twinkling light showed at SHQ — that meant the ambulance — must warn the guard to undo the gates and be ready. The guard grunted as I ran by him. He knew me. I shouted to him the ambulance was behind. I kept running hard and came to a RAF policeman. He tried to prevent me from climbing the fence — men were shouting for doctor, ambulance. I yelled "Coming." There was a blazing fire started. The nettles stung me in the ditch on the other side. A figure panted up and I saw another silhouetted against the light. A man was dragging a harnessed figure — told him to race and get the fence down for the ambulance. I tried to drag the pilot further away from the blaze, but he was groaning and so decided to render first aid immediately in case of further damage. I took his

Corporal Joan Pearson GC (This England).

Left *An award certificate.*

The Under-Secretary of State for
Air presents his compliments and
by Command of the Air Council
has the honour to transmit the
enclosed Awards granted for
service during the war of
1939-45.

Below right *LACW
McKinlay BEM (Mrs
Harding).*

Far right *Corporal Holden
after her BEM investiture
(Mrs Horton).*

parachute harness off and found his neck was causing great pain. He told me to
keep clear as he had a full load of bombs aboard. The petrol tanks blew out and
so I lay down and tried to shield the light from his face as he was suffering shock.
A huge bomb went off, but I was holding his head to prevent further dislocation.
He was very concerned about a small cut on his lip in case it showed. A soldier
crawled up and lent me his handkerchief. The bomb took all the oxygen. As
there was another bomb to go, I ran to the fence to help the Medical Officer over
with the stretcher. We got aboard the ambulance and into camp. The other
bomb went off worse than the first. The Sick Quarters was all ready and we
finished our work about 03:00 hrs. Sick Parade was as usual 08:00 hrs.'

The George Cross was given to Corporal Pearson, but her award was followed
by many other honours and decorations not all for courage but usually for some
outstanding devotion to duty. Thus in the Second World War WAAF were
credited with 2 GCs, 2 DBEs, 3 CBEs, 20 OBEs, 97 MBEs, 93 BEMs, 6MMs, 8
Commendations and 2,497 Mentions in Despatches. As an example of these,
here are the stories of the three British Empire Medals (BEMs) given for
Special Gallantry.

LACW Kathleen McKinlay was duty Balloon Squadron ambulance driver in
Dover, when the allied troops in 1944 were taking the French Channel ports,
and Dover was shelled almost continuously. On 26 September 1944, the Medical Officer (MO) and she 'had been out all morning and went back to HQ to get

something to eat. Just as we parked the ambulance there was a thud. We shot behind the blast wall and there was an almighty blast and glass, dust and rubble flew everywhere. The MO put his arm around me and said "Hold tight". We both ended up on the floor, and when things cleared I got up and said "Are you all right?" I got no reply. He was dead. After covering him up, I didn't have a great deal of time to think, as there was a yell for the ambulance, which fortunately was in one piece. The Medical Orderlies were busy, so one of the RAF Sergeants dealt with my wounds [in the hand and thigh] and as I still could drive, we started getting the injured to hospital [one and a half miles away]. I don't really remember much about the journeys as I think I was just acting like a robot, but the Sergeant told me later that I scared the hell out of him. I remember creating at the hospital, because all the stretchers had been taken into casualty and I couldn't get them back — I was worried that if they got lost I would have to pay for them. The next thing I remember was waking up next morning in hospital myself and demanding to know what they had done with my uniform.'

Another to win this special BEM was Alice Holden, a 22-year-old Corporal who was on Radio Telephone duty in October 1943 when a Wellington bomber crashed and caught fire. Hearing cries for help, she ran towards the wreckage

Left *Flight Sergeant Turner (on the left) in 1942 (Mrs Grose).*

Below *Section Officer Syers in her office at HQ RAF ME Cairo, 1942 (Mrs Bisdee).*

through the flying debris from exploding petrol tanks and ammunition. Despite the searing heat she managed to wrench open the escape door to the burning turret of the rear gunner, freed him and dragged him out. The others were beyond help.

The third was LACW Lilian Ellis in charge of a balloon site during a raid in 1943. A bomb killed three and wounded four of her airwomen, and although severely wounded herself, she kept the balloon flying till help arrived. Then she organized relief parties and administered first aid, by which she undoubtedly saved the life of at least one airwoman.

Six airwomen won the unusual award of the Military Medal. Here are the stories of just two. When enemy bombers attacked their station in September 1940, Sergeant Helen Turner and Corporal Elspeth Henderson, Telephone Operators, were working in the Exchange which suffered a direct hit. Despite the falling bombs and knowing there was only a light roof over their heads, the girls continued with their work, only stopping when the building was aflame and they were ordered to leave. Later Joyce Grose worked with Flight Sergeant Turner as Telephonist on the Green Line Switchboard in King Charles Street, and said of her, 'She was always known as Jimmy Turner and a great person she was.'

So the tally of coolness, devotion to duty, selflessness and leadership illuminates the WAAF annals of courage. Let these stand for the many others.

However, those actions could be spoken of and their names given because the girls worked with a regular uniformed force, but such was not the case with WAAF on secret work. The Secret Service in Britain was split into many sections and in many places, ranging from MI5 under the Home Office and MI6 under the Foreign Office, to a whole row of others into double numbers. Each had a different function, although sometimes these overlapped.

The Special Intelligence Service, SIS, generally known as MI6, gathered information, some of which was provided by the listening service 'Y', Photographic Interpretation and Codes and Cypher work. Experienced in Serbo-Croat languages and sensitivities, Pamela Syers had been posted to Egypt as RAF Liaison Officer to the Royal Yugoslav Air Force, during the time when the Germans were bombing the Suez Canal nightly, and Yugoslavs' loyalties to King and Communists were, to say the least, confused. Here she shared an office with colleagues responsible for the French, Greek and Polish Air Forces in the Middle East. Then in October 1943,

'I was seconded to SIS Intelligence Work with the Yugoslavian partisans in Bari [Italian HQ of the Balkan Air Force]. Life with the Yugoslavs was never dull. One evening in the flat in Bari, which served as our Mess, I was reading a detective story, when a shot did actually ring out. I went to the kitchen where I found a young partisan showing off to the cook by shooting at the pans hanging on the walls. This was very dangerous because of ricochets in a confined space. I was very angry and told him to save his bullets for the enemy and threatened him with the Yugoslav Colonel if there was any more nonsense. The cook had an Alsatian dog whose proudest trick was to help her lay the table by carrying the cutlery in his mouth. She couldn't understand why I protested! By this time, the

Section Officer George in the Operations Room of the Balkan Air Force, Bari, Italy, 1944 (Miss George).

Royal Yugoslav Air Force had been transferred (by their own wish and against that of their government in London) to Tito's forces, and occasionally appeared in Bari sporting red stars in their caps. When finally allowed to fight, they did so with such fury and intensity that very few survived.'

As Liaison Officer between SIS and SOE, Yvonne George was in London, then Algiers and Bari. Here, on one occasion a group of Italian partisans, bristling with arms, broke into the requisitioned office where she slept, looking for evidence of the collaboration of one of its former inhabitants, in the desk she was using as a dressing-table. 'The leader was a tough looking female Corporal with a full mouth of silver teeth.' Fortunately nothing happened.

1940 had seen the emergence of an independent, inter-service and civilian, Special Operations Executive (SOE), formed to give aid to those resisting enemy occupation. Its headquarters became collectively and appropriately known as Baker Street, where part did indeed exist. Over 300 members of the RAF and WAAF worked for SOE, at home and abroad, and several WAAF held key positions.

In the Air Section Baker Street worked Faith Townson and Jean Woolaston who were part of the organization which arranged the dropping of armaments and agents into occupied Europe, including France, Belgium, Holland, Denmark, Poland, Yugoslavia and Czechoslovakia. At one time Faith was with the French Section. Then she moved on.

'I also worked for a time in the Danish Section in Baker Street and then with Force 136 Office in Calcutta. From there I was in the Ceylon Office where we were operating Liberators flying agents and stores to occupied Malaya. I was there when our submarine picked up two agents who had been working behind the lines in Malaya and brought them back to Ceylon. When the war was over our office moved back to Meerut and our aircraft switched to dropping stores to POW camps in the Far East.'

Peggy Robinson was an Intelligence and Liaison Officer between Air Ministry and SOE. 'With such abnormal, detailed, secret and individual work carried out in SOE, this was sometimes a difficult job' — probably a vast understatement! Those were, however, dealing with perils, mostly known, amid their own kind and in their own surroundings. It calls for a different sort of courage to face unseen dangers in a hostile environment, day after day, death only a step behind.

Agents worked on communications, morale-building and direction of resistance groups, within an enemy occupied country. Along with men, about 50 women were sent to France, many landing by parachute. They were to act primarily as Couriers and Wireless Operators. They included 15 WAAF, among whom six died — five in German Concentration Camps, after endless interrogation and privation. One WAAF went to Yugoslavia.

The women selected to be agents trained with men and learned to be proficient in the handling of weapons, demolition, fieldcraft, map reading, morse, survival and security techniques. They learned the art of living a false identity on false papers, following and being followed, and were shown something of how to resist interrogation. They had to understand the organization of sabotage groups, secret armies and reception arrangements for the dropping of men and materials. Wireless Operators had to master safety codes and checks, the arts of concealing heavy equipment, bulky enough to fill a small suitcase, how to avoid traps and the finer art of message giving and taking.

They all did hard physical training near Inverness, espionage in the New Forest and parachuting near Manchester. Those destined for France were usually bilingual, often with one parent of foreign origin. Although Winnie Field often saw the French women who trained as paratroops, 'we did not know they were all to be dropped over France. They were brave women and still took time to wear their make-up.'

One pretty young woman who volunteered to be dropped into France was remembered by Audrey Ririe.

'I later heard she'd died of pneumonia. [See Muriel Byck, page 222]. I always shudder when I think of those vast empty fields of Germany and France and how they must have looked to a young woman dropped into enemy territory.'

Training lasted several months, though compared with present ten-year training for Russian agents, this was short. It ended with tests and dry-runs in this country and then, if successful, waiting in Holding Schools or flats for the night call to Tempsford or Tangmere airport, and the ghostly flight in a Hudson or Lysander aircraft, through the flak, to a tiny French field.

While in Baker Street, Faith Townson records, 'For a time I worked in the Pick-up Section, which meant taking agents down to RAF Tangmere and waiting for the Lysander to return with agents who had to be got out of France urgently. Then drive back to London in the early hours and hand them over to be debriefed.'

This could have been done by someone like Jean Alexander, another WAAF Officer, this time in intelligence and interrogation.

Radar Operators were usually aware when RAF aircraft were involved in these secret drops or sorties by certain features, but they never spoke of it. Such flights were more than usually dangerous, and the pilots who flew on such missions took their lives in their hands. Pearl Panton recalls what happened to one.

'It was a full moon last night, an essential factor for special mission pilots taking off and returning. At 8 pm I was driven from the Mess to the Happydrome where aircraft were controlled. The Officer of the Watch gave me my orders. I was to work on the Skytron radar. A special mission was going out before midnight, due to return before dawn. P for Peter took off at 10 pm. One of the girls working on the watch was startled to recognize her husband's voice calling to confirm he was airborne. I didn't know her well but had met her and her husband recently in a nearby café. During the night watch, she told me she was expecting her first baby. It was a busy night as usual. P for Peter was due to return at 3 am. There was no RT contact at the scheduled time. I was told to call him and keep calling him at regular intervals. The girl sat next to me watching the Skytron and listening intently for her husband's voice. His call would have included a coded message to be passed on to Air Ministry. It never came through.'

After the war, Vera Atkins, an Intelligence Officer in the French Section, travelled through the German Concentration Camps investigating the fate of missing French agents and questioning Gestapo and others, and to this day she helps those who were in the field. Through her is known what happened to most of the captured WAAF agents, whose actions and adventures would fill more than this book. Many were decorated, though among brave women such awards are only relative. All were well-educated, charming, intelligent, sensitive, self-assured and incredibly courageous in the face of horrible dangers. May these short notes record something of their achievements.

Yvonne Baseden (married Burney) parachuted in, March 1944, to work as a Wireless Operator named Odette, with the Scholar Circuit. Effected large scale supply drops. Was betrayed. Fought, wounded and imprisoned in solitary confinement at Ravensbrück. Survived.

Yolande Beekman (née Unternahrer) landed, September 1943, as a Wireless Operator named Mariette. Worked with the Musician Circuit. Caught. Shot at Dachau, September 1944.

Sonia Butt (married d'Artoise) parachuted in, May 1944, as a Courier named Blanche to work with the Headmaster Circuit. Many dangerous journeys. Arrested, raped, released. Survived.

Muriel Byck parachuted in, April 1944, as a Wireless Operator named Michèle, to work with the Ventriloquist Circuit. Died suddenly of meningitis on mission, July 1944.

Yvonne Cormeau (née Biesterfeld) parachuted in, August 1943, to work as a Wireless Operator named Annette for the Wheelwright Circuit. Lived with Maquis. Effected large scale supply drops. Continuously on move. Survived.

Christine Granville (née Skarbek) parachuted in, July 1944, to join the Jockey circuit as Pauline. Captured and, by cunning, rescued three Resistance leaders from being shot, three hours before Allies arrived. Murdered in London 1952.

Mary Herbert (married Baissac) landed by boat, October 1942, as a Courier called Marie Louise for the Scientist Circuit. Remained working after circuit broken up, 1943. Survived.

Phyllis Latour, parachuted in, May 1944, as a Wireless Operator named Geneviève to work with the Scientist Circuit. Kept on move. Many narrow escapes. Survived.

Cecily Lefort (née MacKenzie) landed, June 1943, as a Courier named Alice also to join the Jockey Circuit. Arrested trying to escape cover. Imprisoned, sick. Gassed at Ravensbrück March 1945.

Patricia O'Sullivan (married Alvey) parachuted in, March 1944, as a Wireless Operator named Simonet to join the Fireman Circuit. Trained two assistants, despite sickness. Survived.

Lilian Rolfe landed, April 1944, as a Wireless Operator named Nadine to join the Historian Circuit. Continued after chief's arrest. Caught by accident. Too weak to walk. Shot at Ravensbrück January 1945.

Diana Rowden landed, June 1943, as a Courier named Paulette to work with the Acrobat/Stockbroker Circuit. After her chief's arrest carried on, till trapped in her sawmill hideout by Gestapo impersonating new Chief. Lethal injection at Natzweiler. Cremated July 1944.

Anne-Marie Walters (married Comert) parachuted in, January 1944, as a Courier named Paulette. Also joined the Wheelwright Circuit. Travelled vast distances. Helped escaping POWs. Returned over the Pyrenees, July 1944.

Lilian Rolfe (IWM).

Noor Inayat Khan (This England).

Pearl Witherington (married Cornioley) parachuted in, September 1943, as a Courier named Marie to the Stationer/Wrestler Circuit. Trained and ran an active Maquis group of 2,000 men after her chief arrested. Led them in sabotage and battle. Million francs reward offered for her capture. Returned in September 1944.

Sibyl Sturrock, only WAAF parachuted into Yugoslavia, September 1944, to collect information and co-ordinate partisans' efforts with those of the Allies. Survived.

The sole WAAF agent to be given the George Cross was Noor-un-Nisa Inayat Khan. Long before that time, Nora Wenman, a Wireless Operator, met her at Abingdon. As both were called Nora, Wenman was asked to change to Wendy, to avoid confusion, which she did.

'I remember well my meeting with Nora Khan. Her slim hand gripped mine in real welcome and her lovely brown eyes shone in a smile. She was a quiet, gentle person, sensitive to the needs of others. She and I often collected the rations for the mid-watch break at 3 am. Our conversation was always philosophical and I felt she really did understand what I was trying to say. There was something 'fey' about her. On my 21st birthday, another friend and she went down town and bought an ersatz cream cake and put a silver Key on it. We all ate a bit when we went back on watch at 6 pm. However she was an efficient operator, despite the fact that her morse key seemed to have a wide gap, and when she used it there was a loud 'clakketty-clack'. This earned her the name 'Bang-away-Lulu', at which she would smile unconcerned.'

There was, however, an unhappy reason for this, as Irene Salter, another fellow-trainee, recognized.

'She suffered very badly from chilblains. For this reason she had to wear shoes two sizes larger than normal and was unable to grip the morse key because of her swollen fingers.'

Later on another station, Stella Cottman remembers seeing 'a strange, dark-skinned WAAF Officer, who appeared for a few days only, spent a lot of time playing the grand piano and then disappeared.' In fact, Noor Inayat Khan was landed in France by the same Lysander as Diana Rowden and Cecily Lefort in June 1943, though Noor went as Wireless Operator to Cinema, a sub-circuit of Prosper, an important organization based on Paris. The Gestapo made many arrests shortly after she arrived, but she refused to return to safety, saying that she was the last link between London and the group she hoped to build. She then hid her set and went into hiding, while the Gestapo, knowing her by her code name 'Madeleine', hunted for her.

Later she thought it safe to resume work, carrying her wireless around in a violin case. Soon afterwards she was betrayed, watched and finally captured. While the Gestapo began to operate her set, she was interrogated painfully and kept in a cell on the fifth floor of the Gestapo Headquarters on Avenue Foch, from which she made two attempts at escape. In one she filed through her window bars and would have escaped over the roofs, when an air raid alarm alerted the guards and she was recaptured. Under questioning she would say nothing nor promise not to escape. She was therefore sent to prison in Germany, first to Karlsruhe and then Pforzheim, where, as a particularly dangerous and uncooperative prisoner, she was held in chains in solitary confinement.

On 11 September 1944, with Yolande Beekman, whom she again met, and two FANY women agents, she was sent to Dachau, where in the prison yard next morning they knelt down in pairs, holding hands, and were shot through the back of the neck and then cremated.

These are a few stories of women for whom patriotic and brave are but weak descriptions. Their exploits will for ever remain a bright star in WAAF history.

Above *The day war ended, May 1945. High jinks in the Station Orderly Room, RAF Andover (Mrs Poulton).*

Left *Belgium, 1945. WAAFs enjoy the first bananas since before the war (Mrs Hiden).*

Chapter 17

Survival In Peace Time?

'The WAAF was started, I believe,
Six years ago today.
They couldn't do without us now
Despite what airmen say.
I can't think what the airmen did
Before the women came
To cheer them up and mend their socks
And join in work and game.
When all we WAAF are WAAF no more
And airmen work alone,
They'll think with sighs of girls who made
The Service home from home
They'll wish that we were back again,
And talk of "Good Old Days",
Instead of laughing at our trials
And lack of service ways . . .
The NAAFI and the Sally Ann
Will look a trifle bare,
With only airmen hanging round,
No WAAF to meet them there.
We know that you will miss us girls
Whatever you may say,
Because we've shared your service life
In every kind of way.
But when we all go home once more
And are no longer WAAF,
I'm sure we shall look back with pride
On serving with the RAF.'

Jackie Poulton, June 1945

Even though discussions about the future of the WAAF had been going on at the Air Ministry since 1943, airwomen still believed that they would be disbanded at the end of the war.

Meanwhile the war machine rolled on. When Belgium was freed in 1944, Josette Demey will always remember being sent to join the Belgian Recruiting Mission at Brussels. For her, 'Going back home after four years was indescribable. A large Dakota flew me over and a nice father-type American VIP helped me with my kit — it was my first flight.'

One can imagine her feelings when she met her own family again after so many years. Belgians obviously went out of their way to welcome the forces. One family answering a thank you note from the mother of a WAAF they had befriended, wrote:

'We are very glad that Pam enjoyed her stay in Malines and especially in our little family. The whole Belgian population liked to show its gratitude to the British nation for our liberation, and everybody did what he could. So did we! For a few months we have tried to be for Pam, what you would have been for our daughter in a similar case.'

Others posted into Belgium with the Second Tactical Air Force (2TAF) endured machine-gunning and bombing during Hitler's desperate December 1944 Ardennes offensive to hold up the allies. When this failed, the Allied advance into the heart of Germany was inexorable.

Victory in Europe day (VE day) was celebrated in the Western World on 8 May 1945, the day after the Germans officially surrendered to Eisenhower at Rheims. It was a day long to be remembered, and in England discipline went by the board. Tess Gilbert's station 'lit a huge bonfire on a hill overlooking the

Below left *London cele-brates on VE Day* (Mrs Craufurd-Stuart).

Right *WAAF marching from a Thanksgiving for Victory Service at York Minster* (Mrs Beasty).

NAAFI and sang and danced all night. We roasted potatoes on the fire, which we had acquired from the cookhouse. It was wonderful to see the lights shining out of all the windows after so many years of blackout.'

RAF Oakley's New Zealand Squadron, in full Maori dress, descended on the billet of the WAAF SNCOs and carried them out on their beds, to the accompaniment of chanting, singing and banging dustbin lids. On other stations, great snakes of personnel did a mile-long conga through the houses and Messes, while in several places bonfires got out of hand and celebrators had heavy bills to pay. Those near enough slipped out to London — often against orders — to join the crowds and cheer the King, the Queen and Winston Churchill. Poor Joan Slater recalls that her good intentions for the festivities suffered a slight set-back:

'I'd stitched together strips of red, white and blue bunting into a large flag, which I hung out of the window. The WAAF Sgt wanted to know why I'd hung out the French flag. The truth was that I hadn't a clue at that time what the French flag looked like! I remember the CO announcing over the tannoy that

Left *Airwomen with Soviet slave workers and Red Army men from a German Prison Camp* (Mrs Hiden).

Below right *Returning POWs from Europe welcomed by WAAF, May 1945* (Mrs Reimer).

there was peace in Europe, but not to forget BLA — Burma looms ahead.'

A salutary reminder, as the war with Japan still continued. Indeed there was a darker side amid all this celebration as Pat Sparks felt.

'I spent VE day in the hut feeling sorry for myself, thinking of my family, my husband so far away and the friends who had been killed — all for what? (I'd had a whitlow lanced that morning and the M&B tablets made me depressed.)'

Sadder still was the sight of Prisons and Concentrations Camps overrun by the advancing allied troops, where the Germans had confined opponents of their regime or captured prisoners of war. There were also other, more terrible, camps which yielded up secrets of slave labour and mass extermination.

The VE day celebrations in Brussels were watched by Eileen Younghusband. Afterwards she was seconded for three weeks 'to Breendonck, the Camp of Silence and Death, a Belgian medieval fortress prison used by the Germans. I acted as interpreter and guide to show parties of RAF personnel over the camp where many fearful acts of terror and torture had taken place. It was by then occupied by our forces, who imprisoned there Belgian collaborators — "The Black Ones" — mostly young boys and men who had joined the SS.'

By May 1945, the repatriation of prisoners of war (POWs) from their prison camps to the UK became a torrent, during which planes of the RAF and USAAF co-operated in Operation Exodus, the humanitarian task of bringing as many men home as quickly as possible. Lancasters, Fortresses, Ansons, Dakotas and other aircraft were used to ferry the men to various stations, one airfield logging as many as 5,400 arrivals in one day. As SNCO, Lydia Wilcock was put in charge of the catering and reception arrangements on one station, with 14 others, 'all terrific girls. We worked in a big hangar in which half was used for feeding. Outside were 12 boilers filled from water bowsers. Stoking them regularly was hazardous work on windy days. Tea was brewed non-stop and water provided for washing crockery in tin baths. We called this "the Burma Road". As troops were arriving all daylight hours, it was hard work, done with no grumbling, no clockwatching and little off-duty. An area was set aside where the men could sit in comfortable chairs, listening to piped music and read the latest papers. Women from the village used to trudge up to lend a hand, and when the forsythia and wisteria were in bloom they would transform the hangar. Two Salvation Army ladies used to distribute preprinted cards to say "arrived safely". It was a really worthwhile job for me and I remember many happy and bewildered men. When the runways cracked up and no more troops could be brought in, the reception area was disbanded after ten months of hard work.'

In accordance with the terms of the Geneva Convention, which most European countries, including Britain and Germany, had signed, many of the returning Prisoners of War had been reasonably well treated. Among the WAAF Personnel at Tangmere was Margaret Marsh.

'[Everyone] was called by tannoy to the camp cinema where POWs were fed, processed by documentation clerks and sent on to the other centres. Each day the men had to be cleared from Tangmere, ready for a further wave of aircraft next morning. Memories include WAAF sheets used for table cloths, the station dance band playing for hour after hour to lighten the atmosphere, the weird dress of the men — bits and pieces of uniform, the cheeky chat from aircrew as compared with the rather strained, indeed stunned response from the other services, the typists who typed till their hands were sore and cramped, and finally sitting with the men and letting them talk, talk, talk and talk.'

At her station Molly Reimer 'heard many sad and happy stories and many "Dear John" letters were read to us [telling the man that his wife or girl-friend had left him]. It was most rewarding work.'

Other Prisoners of War had not been so well treated, although by the end of the war even the Germans themselves were short of food. Doreen Compton doubts whether she could ever forget the sight of her POWs.

'They were like walking skeletons. Thin, grey-fleshed, their bones showing, their poor bits of clothing, and worst of all, the awful smell which came from

Left *Cartoon,* Victory Viewpoints (Mirror Group Newspapers).

Right *VJ Parade Day in Columbo,* Ceylon (Mrs Whyatt).

their poor dirty bodies.'

After a medical, delousing, food and talk, 'a fleet of RAF buses drove them away to a secret destination to be re-equipped with clothes and rested, before their relatives could be permitted to see them'. Some had also to be interrogated, much as aircrew after a mission, a task carried out by Intelligence Officers like Pamela Craddock of MI9, who was stationed at Cosford in May 1945.

Half a world away in Ceylon, Doreen Mills 'worked hard and sweated in a very unladylike manner, while the war in Europe ended and then it was all out for the Japanese Campaign (10d a day JCP)'. Joyce Pilgrim, finding her job had finished once our forces were established in France, managed to obtain a posting to Intelligence Delhi, 'where I worked on the Malayan invasion, which fortunately did not take place owing to the dropping of the Atom Bombs'.

The formal Japanese surrender, signed aboard the battleship *Missouri* on 2 September 1945, was designated VJ Day. Everywhere it was marked with widespread rejoicing, but nowhere more fervently than in the Far East. An amusing incident in India is recalled by Pat Bracey when the WAAF were taking part in the huge VJ Victory Parade in Delhi.

'I was in the front row, and we were formed up in a hollow square with VIPs, Mountbatten, Wavell — the lot. Thousands of spectators. Suddenly a Holy Man wearing only the traditional orange loin cloth, lost his way and wandered aimlessly in front of us. His very loose loin cloth kept falling off his bony hips and after several attempts to preserve his modesty, he gave up the struggle and slung it round his neck. A stunned silence all round was then broken by an American in the crowd. "Gee, would you look at that dirty old man there, right in front of those poor WAAFFLES." The effort of suppressing our giggles was enormous, but to our everlasting credit we made not a murmur nor did we bat an eyelid. The Military Police hastily escorted the poor man away and the WAAF Officer turned round to give us our next command with a whispered "Well done girls. Congratulations," and the ceremony proceeded.'

The overseas forces had worked tremendously hard, very often in terrible conditions, and now suddenly and almost unexpectedly everything had stopped. Relief was replaced by an emptiness which bred discontent. Betty Hunter was in Kogala, Ceylon.

'Walking across the runway to lunch, I heard a jeep approaching. It was our

Station Commander and a plump, small man in black pin-stripe trousers, black jacket and tie, immaculate white shirt and collar, and looking as if he had come off the floor of the House of Commons (the temperature was about 100° F). He had come from Mr Attlee's Government to speak to station personnel. I cannot remember what was said, but in my opinion he turned a peaceful protest into a near mutiny. The war was over and all we wanted to know was when we were going home. [There were also accusations of vote rigging in the recent elections.] However, in my heart I felt very sorry for him. The perspiration was just pouring off him. He could not stand the heat.'

It was unfortunate that difficulties of transporting the huge forces that had built up in the Far East back to the UK in an orderly manner were compounded by the task of repatriating vast numbers of Prisoners of War, now being released by the Japanese. Many were in a far worse condition than those in Europe and had to be given priority. For Doreen Mills, 'The sights and stories I saw and heard when the first Prisoners were released from Japanese camps and brought to Colombo Hospital would make your hair stand on end. They looked dreadful — some were in wards we weren't allowed to visit. Except for the bomb, there would have been so many more. I don't think I will ever forget.'

In Europe, the sad debris of war was also encountered. In January 1946 Queenie Lee went to Calais to work at a Transit camp.

'Our work was putting WAAF on homeward boats, meeting drafts and seeing the girls caught the correct trains. Then the European wives started filtering through and we found that a slight knowledge of French was a boon.

WAAF escorts in Ceylon for the earliest POWs released by the Japanese (Mrs Whyatt).

'The displaced persons (DPs) then started coming through in their thousands from Poland. It was a pitiful sight seeing so many homeless people — particularly the old ones. They were so grateful for everything we did for them, it seemed such a worthwhile duty.

'In December 1946, I was posted to Wahn in Germany. There I was terribly sorry to see the children and the old people so ill-fed. I also visited some DPs outside the camp, but was appalled when we got there. Sixteen of the children had been ill and had been placed in a disused restaurant; the room had no light (electricity was cut off during the day). There were some old people in the restaurant too — they had scarcely any clothes, only old striped pyjamas, one old lady had the tattered remains of a blanket tied with string to make it fit and a blind lady just sat patiently with folded hands. We gave them lanterns, oil and sweets for the sick children. We knitted comforts for them and arranged for food scraps from the Messes to be collected for them. From the Girl Guides I was able to send sacks of clothing and toys. At Christmas we collected all the free chocolate, oranges and food we could scrounge. It was surprising how much happiness we WAAF were able to bring into their lives.'

For some WAAF at home, the RAF offered flights over Germany, much as they were organizing for RAF ground staff. Enid Bayliss was on one of these.

'I sat next to the pilot, but two of the girls were lying on their stomachs in the nose of the Lancaster, looking frightened and very green at the sight of the ground rushing past. We were flying very low the whole time, so missed nothing. The devastation was shocking, far worse than we ever imagined it could possibly be.'

Now that the war was over, most RAF and WAAF wanted to leave behind the discomforts and restrictions of the past six years and return to civil life, so to fit its members for peace, the RAF began a world-wide Educational and Vocational Training Scheme, popularly known as EVT. It aimed to prepare them for employment, by brushing up half-forgotten trade skills, often by day-release at local colleges, while for airwomen there was housecraft and citizenship as well as joint classes in educational subjects and hobbies. For this crash programme, mobile classrooms and 10,000 instructors were made available.

Training also went on overseas on much the same lines, except that, save for a series of courses run by the Women's International Zionist Organizations at Tel Aviv for Palestinian WAAF, civilian help could not be called on. In Ramleh, for instance, home management classes were run in a bungalow fitted out like a modern home, and though attendance was voluntary, there was still a long waiting list for the two-week courses.

At home in England, Pat Pattison found, 'Life had been rather dull workwise, and we spent our time in Ops doing the Times crossword, or just talking and were given classes in dressmaking, cookery and so on, to fit us for civvy life.'

Phyllis Hope-Bell felt quite rightly that, 'When the war finished no-one knew what to do with Plotters. I was posted to Records and hated it. EVT was the thing then, to keep us occupied. I taught Drama in a hangar at Biggin Hill. Afterwards I

was released to join the Drama Section of ENSA. We were the first company into Berlin and Copenhagen.'

Indeed entertainment became a very important part of WAAF life, as Pamela Craddock was to discover in 1946 when she took the WAAF Gang show on tour in Italy and Austria, to great acclaim.

In the Far East it seemed to Doreen Mills that after the Japanese surrender, 'Almost overnight everything stopped and we were left hanging in space. There was very little to do except wait to come home, so we had parties and picnics. Then comments were "good time girls". Nobody seemed to realize that we had worked hard and were prepared to go on doing so. We were demobbed in Bombay, so for a while we were neither fish nor fowl. When we came home, what hurt was the reaction. We obviously looked different — middle of January 1946 — sunburned (not known then) and wearing Glengarries [Highland caps] like the men, all of which seemed to be resented. We ended in Birmingham just for final clearance.'

In fact demobilization had begun for the WAAF on 18 June 1945, but even before the war ended, stations were making themselves ready for the expected exits. At Stanmore, Pat Sparks with the other married WAAF was put into one hut, as it would be easier for demob time.

'We had a set of quads born there, as the station cat thought she would become respectable and joined the married women.'

The actual demobilization was preceded by a pre-release medical, usually either at the girl's own or a central station. Hazel Williams had good cause to remember hers.

'As I had married in June, I came out with other married WAAF in September 1945. For our pre-release medical we had to present ourselves two at a time to the Medical Officer. My companion was a very large, red haired Yorkshire lass, bursting out of the undress in which we waited. We stood to attention as the MO entered the room. He was a Polish Flt Lt, who spoke little, heavily accented English. He asked us in unison to show various parts and answer questions about our insides and outsides. Then came the last request "And now airwomen, your Tith!" To my horror, the red haired WAAF unhooked her bra and stood baring all. The MO, a small man, jumped several feet it seemed, and pointing to his mouth said, "No, No. Your teeth, teeth!"

'Then came the day spent in Birmingham, being demobbed. From the floor above I looked down on the great snake queues of hundreds and hundreds of WAAF, from all walks of life and countries, all married, the first to leave the service.'

Starting at releases of 60 a day, the ex-Balloon Centre at Wythall, Birmingham, under its WAAF Commanding Officer, one of five then commanding different units, had by 20 June 1946 released its 100,000th airwoman. In July 1946 with

Left *EVT Homecraft training for the WAAF in Palestine* (Mrs Fox).

Demob at an all male station!

Right *Cartoon*, Demobilisation at an all-male station (Mrs Sturgeon).

the daily release numbers tailing off, 105 Dispersal Centre closed and its work was removed to the joint RAF and WAAF Release Centre at Kirkham.

Something of how this massive undertaking worked, and reduced well over 150,000 WAAF in June 1945 to just over 25,000 by December 1946, is described by Phyllis Smart.

'In Birmingham we were taken to a large hall. Tables were arranged along the walls and we worked our way clockwise around. At one table we were given 56 clothing coupons, at another a ration card for 14 days, another pay, leave passes and so on.' The money she received included any credits from her last station, 14 days' pay and allowances, postal drafts for two further periods of 14 days, and £12 10s for the purchase of civilian clothes. This latter was won in the teeth of opposition from a Treasury woman adviser who was convinced that a very good outfit of civilian clothing could be bought for £8 15s! Many an airwoman had already had lectures and fashion shows by various companies on how to spend her grant. In addition, she received unemployment and health insurance cards, her Service and Release Book and could purchase 320 cigarettes and 7 oz of chocolate ration at the nearby NAAFI canteen.

'After about ten minutes we emerged from the room as civilians, then I entered a small office where a young WAAF Officer sat. She was probably about 18 and I was 32, but she solemnly shook hands with me and said "Thank you for coming." I was out! I have never felt so forsaken in my life. After being part of a huge family for so long, I was on my own. I lay in bed that night and cried.'

The reaction was much the same for Hazel Williams.

'I remember the end of that day leaving Birmingham railway station clutching my holdall and other bits and pieces, and crying solidly all the way to Guildford, where my husband of just three months was awaiting me.'

Most girls had lost their youth in the service of their country. It had left a huge gap in their lives but they were now more sociable, adaptable and mature, a generation better able to stand up for itself in the new post-war world. They also carried away friendships which in many cases were to last the rest of their lives.

Victory in 1945, however, had brought little joy to the Allies, whose divisions were already apparent before Churchill's 'Iron Curtain' speech in 1946. The so-called Cold War between the Communists and Democracies had begun, and small and efficient peace-time forces had to be retained. Large scale demobilization of men and women after the war had thrown all the services into disorder, so that new rebuilding had to take place.

In 1946, Parliament announced that it was planning to retain women in the Armed Forces of the Crown on a permanent basis, but as an interim measure an Extended Service Scheme was produced to provide the nucleus of trained Officers and NCOs to bridge the gap and start a permanent force.

Home from Egypt in January 1947 for demob was Kay Farrington.

'I had extended my service for two years on volunteering for overseas at the end of the war. Consequently I had one month disembarkation leave, 28 days re-engagement leave and one month terminal leave.'

In April 1947, she signed on for a further four years, 'and was posted to

The oldest and youngest WAAF celebrate their 1948 last WAAF Birthday, before the coming of the 1949 WRAF (Miss Coulthard).

Wilmslow for a refresher course along with other familiar faces doing the same as myself.

Then, on 1 February 1949 the permanent service was inaugurated, reverting to its original First World War title of the Women's Royal Air Force (WRAF). On the previous day, an epoch-making ceremony was held in the Air Council Chamber in which Air Commandant (Bunty) Hanbury — who had taken over as Director from Lady Welsh — received the document of Constitution of the re–formed service from the Secretary of State for Air.

During the congratulatory speeches, Lord Tedder, then Chief of the Air Staff, summarized the past, present and future well.

'I was going to say "welcome", but all of us in the regular Service throughout the war and since have always, I think, regarded the WAAF as very much an integral part of the Service. There is no doubt that the women Mechanics I saw working in Berlin in the Air Lift last week are very much in, and part of, the Royal Air Force. Still, the ceremony does mark a milestone. In addition to being part of our Service in the workshop, on the tarmac, in the air and in the office, you are now part of our Service in the book. Good Show!'

Thus the WRAF became commissioned or attested members of the RAF, unlike women in the other two Services; the WRNS retained its civilian status and the WRAC was set up as a self-contained Army Corps. Spare-time women members could also join the existing RAF reserve forces as Women's Royal Auxiliary Air Force or do flying duties as the WRAF Volunteer Reserve. By the new Constitution, serving WAAF were given the choice of completing their service as WAAF or transferring to the regular force. Their pay now became about three-quarters of that of men, but the new pensions were only two-thirds. Ration money and accommodation allowances were to be the same as the RAF.

The Air Force Act now applied to them fully in discipline and scales of punishment except for field punishments, since the restrictions on combatant duties and flying still remained. WRAF Officers and NCOs had the same powers of command over airmen as RAF, saluting became compulsory instead of a matter of courtesy as formerly, and the names of the first two Officer ranks were changed in line with the RAF from Assistant Section Officer and Section Officer to Pilot Officer and Flying Officer respectively. Even then it was hoped that these differences would eventually disappear!

Thus, except in matters affecting their welfare as women, WRAF employment in the RAF was now to be treated not as a separate issue but as a matter affecting the Service as a whole and the democratic system which it existed to defend.

Chapter 18

Into A New Age

'I swear by Almighty God (or I affirm) that I will be faithful and bear true allegiance to Her Majesty Queen Elizabeth The Second, Her Heirs and Successors and that I will as in duty bound, honestly and faithfully defend Her Majesty, Her Heirs and Successors, in Person, Crown and Dignity against all enemies, and will observe and obey all orders of Her Majesty, Her Heirs and Successors, and of the Air Officers and other Officers set over me.'

With this Oath (or affirmation) today, a girl becomes part of the RAF. This is what she promises at her solemn Attestation.

For airwomen between 1943-60, whose recruit training took place at Wilmslow, attestation usually was delayed three days, until they finished further trade selection tests and interviews at the Wilmslow Reception Centre, although they could defer their final choice of trade as long as three weeks. They could still enter at age 17½ years, but for most trades in the new WRAF for a few years the upper limit was 37, today 39.

Life in No 31 S of (W) RT, Wilmslow, had not noticeably changed in the years after the war. Airwomen still trained on the same station as the airmen but remained separate and autonomous. To Joyce Mylan, 'It all seemed very noisy at first because of the size of the huts — about 20 girls. We had to go outside in all weathers to the ablution block for wash, toilet or baths. We thought the Corporal Drill Instructors were gods and were terrified of them at first. The food, particularly cheese and onion pie, was marvellous and we had plenty of it. Because of the marching and Physical Education we were always hungry and we had plenty of PE, especially after having injections.

'The uniform seemed bulky, especially the shoes. It was funny seeing girls in city-type suits, grey lisle stockings and big black shoes. We had a fashion show in our hut with the RAF issue pink bloomers and shapeless bras, which was hilarious. We spent hours writing our name tapes in Indian ink and then sewing them on to our uniforms and tried shrinking our berets to two sizes smaller. One

Above *Aerial view of part of RAF Wilmslow, 1948* (Mrs Dyke).

Above right *Airwomen's Dormitory with bedstacks and 'biscuits' 1948* (Mrs Dyke).

Left *1950s uniform. Note the hard, high-top cap then in use. The disc behind the badge indicates a trainee.*

thing I particularly hated was lighting the old coke heaters in the huts — I always had trouble. Once they were lit however, they were lovely and warm.

'I vaguely remember some of our Passing Out song which ran,

On top of old Wilmslow
All covered in snow,
We lost our late passes
For marching too slow.
For marching's a pleasure,
Fatigues are a grief,
And the cold winter weather
It shatters your teeth.'

By the time Rosemary Jones joined in 1958, many things had changed. Mattresses took the place of the three much-hated biscuits and FFIs and cutlery irons were disappearing. She enthuses over the food and company, as well as the fact that she had never been so fit in her life, but some things struck her as amusing.

'I remember that at the reception billet for a week we had pretty curtains with nets, pretty bed covers and rugs. When we signed on, however, and moved into other billets, these were noticeable by their absence. Dark green curtains, no nets, and threadbare rugs.'

But still more change was on the way, when in July 1960 Recruit Training moved to Spitalgate in Lincolnshire. Here, for the first time, girls lived in centrally heated brick-built barrack blocks, freshly decorated in lilac, pink and mushroom with flowered curtains on pelmeted windows. Each bed had a wardrobe, locker, lamp and mirror, with radio and TV for the block. Recruits spent five days in the Spitalgate Reception Centre, when they could leave if they wished. After this, around 50 out of a weekly intake of 75 were usually finally

Catering . . . (Mrs Sturgeon).

attested and began their six weeks' training. Some had bird's nest hair-styles, 'winkle-picker' shoes and coming from broken families sought a sense of security in the service, while others were very young girls of 17 in ankle-socks, straight from school, since in 1959 the entry age had been lowered, with parental consent.

A presently-serving Sergeant describes her first six weeks.

'The whole flight seemed a good bunch. Accommodation was in a large, approximately 14 person room, with highly polished floor. Instruction was adequate, food awful, uniform was "Hairy Mary's" [rough serge battledress top and skirt] suitable for keeping Eskimos warm. We had no problems with discipline. We simply did as we were told and emerged from *most* days unscathed. Drill was enjoyable, until one was sized to march behind the inevitable camel-marcher — every flight has one — the person whose left arm and foot go forward together.'

The verdict by Kay Boucher was that 'the comradeship was great. Everyone helped each other out', but as time went on and timetables became more crammed into the five-and-a-half day week, she found it increasingly 'very hard work. A lot was put into a day'. Another summed it up as 'mostly drill, kit and sleep'.

For the staff looking after the Flights, before their girls left there were often parties, tears, presents and occasionally poems, like this from E Flight.

'I suppose we've been a troublesome crew,
And caused you worry and woe,
But we owe such a lot to you,
We'll all be sorry to go.

You've turned us into a decent Flight,
And your patience is above par,
You taught us our left foot from our right,
You really should go far.
When anyone asks, "Which Corporal's best?"
We let out one single cry,
"Corporal Jeffries, of course!" no less;
So as we all say goodbye,
We hope you'll forgive our many errors,
And wish us the best when we part —
Although we've been a lot of terrors,
We thank you, right from the heart.'

By 1974 the decision to close the station of Spitalgate had been taken so the WRAF Recruit School was moved to RAF Hereford, where the removal of its former craft apprentices released suitable accommodation for it to take over. There each of its six flights had its own brick barrack block of four 14-bed dormitories, with laundry rooms on each floor, washing machines, electric polishers, sitting rooms, TVs and an improved scale of furnishings. There were individual

There's Snobody like our SWO-man, Spitalgate, 1972 (Mrs Scott).

bathrooms, showers, cubicled washbasins and toilets.

Since trade selection and attestation had now been completed by the Recruiting Offices, reception and kitting took less time, and recruit training lasted only five and a half weeks. Uniforms were only worn during the working day, and there was no service underwear. Girls who found that service life did not suit them were allowed to be discharged during their first three weeks.

Except for the once weekly domestic nights, and study for the three major Progress Tests of the course, girls could stay out most nights till just before 11 pm at the cinema shows, social clubs, games, dances and discothèques to be found on the station or at the local town. Apart from the drill, sports and PE sessions, courses included talks on General Service Knowledge, Nuclear, Biological and Chemical Warfare, First Aid, and History of the RAF, as well as air-experience flights and two-and-a-half days of outdoor Resource and Initiative Training.

Again there was a tremendous amount to put into such a short time, but the recruits took everything in their stride, gaining 'a lot of laughs, learning and satisfaction from it. All our activities, whether social or otherwise kept us occupied, motivated and involved,' says Valerie Stevens. Flights also seemed to be growing taller; at least one comprised of girls 6 ft or over.

But the tide for greater integration of WRAF training was becoming hard to resist from both financial as well as social grounds, and eventually, after long discussion, the girls joined the men at Swinderby, Lincolnshire, where they became part of the RAF School of Recruit Training, although still housed in separate H-shaped barrack blocks. They appeared in their first combined Passing Out Parade in 1982. The six weeks spent there in 1984 by Kim Matthews were the most enjoyable but also the hardest in her career.

'All the other girls were in the same position, and we soon rallied around and clubbed together to help pull each other through. For the first two weeks we had a "Bull Night" every night, fatigues to do in the mornings, parades and drill every day. But if there was one thing I could not do, it was make a bed pack. The number of times I had to retrieve my sheets and blankets off the trees outside the block, was unbelievable. But it was also the most enjoyable six weeks I have ever had and when it came to the Passing Out Parade and I was front marker for our flight, I don't believe there was anyone prouder than I on the square. Swinderby had thrown everything they could at me, drill, bull, kit inspections, combatancy course, the lot — and I had come through it all. And what made everything worth it, was the sheer look of pride on my father's face afterwards.'

Officer Training for women also underwent considerable changes both from the three-day selection procedure first at Uxbridge and then at Biggin Hill, which later became known as the Officer and Aircrew Selection Centre (OASC), to the stations where they were trained. The four years spent in the Women's Junior Air Corps by Chrystine Lord in the late '50s 'gave a good introduction to service procedures. It helped too with Officer Selection at Uxbridge, when it came to how to cross rivers with three planks and a bit of rope.'

The trauma of girls intended for commissioning, who all started with initial airwoman training, is well illustrated by Keeta Weale who went to Wilmslow in 1954.

'I was in a hut with about 17 other girls and the only one going on to become an Officer cadet if I passed the course. I really was something of a disaster area and always seemed to be in trouble, particularly as I was continually told I was supposed to set an example and show qualities of leadership.'

This practice changed in time, although the RAF still strongly encourages commissioning from the ranks.

In 1947 a small band of Officers and airwomen had been sent to the former Kentish fighter station of RAF Hawkinge to reopen it, after it had been closed for

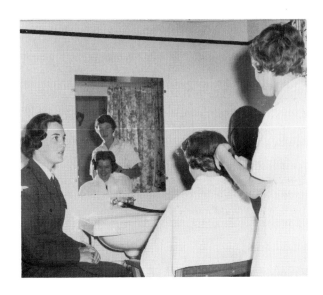

Above left *Airwomen having a party in the NAAFI at Spitalgate, 1973* (Mrs Stevens).

Right *Hairdressing allowances were given to girls from 1940. Airwomen were found as Station Hairdressers at Recruit Training and many other large camps* (Mrs Scott).

nearly two years. They cleaned, refurbished and re-equipped it ready for the revived Officer Cadet Training Unit (OCTU) to move in. The cadets were trained in an old operations block, drilled in an old hangar and lived in tiny study bedrooms in wooden huts with adjoined ablutions for the three months of their course. Of course, here as on other stations where all WRAF were trained, they did not operate in a totally female world. Other predominantly RAF units were also present, with their own particular tasks.

After passing Wilmslow, Keeta Weale went to Hawkinge to complete her training, as did other intended officers during that period. It was hard work but she found, 'Amongst our OCTU lectures was one by a Padre who assured us he would not let any daughter of his mix with the ravening wolves of the RAF. By the end of his lecture we were all looking forward to the rest of our service lives immensely.'

However, the station was destined to be closed again, and late in 1961 Diana McCall was one of the staff who accompanied the final 14 WRAF cadets from Hawkinge to join the first integrated RAF and WRAF OCTU at Jurby, Isle of Man. There they became part of the Blue Squadron and she was the Senior Training Officer. Courses were lengthened to six months and now airwoman training was omitted. Certain specialists and former airwomen did not take the WRAF Junior Term comprising the first three months of PE, station visits, grooming, RAF etiquette, public speaking and business administration, once

described as the 'best finishing school in Europe', but instead joined with the RAF in the last three months 'Officers Initial Training Course', where subjects like drill, man-management, Air Force Law and administration were studied.

In 1986, Anne Barker was indignant to read in a newspaper that since "WRAC Officer cadets had begun to train alongside their male counterparts, the army was in the forefront of Officer training and equality for women". She points out that no mention was made of the fact that the RAF had been training RAF and WRAF Officer Cadets together for over 20 years and that all new WRAF must now be given weapon training.

Although the Isle of Man were perfect for expedition training, it was too remote. In September 1963 the combined OCTU therefore left Jurby, now destined to close, for Feltwell, Norfolk. There it remained while awaiting the removal of the RAF Technical College to Cranwell, so that the OCTU could then take over the post-war Messes and accommodation at Henlow. Elizabeth Kibart followed these changes through as Junior Flight Commander, and saw the OCTU finally established at Henlow in July 1966.

By now the OCTU had again slightly changed its form. Men and women from civil life did a short preparatory course together, before embarking on the 17 weeks' main course. Women made up about a third of the total numbers at the rate of about 80-90 a year, working in mixed Flights of about nine cadets with a RAF or WRAF Flight Commander. The accent was much more on leadership

Elizabeth R

Elizabeth II, *by the Grace of God* OF THE UNITED KINGDOM OF GREAT BRITAIN AND NORTHERN IRELAND AND OF HER OTHER REALMS AND TERRITORIES QUEEN, HEAD OF THE COMMONWEALTH, DEFENDER OF THE FAITH.

To Our Trusty and well beloved   Greeting :

WE, *reposing especial Trust and Confidence in your Loyalty, Courage, and good Conduct, do by these Presents Constitute and Appoint you to be an Officer in Our Royal Air Force from the*   *day of* 19   . *You are therefore carefully and diligently to discharge your Duty as such in the Rank of Pilot Officer or in such other Rank as We may from time to time hereafter be pleased to promote or appoint you to and you are in such manner and on such occasions as may be prescribed by Us to exercise and well discipline in their duties such Officers, Airmen and Airwomen as may be placed under your orders from time to time and use your best endeavours to keep them in good Order and Discipline. And We do hereby Command them to Obey you as their superior Officer and you to Observe and follow such Orders and Directions as from time to time you shall receive from Us, or any superior Officer, according to the Rules and Discipline of War, in pursuance of the Trust hereby reposed in you.*

GIVEN at Our Court, at Saint James's

the   day of   19   in the   Year of Our Reign

By Her Majesty's *Command*

It is worth noting that in the wording of the Royal Commission, a WRAF, like her male counterpart, is recorded only as an Officer of the RAF.

and practical training, with six-day and then eight-day camps in Norfolk being planned and administered by the cadets themselves. It was stimulating and in 1967, according to Lynn Child, 'wonderful, hard work but fun'. This was the same verdict as that of Michele Codd, who graduated from Henlow in 1978.

'I will always remember bivouacking on the training area in a para-tepee containing four women and six men in a February blizzard, huddled together for warmth. Nice to find that we could keep up with the men physically and live in the field on equal terms.'

In 1970, the RAF College at Cranwell, Lincolnshire, replaced its flight cadet system by a special Graduate Entry Scheme designed for three months' General Service Training and nine months' specialist courses. The first course included the Prince of Wales and women University graduates entering under the scheme. It became redundant when in 1979 it merged with the OCTU, which now moved to Cranwell, where the resulting course then became known as Initial Officer Training or IOT. It included many graduates and was 18 weeks in length. Squadrons of 90 usually contained 6 to 8 WRAF cadets and they lived in the same corridors as male members of their flights in single study bedrooms — similar to what happens today in hotels and Sergeants' and Officers' RAF Messes throughout the country. Students were subjected to office simulators and the searching eye of closed circuit television in oral communication sessions, with an even greater emphasis placed on leadership exercises, endurance marches and battle scenarios in field conditions.

'It is tough, strenuous and, as in all training, many do not pass'. However, Christine Oxland felt that 'With the girls treated exactly the same as the men, it is hard going at the time, but it pays off in the long term as you are accepted as equal.'

NCO training divided into many different types of courses as trade structures changed, and more emphasis began to be placed on promotion examinations and management and organization skills. For the most part these courses remained on the stations with Recruit Training, because of the availability of accommodation and instructors, so they were to be found at such stations as Hawkinge, Spitalgate and finally Hereford.

Hawkinge also was selected to start the training scheme for Local Service airwomen, who lived at home and worked on station in uniform during the day. This scheme began in 1959 to replace future RAF losses from the ending of National Service for men. Intended as a short term expedient, the practice of recruiting small numbers of local service airwomen in a limited number of trades and stations was later discontinued.

Chapter 19

How Times Have Changed

'Half a trade and half an art.'

W R Inge

With initial training successfully passed, before the long desired posting to work on a station (perhaps it will have real aircraft!), a WRAF must next go through a thorough basic training in her chosen trade or branch — and what a choice of career is open to her! In 1984, out of the 100 or so ground trades for airmen, over 75 were open to airwomen and no doubt these will increase. On the other hand there are some trades reserved solely for WRAF, as with kennelmaids and typists.

When the Second World War finished, after working in so many and varied fields, women found that at a stroke many of their horizons had narrowed, if not totally disappeared. On paper at least, in 1946 new entrants to short service or 'the duration of the present emergency' — as the Air Ministry Recruiting Pamphlet 103 so engagingly described recurrent world crises and the interregnum before auxiliary WAAF became permanent WRAF — could choose from 79 trades, 10 of the highest being in Group I. However, airwomen electing to stay on under Extended Service terms, often found as did Mary Lloyd that ' they were forced to move out of the wartime trades they had loved' into a much more limited 31, unless they were already in the few highly-skilled trades the RAF still wanted. The cause was less the desire to cut WAAF numbers than the ever-present necessity to match new skills with fast progressing technology, in which race the RAF will always be peculiarly and continuously vulnerable.

Then the Cold War, the Malayan Emergency and the Berlin Blockade erupted, where incredible though it seemed, the armed forces still had a role to play. Unwillingly, in 1948 the Government introduced two-year National Service for men, to bolster up numbers in its largely demobilized and depleted services. Nevertheless much more was needed to encourage the best personnel to sign on and stay, because outside employers were man-hungry and in direct competition. Consequently improvements had to be considered.

Already 1949 had brought in the reconstituted WRAF with about 70 trades. Their restructured pay was quoted not by the day but by the week — a comment on changing times. Away went Trade Groups 1–5 and M, and in came a simplified four, labelled A–D. Permanent careers were opened and positively encouraged, with gratuities offered for airwomen after 10 years' regular service, and pensions for service over 22 years (16 for Officers), although this was looking a long way ahead.

1951 saw the first of the big changes in trade structures of the RAF. Trades were now distributed into a more commonsense and comprehensible 22 functional groups with women in 18, and pay again rose slightly.

By 1964 there were effectively 19 Trade Groups, with WRAF in around 15, and the old promotion ladders were replaced by two lists: List I for engineering and allied trades looked for time promotion, while List II, mainly for administrative trades, had to wait for vacancies. The basic pattern has remained, though there are now 18 Trade Groups.

Inevitably the years have also marked many firsts, as girls extended their skills. Higher ranks came with time and experience — factors unavoidably lacking during the war — and in direct competition with male colleagues.

In the 1960s Rosemary Boot, formerly a Physical Training Instructor, remembers trecking off with 200 other hopefuls to be considered for Air Quartermaster, a new trade open to women since 1959. She was lucky enough to be one of the two selected.

'I did my training at RAF Thorney Island and from there I was posted to Lyneham and joined 216 Squadron flying Comets. We became affiliated crew members as it were after a few months. The work was always extremely interesting, varied and often very amusing. I did many VIP trips, off-route trips as well as

Air Quartermasters with luggage (Mrs Boot).

Left *Air Loadmasters taking the weight off their feet, while loading up a Hercules transport, 1982 (Miss McArthur).*

Below right *An Operations Room Clerk on practice interceptions (PI) at a Flight Controller School, 1984 (RAF Halton).*

the bread-and-butter runs down the Med.'

In fact 1962 saw the trade awarded aircrew status and the ten women then in training were the first to wear the flying brevet. In October 1970 they were renamed Air Loadmasters, and in 1973 the first woman Air Loadmaster was commissioned in the General Duties (Flying) Branch. Until 1981, the RAF had insisted that the job of Air Loadmaster on Hercules transport aircraft was a man's job, but in that year three WRAF went on a conversion course at Lyneham and were subsequently posted to an operational squadron. One of these was Joy McArthur, who was involved in checking and supervising the carrying of dangerous cargoes to Ascension and the Falkland Islands during her tour of duty.

Radar was just as much needed after the war as during it, and airwomen still continue to work with it. As Radar Operator at Bawdsey in 1950, Margaret Stacy was there during the 'visit of a Government team to assess the amount to be paid to Sir Robert Watson-Watt and his team for the invention of radar. The radar site was polished and we were all in our best blue. Our "difficult" WRAF was kept out of the site, but managed to appear in the Operations Room with a vital piece of equipment for Sir Robert!'

A few years after the war, WRAF Officers were accepted into the Fighter Control Branch, which had taken over all three Radar Control and Reporting operations. Today they control Aerospace Defence Systems by using modern electronic equipment following very small dots of light on a dark screen to compile a split-second picture of the air situation. As Sector Controller responsible for the Air Defence of Southern England and its sea approaches, Joan Hopkins took command of RAF Neatishead in November 1982 — the first post of such a nature to go to a woman. Even then she had broken new ground as Deputy Chief of the Air Defence Component at SHAPE headquarters Brussels and was again to do so in 1987, when she became the first WRAF Air Commodore in the Fighter Control specialization.

In 1963, when Area Radar had just started, there was a shortage of Controllers and so some Fighter Controllers were seconded to it. Chrystine Butcher was one.

'Thus we could be Area Radar Controllers, because we were Fighter Controllers, but couldn't do Air Traffic Control of which Area Radar formed a part, because we were women. After much battling the first three women were finally allowed onto the Air Traffic Course at Shawbury. We came first, second and fourth of fourteen. Things have so much changed, that the route today is to be airfield Air Traffic Controller before going on to Area Radar Control.'

To them is entrusted the landing and take-off of fast moving civil and military aircraft worth many millions of pounds, and taking emergency action when necessary. Pilots find a girl's voice talking them down 'more relaxing and easier to understand', but the girls are under very heavy pressure. They work on airfields, Radar Units and Control Centres, in whatever part of the world they are needed.

The daily schedule for Rusty Reeves in 1960 ran like this.

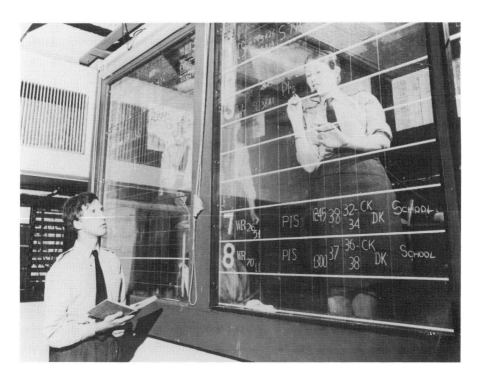

'Cycle to underground bunker in my special issue white duffle coat — always cold down there. Show my pass and then down to work as an Operations Clerk. I had two Squadrons each calling me with aircraft movements of take off and landing times, places of destination, amount of fuel, how long at destination, pilots' and navigators' names, all of which was written on a huge Perspex board for all to see. I had to keep an eye on the times in case of accidents or break-downs, and I had to notify the appropriate people if they were late. A great deal of telephoning went on. I also had a squawk box to the Control Tower and both Squadrons, which was sometimes red hot. At the end of my shift I handed over to another Operator, complete with the log which I had kept.'

Others, frequently in the Signals trade, also work underground. In the so-called 'hole' at High Wycombe in the '60s, Alma Churcher remembers strange stories of the Met men hearing footsteps in the corridors and doors opening and closing, said to be the pilots who died in the war. As a telephonist, 'one night I had calls set themselves up on the switchboard, but it never worried me — all in the night's work!'

Engineering is yet another trade where women are represented, not in such numbers as their wartime past would indicate, but their immediate post-war decline is now in reverse. Janet, an Aircraft Technician (Electrical), enjoys servicing and maintaining the complicated electrical systems of today's aircraft and has found that 'airmen take me as another Electrician and even try to cut down their swearing'.

In 1972 Suzanne Jones was the first woman Engineer to graduate from Cranwell and won the sash of merit for her entry, while in 1975, Joan Peck became the first woman Engineer to reach the rank of Group Captain and become Deputy Director of the Signals Branch.

Left *Ground Electricians carrying out adjustments to a ground power unit (RAF Halton).*

Right *A Supplier working with a Visual Display Unit (VDU) on stock control within SCAF.*

Early post-war Equipment Depots abroad were sometimes reduced to a quarter their size due to the repatriation of RAF, and in Egypt many sections were mainly kept going by WAAF and German prisoners of war who replaced repatriated Italians. Even in 1949 it was not unusual for airwomen to work single-handed on particular jobs. At RAF Fayid, Billy Grigg did not have the most exciting of posts as an Equipment Assistant. She spent most of her time attached to its Hospital on her own, issuing shrouds and coffins.

In Equipment Sections at home also, the day's work sometimes brought strange things. To one, on an afternoon in 1957, the local Police delivered a rusty object. Next morning on her arrival at work, Paula Muldrew decided that it looked shell-shaped and called her Flight Sergeant.

'We stared at it for a bit and then I called the Gunnery Officer around. He stared and sent for his Flight Sergeant who called in the Sergeant, who in turn sent for an airman. Half an hour later they were back with a 10 in piece of shrapnel, jagged beyond belief. We called the police, who said it had been discovered by a farmer ploughing a field. They rushed round to find he'd dug up 15 or so more. They were unexploded shells used in manoeuvres during the First World War — and still live.'

Women also shone in their handling of people, so as early as 1947 they were working as Movements Officers at seaports. Later came the task of Air Movements Officers, deploying both military passengers and freight. WRAF in the Supply Branch won their final accolade, when in 1973 one of their number, Molly Allott, was not only promoted to Air Commodore, but also became the first non-Secretarial Officer to be WRAF Director.

The advent of computers has revolutionized the work of many sections. Equipment work has now become known as Supply, and has moved from the

Left A Station Photo-
grapher in Germany, 1948/
49 (Mrs Roberts).

Below right *The WAAF
Central Band rehearsing
for the Farewell Parade in
Brussels, 1945* (Mrs Irwin).

Below far right *1960,
Ceremonial Dress of the
WRAF Band* (Mrs Jones).

manual equipment accounting procedures of EPAS (Equipment, Provisioning
and Accounting Section) to the Supply Computers Mark I (1965) and Mark II
(mid 70s) of SCAF (Supply Control and Accounting Flight). Their introduction has so speeded up processes of demand and supply that automatic
requisitioning has become a reality, and functions all the way from clothing and
furniture to petrol and aircraft parts. With Operation Corporate in the Falklands
in 1982 the RAF system really showed its worth, maintaining a supply line of
8,000 miles.

Sally Ingram was employed as Station Photographer in the '60s — still a popular trade — where she remembers a lot of mundane work. On other stations it
could include the mass production of reconnaissance prints.

'In 1962 at Seletar, well into the Borneo confrontation, I could recognize from
some of the photographs where the guerillas were clearing jungle to land illegal
aircraft — some even showed wreckage of forced landings.'

The trade of Musician is now unfortunately closed to WRAF since its Central
Band, formed at Stanmore Park in 1944 and based at Uxbridge in 1950, was
finally disbanded on 31 December 1972. Many regret its passing including Diana
McCall, its young Officer in charge in 1946-7. However, with the Band she
travelled extensively over Europe and the United Kingdom, playing at Victory
Parades, Olympia, the Albert Hall and the Lord Mayor's Show, while in Brussels
her Drum Major and a few NCOs taught the all-male Belgian Air Force Band
ceremonial drill movements. Rosemary Pope, a trombone player, recalls that in

1960 bandswomen were issued very smart new ceremonial uniforms, 'complete with a dashing cape lined with red satin, to be thrown over the shoulders. However, in very cold weather we wore ordinary greatcoats, which made the arms ache if worn over a ceremonial jacket, so I often left mine off.

'Anyway, one day we had a job to do and left about 5 am on the coach in the cold but by the time we arrived the sun was out. Ceremonials were now to be worn. I, of course, had only my shocking pink sweater on under my greatcoat and hadn't brought my 'cerries' with me. This meant that the whole band had to do the parade and sweat it out in greatcoats. The girls were unhappy to say the least and I got a rocket.'

In the 1950s WRAF joined the domestic staff at the Prime Minister's country retreat at Chequers, previously a privilege of the other two services only. In 1956 Dorothy Isbell went there as a Stewardess.

'The big doors opened to this magnificent house and there stood lots of smiling faces. A friendly Flight Sergeant asked one of the girls to take my bags and then invited me in for a most welcome cup of tea. I was allowed to wash and change, then I was taken on a full tour of this beautiful historic house. Everywhere was spick and span. My quarters were at the back of the house and I shared a room with three other girls. We soon became good friends. I was also taken to meet the Head Housekeeper, such an inspiring friendly lady. She had been one of Sir Winston's private secretaries during the war. We all came to love and highly respect her as she was a friend and mother to us all during our stay there.

Left *WRAF Cook and Stewardesses in the grounds of Chequers* (Mrs Lone).

Below right *The air-sea rescue of the survivors of the crashed aero-medical Anson, 1950* (Mrs Stewart).

'My years at Chequers were really memorable ones, waiting on Prime Ministers, Presidents, Lords and Ladies of all nations. If I had my time again I wouldn't change any of those years.'

The Administrative Wing of stations had a rash of name changes, ushered in by the Binbrook Scheme of the late 1950s. Airwomen might now be working for the Officer Commanding Station Services Squadron, instead of the Station Administrative Officer. The Senior Secretarial Officer, a large part of whose staff is still airwomen, changed to Officer Commanding Personal Services Squadron and then in the mid '70s to OC Personal Management Squadron, while his former P1, 2 and 3 became Clerical Services and then Personal Services Flight. Very often, too, these Officer posts are filled by WRAF. Typist and shorthand typist are now limited to girls, mainly airwomen, and new posts have appeared in such tasks as Work Study and Computer Programming. As a Data Analyst working in Statistics today, Kim Smith is glad to use her skill in mathematics for a worthwhile cause and finds her work very rewarding.

Post-war WRAF Administration Officers devoted purely to watching over the welfare of their airwomen formed a very small part of the Secretarial Branch, both on stations and in senior posts at Group and Command Headquarters. In the '60s, Officers from other branches were tried out in these senior posts. Mary Crichton had a varied career spanning three decades, starting as a Met airwoman and ending as a Wing Officer.

'Meteorology was fun, punctuated by anxieties; education was a mixture of adult instruction — more my scene than children — and varied administration, and then my unexpected plunge (pushed from on high) into WRAF Administration was educative for me. An almost complete mental rest, but demanding physical energy and stamina — night inspections and those hockey side-lines with the snow going past horizontally!'

Gradually these posts dwindled and disappeared, the duties becoming secondary, and in 1968 the post of WRAF Inspector was abolished. The WRAF Director remains, though her staff is down to only two WRAF Officers and a SNCO, and welfare matters for both men and women have been added to her task. Problems relating to WRAF Officers and airwomen are now handled by the appropriate specialists, and Queen's Regulation 2064 'WRAF Channels of Communication' vanished in 1979. As a result, WRAF Secretarial Officers share common promotion lists with RAF, although as early as 1971, Bridget Martin became the first woman to achieve Air Rank in open competition with other RAF members of the Secretarial Branch.

A similar change has taken place in the airwomen's trade. In 1984 it was decided to amalgamate the WRAF and RAF Administrative trades in the General Service Group, thus broadening WRAF SNCOs' chances of promotion. As a result the same year saw Jenny Winspear becoming the first Station Warrant Officer. Now only two female posts have been retained for work in WRAF accommodation blocks.

The passing years have also seen the loss of many RAF Hospitals and special medical units, owing to greater need for economy. In the '50s and '60s Lydia Wilcock spent nine of the happiest years of her life working at the Rehabilitation Medical Unit at Collaton Cross in Devon.

'Patients from all the services came, and the work done by the Doctors, the Medical staff, the Remedial Gymnasts and Physios was terrific. I liked to think that the Catering section played its part, too, in the well-being of the patients and I did my best to encourage the staff and ensure that a high standard of cooking and presentation was maintained. When the unit closed I was posted to RAF Weeton and worked there as Catering Officer until that too closed.'

In the medical field, airwomen are found in clerical and administrative work in RAF Hospitals and medical centres as well as some specialist work in such

places as laboratories and dispensaries, in radiography, physiotherapy and operating theatres, and in the recent fields of environmental, occupational and community health.

Nursing has always attracted girls. Sergeant Dixie Ferris was awarded the King's Commendation for Brave Conduct in 1950; she was engaged in aero-medical evacuation duties when her Anson aircraft ditched in the Channel off Felixstowe. Using great presence of mind and with the navigator and pilot, she calmly assisted her two tuberculosis patients, an Army Sergeant and a woman, from a stretcher into a dinghy, where she tended to the Sergeant's head injury and comforted them until they were eventually picked up and taken to a UK hospital.

Women Medical Officers are still categorized as RAF. In 1968 Elspeth McKechnie became the first woman Doctor to be CO of the RAF Hospital at Cosford, and in 1972 she became the first woman Doctor to make Air Commodore. Josephine Kingston also scored a first, when she took RAF pilot training to become a Flight Medical Officer. Polly Arnold is a woman Dental Officer, but, like the Doctors, a member of the RAF. She enjoyed 'being able to practise dentistry with complete clinical freedom to an excellent standard and to treat the patient as well as the mouth. The nursing was of a consistently high standard without exception. But one of the snags of operating on the people you share a Mess with, is watching while they eat porky scratchings on your fillings . . . and praying! Also for fillings on fighter pilots, one has to compact the silver amalgam

Below left *The first woman doctor for Aeromedical Flying Training (RAFSC).*

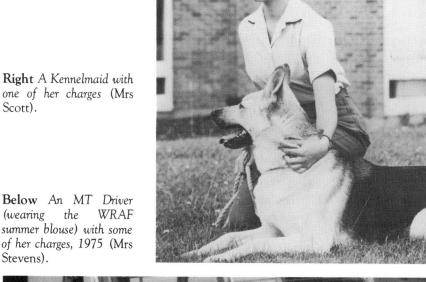

Right *A Kennelmaid with one of her charges (Mrs Scott).*

Below *An MT Driver (wearing the WRAF summer blouse) with some of her charges, 1975 (Mrs Stevens).*

correctly, or it could result in great pain to the pilot causing an aborted sortie, even a lost aircraft.'

There are of course still airwomen acting as Dental Technicians, Hygienists, and Surgery Assistants.

Airwomen may only join one of the three specializations in the Security Group. Firemen and Regiment are ruled out, but they may train as Policewomen in Special Investigation or Counter Intelligence duties.

There is also a very small and select trade of Kennelmaids, who have proved their worth since their appearance in 1957 and their début overseas some eight years later.

Airwomen are still much in evidence in the Telecommunications and Mechanical Transport Groups, and even the latter have their 'firsts'. Marjorie Blake was the first woman driver to be appointed to drive DWRAF in 1948-9.

Also, where would the RAF be without its survival equipment, lovingly checked and packed by the nimble-fingered airwomen of the Safety and Surface Sections?

However, this is the era of cut-backs. Greater economy sometimes makes for a greater move towards rationalization and the 1980s have seen many changes. Officers doing Secretarial, Catering, Education and Physical Education work, woke up one day to find that they were all in the one big Administrative Branch, though they continued to practise their own specialization up to Squadron Leader. A number of the support functions are also under the microscope, including Physical Education, Education and some medical services, while already the RAF is using the same buildings as the Army at Aldershot for Catering training. It is to be hoped that whatever else alters — and because of its history the RAF can adapt more quickly than most — the high standards and quality of work, which is the pride of both WRAF and RAF, will continue to be maintained.

Chapter 20

Going Places

'Hope and fear and peace and strife,
In the thread of human life.'

Sir Walter Scott

To call these days peace is only relative. Everywhere there is conflict. The Second World War did not end war. Even at home, there were difficulties. In 1949, out of the blue came orders for Ruth Higgins, an Equipment Assistant, to be detached to Aldergrove, Northern Ireland.

'It was interesting in that it had 202 Squadron there, doing the Bismuth (weather) flights over the Atlantic. The accommodation wasn't good and it rained most of the time, or it seemed to. Belfast was a once a fortnight trip on pay day. Even then we could sense the unrest there, as we marched through the streets in uniform to the Cathedral. Lots of roads and certain areas were out of bounds.'

Airwomen who volunteered to go overseas hoped to find something different from life at home, and often ran into much more than they expected, though with their refreshing mixture of enthusiasm, idealism and practicality they took it all in their stride. At New Delhi, Pat Martin having arrived with the first WAAF Draft in 1944, 'saw VE and VJ Days come and go, the approaching end of the Raj in India and our eventual evacuation when trouble arose'. India and Pakistan were given their independence in 1947.

Egypt was the destination of around 100 Signals WAAF sent to Telecommunications Middle East in November 1945 to take over from the by now, all-male, time-expired personnel awaiting repatriation. With them was Sergeant Kay France, who recalls it vividly.

'Morale was low, working conditions terrible, discipline non-existent. The Flt Sgt soon got things sorted out workwise. I had accommodation, welfare and the admin side to sort out. My nearest WAAF Officer was at Cairo HQ, some 12-15 miles away.

'On my first day I saw the Station Commander and told him that I wanted the tented camp of WAAF Quarters fenced round into a compound, a solid-built

Above *Interior of a Signals Sleeping Hut, TME 1946. Note the bomb boxes used for storage* (Mrs France).
Left *Poster* (RAF Museum).

guardroom and office with sleeping accommodation for two, and at least three huts of some sort for the signals shiftworkers. I also asked for daily labour to keep the compound and ablutions clean. He passed me on to the Egyptian in charge of the local labour gangs, with instructions that he was to get everything I wanted done at once. Being briefed on the attitude of Egyptians to women, I had to make my demands rather forcefully.

'Eventually all WAAF moved into huts, leaving the tents empty. During early 1946, I had 30 locally enlisted Palestinian girls as Teleprinter Operators, and they were delighted to live in the tents. When the Palestinian troubles started later in 1946, I had instructions to get them all demobilized and off the camp within 24 hours.

'The coolest place at mid-day was the covered verandah of the Sergeants' Mess, looking out on to a small but beautiful man-made garden. When we WAAF arrived there were about 50 RAF members, so it was rather a shock to have three WAAF SNCOs disturb their bachelor existence, but we all soon settled down to a very happy time for us all. An Arab gardener looked after the garden. When we arrived it was a blaze of colour with flowers, shrubs and trees full of blossom. The pool even had goldfish in it. This oasis was surrounded by sand, sand and more sand.'

A sign that post-war work was almost back to normal on all camps in Egypt could be seen in service activities like sport. In Kasfareet in April 1949, Olivia Ayres was 'called early — the Netball Final at Abyad. We had to win today against the WRAC. We didn't have any work as we had a fair way to travel. Couldn't eat much — too excited. Set off in convoy to Abyad with all our fans and mates to cheer us on. Game was early, but even then it was hot. We met the WRACs and got ready for this third and final game. (We played a blinder.) We didn't put a foot wrong. Even the Egyptian spectators clapped. We beat the

WRAC 13 goals to 8, and I was assistant shooter. They went into the net a treat.'

Anti-British feeling, riots and demonstrations still continued. By 1950 WRAF numbers had been reduced to just under 400 and in 1952, the year of the coup replacing King Farouk by General Neguib, they were down to 262. In the Canal Zone with other WRAF, Barbara Joy experienced the gathering storm.

'There was trouble in Ismailiya and the married families were attacked. They were brought into our station and we vacated our billets and went to live in the children's school. The Egyptian mob attacked our cinema, which was situated outside the camp, just as the film show ended [as well as a nunnery, killing one nun]. At night we could hear the machine-guns going. All the native labour vanished and we had no fresh food for quite some time. Water was very scarce and we just had small amounts to wash ourselves.'

Most British troops had left Egypt by 1955, but in 1953 when Britain was considering running down its bases, Myrtle Devine noted, 'Suez had lots of curfews. We were allowed to play sports against other WRAF in the Canal Zone but we always had armed guards, because it was not unusual for people, buses and everything to just disappear.'

From there she was posted to Aden in 1954, another trouble-spot, where Britain was co-operating with Aden's own levies to counter Yemeni attacks and local unrest. This posting was shortly followed by another to Cyprus to accompany the first airwomen sent from the Canal Zone into Nicosia. It proved to be a case of 'out of the frying pan into the fire', as they ran into 'curfews, lots of bars in Nicosia were being bombed by Eoka terrorists'.

Above far left *TME 1946. Making demands rather forcefully* (Mrs France).

Above left *Man-made garden at Kasfareet, 1946* (Mrs Winstone).

Above *Three-legged race in the 1946 Sports Day at Kasfareet* (Mrs Winstone).

Right *An official inspection of the WRAF Compound just after the arrival of the first WRAF in Nicosia, Cyprus, March 1955* (Miss Devine).

Left *The Station Riding School at RAF Habbaniya, 1946* (Miss Acheson).

Right *A Comet on Gibraltar, transporting families. Air Quartermasters near the steps* (Mrs Boot).

Indeed the serenity and beauty of Cyprus, the island of Venus, was constantly disrupted. Although given independence by Britain in 1959 with Archbishop Makarios as President, there were internal troubles.

In 1959-61 Edith Bray found 'travel in Nicosia was restricted, a curfew remained in force and only volunteer WRAF were posted in. There we were issued with soft rations for self-catering, due to poor messing facilities — which was advantageous in that it enabled us to provide chips with everything to the soldiers who lived next door, in return for gardening duties.'

The attempted Greek coup followed by the Turkish invasion of 1974 caused a vast influx of servicemen and their families, civilians and Turkish and Greek refugees into the relative safety of the RAF Camps at Akrotiri and Episkopi. Airwomen squashed up and anyone not on essential duty went to help in Reception Centres. The result was partition of the island, an uneasy peace, and reductions in all but essential personnel assisting the United Nations, amongst whom, of course, there continue to be WRAF.

WRAF were also to be found at Habbaniya in Iraq, on whose borders lie Turkey, Syria, Jordan, Saudi Arabia, Kuwait and Iran. The RAF handed over this useful base to Iraq in 1955. Barbara Rayner was there in 1952, when the Arabs went on strike and filled fire extinguishers with explosives, but the trouble quickly died. She describes this prestige camp as having 'our own hospital, sailing club, race course and tote. As the camp is eight square miles, we also have a taxi service. Our bearer, called Rosa, who does our washing etc, and to whom we pay 5s a month, shrinks our woollies and then with regret states that they wouldn't fit memsarb any more but would fit her chico. She has the best dressed children around the civilian cantonment.'

Barbara also quotes a poem which was 'doing the rounds' at that time.

I think it was Lord Balfour, who chanced to come this way.
To inspect the camp Habbaniya, one cool and sunny day.
He came when all was pretty in the scented winter air,
He saw it from the angle which made it sweet and fair.
So good was the impression — it filled him full of awe,
And when he returned to England, he wrote of what he saw.
I do not know what the Premier said, neither do I care,
But I know what I'd have said if it happened I'd been there.
I'd ask her if she'd ever been in a storm of windswept sand,*
Or if she'd ever lived in this God forsaken land!
Had she ever felt the heat at a hundred and twenty degrees,
Had she ever been in bed overrun with bugs and fleas,
Had she ever been under canvas by the Great Habbaniya Lake,
Where it is a common sight to see the scorpion and the snake.
We hope that if you come this way, to Habb your way you'll wend,
And then the sticky climate here will send you round the bend.
And in future, don't forget, it needs two years at least,
To realise what life is like in this "Lido of the East".

On the coast of Spain, the Rock of Gibraltar has always been a determinedly British enclave, with a small Armed Services presence, and its RAF camps have been a favoured WRAF posting, but only for a few. In 1959, Queenie Lee was sent there, a live wire running the 8th Gibraltar Air Cubs and the Rangers for the Gibraltarian Guides, which a number of airwomen also joined. She persuaded the Admiral to let her run weekend camps on his grounds, and with her air-

*Lady Astor complained to the Prime Minister about the RAF's life of ease . . .

Left *Guides cooking a meal at a Gibraltar Weekend Camp* (Mr Chilton for Miss Lee).

Below right *A P3 Section at RAF Changi, 1953* (Mrs Green).

women performed plays and attended evening classes at the top of the Rock, some of their pottery work being displayed at exhibitions.

The little Mediterranean island of Malta, midway between North Africa and Italy, was also an attractive posting for WRAF, but there were troubles which led to the island being given independence in 1964. A handful of WRAF were still to be found there on such work as Air Traffic Control or as Aircraft Fitters until the RAF finally left in 1979.

Another strategic island, once very popular as an overseas posting for WRAF, was Singapore. Off the coast of Malaysia, and granted independence in the '60s, it retained a British naval base until 1971. Girls found themselves mainly at RAF stations near the towns of Changi in the east, Seletar in the north, and Singapore city in the south, and there was considerable rivalry between them.

After the long sea journey in 1954, Brenda Pashley thought Singapore Island very green and very hot.

'There were open sides to our accommodation block, so we virtually lived in the fresh air. The advanced telephonist course for FEAF [Far Eastern Air Force] was held in Changi and I was made instructor. Pupils came from Taiwan, Labuan, Ceylon and Malaya. Every two weeks, an air-conditioned train took girls to the cool and relaxing rest camp at Frazer's Hill and many went to Penang, a jewel of an island.'

Years later, WRAF on a survival course in the Malayan jungle hacked out an escape route to Frazer's Hill village.

There were continuing troubles, and although Doris Cook found Singapore exotic and loved the Chinese inhabitants, she was fully aware of the quiet little war on the doorstep, with the Communist infiltration into Malaya. Between 1954-55, Dorothy Ainge fetched stores from Changi to Singapore town during the Chinese riots, with an airman in the back of her lorry holding a rifle.

In 1965 nurses in Changi hospital tended patients from the Indonesian confrontation where according to Jane, a nurse, one had been making bombs for the

Chinese. The hospital also received casualties from Borneo, resulting from guerilla action. Despite, and sometimes because of, these dangers, airwomen found time to think of others less fortunate than themselves. In 1965, Saletar girls adopted the education costs of a little Malay boy, and the Red Cross Crippled Children's Home, on their departure, must have missed the Changi girl's long, loyal support.

As was usually the case, WRAF made the most of their leave while in the Far East, visiting many countries in that area, even going as far afield as Japan and Hong Kong, although a few individuals actually go to Hong Kong on duty.

The RAF camp of El Adem lay in oil-rich Libya near the Mediterranean coast of Africa. Independent in 1951, its monarchy was overthrown by the military coup of 1969, which closed the base. In 1966, Maggie Dawson was posted there.

'I looked out of the window as we came in to land. All I could see for miles and miles was an expanse of brown land and in the middle a few dots next to a long black line, the dots and black line being the runway and buildings of El Adem. Temperatures were often over 100°F. It contained about 2,000 troops, 70 families, 6 airwomen, 3 nursing sisters, 1 WRVS lady and me [the Accounts Officer].'

She also took the chance of seeing the country, its oases and Greek and Roman ruins. She found the desert 'utterly fascinating — dry shimmering heat from the relentless scorching sunshine and absolute silence. This was compensated for by the magnificent sunsets and flashes of brilliant colour from the

flowering plants which appeared on the only day it rained during my eleven month tour.'

Aden on the southern tip of Arabia was another of the places where WRAF were to be seen, though there were other RAF bases up and down the coastal areas, like Bahrain and Masirah, where Britain had treaty obligations to fulfil and where the occasional WRAF was found sometimes as a RAF wife. In 1956, Kate Clark, as Catering Officer at the Aden RAF Hospital, hardly noticed the Suez Campaign of 1956.

'It had no immediate impact on life in Aden, except for the departure of those taking part. The subsequent closure of the Canal meant that seaborne re-supply had to come via the Cape, but stocks were more than adequate. The harbour and Steamer Point shops became very quiet without the normal commercial shipping.'

Twelve years later, Dorothy Finney came to work at RAF Khormaksar, nine miles' drive from Steamer Point, where WRAF personnel lived.

'There was wonderful, constant sunshine, air-conditioning, free afternoons to sunbathe, a superb social life and some strong friendships. Females were so few that the WRAF and WRAC were enclosed in a compound of high netted walls with only two padlocked entrances. In our Mess, we had a special trellised area of our own in which to eat, nicknamed the Birdcage.

'But Aden was a dangerous place to be at the time of the British withdrawal — shopping expeditions had always to be accompanied by an armed guard. One morning my office at Joint Movement Services was mortar bombed by the Arabs. I was the only female in the place and all the men came rushing in to protect me

Left *El Adem Station from the air* (Mrs Pleasant).

Right *A church in the Falklands* (Miss McArthur).

— to find me sitting calmly cross-legged under my desk.'

In September 1967 the last 30 WRAF boarded a VC 10 bound for the UK to the strains of Auld Lang Syne. Britain was pulling out of the area, a move completed throughout the Gulf by 1971.

The most recent active involvement of the RAF has been in protecting the British inhabitants of the bitterly cold, storm-tossed Falklands, off South America, from Argentinian attack. In 1982, just as the Falkland Campaign started, Michele Clare arrived at Odiham.

'I was terribly busy sending people to war. I remember our horror when we thought we may have lost some men on the Atlantic convoys.'

Afterwards a few WRAF were flown out, on four-month tours, and there are larger detachments in Belize and Ascension Island. For one or two Officers, also, there is a much envied tour in the United States.

The RAF has remained in Germany and the WAAF/WRAF with them, since the end of the Second World War. It was a strange experience, as Paula Warren, who recently wrote a book about it, relates.

'When our unit first arrived at Buckeburg in July 1945, we WAAF were not allowed out of our billets unless accompanied by armed airmen. They carried rifles and Sten guns and all Officers wore pistols in holsters. Although the war had just ended, Germany was still regarded as enemy territory. We had lovely billets. A small orchestra played at mealtimes and we were served by waiters! The unit was one big family.'

The Potsdam agreement divided Germany into four administrative zones of the UK, USA, USSR and France. Berlin, however, lay inside the Russian zone,

but it too was divided into four sectors to which the three western powers had limited access. The airfield of Gatow was in the British sector. In 1948, Doris Darrant remembers returning from a detachment at Gatow on a train stopped by the Russians.

'They claimed that there were German scientists on board, whom they wanted to take into custody. The crew stood firm, closed all doors and windows, and after many stifling hours of negotiations in the hot summer, the train completed its journey. This was the beginning of the closure of all rail, road and canal links to the capital — putting the two million or so inhabitants of West Berlin into a situation of virtual blockade.'

The air alone remained free. So began the massive Berlin Airlift, operated continuously, round the clock by the western powers, flying in all the people and supplies needed to keep this vast city alive. 'We had squadrons at Gatow, from all countries of the British Commonwealth,' says Joyce Roberts. At home Kitty Hawkins was awarded the BEM for her work. After a year, because of the allied success, the Russians lifted their blockade.

In 1955, West Germany, now the Federal Republic of Germany, joined the North Atlantic Treaty Organization (NATO) which aimed at mutual defence against the Soviet block's Warsaw Pact. Its separation from East Germany was physically reinforced in 1961 by the Communist-built 30 ft wall bisecting Berlin, a very emotive barrier. The RAF now remained as part of the NATO shield for the west, and the WRAF continued their two-year tours as before. Memories are short however. During the 1956 Suez crisis Joyce Greason discovered that any

Above left *'Liberty' trip to Hanover, 1945. Note the ex-Luftwaffe coach in front* (Mrs Irwin).

Left *The Director surprises a Wireless Telegraphy Operator in the Flying Control Tower at Gatow during the Berlin Airlift, 1948* (Miss Sibley).

Right *A visit to the East-West German border* (Mrs Stevens).

WRAF in uniform was jeered and spat on by the locals.

In the '70s Pat Wheatley was in one of the regular NATO exercises, involving all services and countries, both at home and abroad. There were several small ones a year and less frequent large scale ones, to test the alertness and efficiency of NATO to defend itself against attack.

In this exercise I had to go to the Operations Bunker to help log the exercise, but the Bunker was invaded by enemies and I was handed a paper saying I was a casualty with a broken leg. Along came the medics and bandaged my leg to the chair leg. They then carried me and the chair to the entrance, whereupon some bright spark produced a wheelbarrow and trundled me along to the ambulance — an ordinary lorry. Then they quite literally threw me into the back with the other casualties, complete with make-believe blood and everything. When the whistle went and the exercise ended, everyone whizzed off, leaving me to unravel my leg from the chair.'

At another practice, the Nuclear, Biological and Chemical Warfare (NBC) kit that Corporal Valerie Walter wore in 1976 'was a suit of two pieces, in heavy itchy material and one got extremely hot whilst wearing it. Additional items like gloves, hood, mask and respirator were kept in the haversack. The steel helmet was often too large and painful to wear for long periods. You lost all femininity in the suit, totally clumsy in all movement and to add to this everyone, male and female, looked alike. Hence a WRAF had to have "W" taped on her for occasions of individual searches and so on.'

A visit in 1977 reminded her of why the RAF was there, despite the seeming normality of camps that resembled an English town.

'On the border of East and West Germany there was a daily border patrol. Patrol Officers wore black uniform and white caps, much like the Navy. We were issued with khaki dress. We were there to observe and learn how the border was patrolled from both sides. We saw the fences, watch towers and soldiers; east and west villages were deserted and we saw no young people. In all we travelled over some 100 miles of border. I found it very disturbing, as you could see how villages had been broken and people separated from relatives, also the graves of those who had tried to escape over the wall. On the border there was an air of fragile hostility and it was so quiet. It was kinda eerie and chilling. Fortunately, having been to Berlin as well, I was able to relate the two visits. Travelling up to Berlin on the train was quite frightening.'

The WRAF are still in Germany, working and playing hard, taking an increasingly important part in what happens. Maggie Docherty found the language barrier a challenge and fun to overcome, and in 1984 she went as Ski instructor to Oberammergau in Bavaria with an all-male party, all reasonable skiers, ranging from SAC to Air Commodore. While at play, many take advantage of the plentiful sports facilities and travel further afield.

The WRAF will adapt and settle in most situations, and are grateful for any opportunity to be posted overseas. Now, however, with the passing of Empire, postings abroad are few, but those who go, usually combine with their work in the RAF the role of first-class ambassadors for their country.

Chapter 21

What Kind Of Evolution?

'A state without the means of some change is without the means of its conservation.'

Burke

A new girl in smart civilian clothes presents herself at the Guardroom of a RAF station. Beyond the barrier she sees brick buildings for living and working in, with perhaps the occasional prefab or wartime hut, and large concrete and steel hangars lurking in the background. She has been through the selection process, is trained in service ways and has learned the skills of the work she has come to do. Now she is starting on a new way of life as well as a new job.

Tomorrow she will 'arrive' officially. Soon, wearing her working dress (not the smart Victor Stiebel suit now kept only for rare occasions), she will meet the people and sections she will grow to know well during her tour of duty. Then she will take her place, proud in the knowledge that she, equally with the men around her, is RAF. Her work and life today will differ greatly from that of her mother and grandmother. How much has it altered?

Over a long career spanning the Second World War and into the '60s, May Beagent saw many changes in accommodation.

'Large huts became blocks designed for either a mixture of single rooms or rooms of four beds. The dividing walls were cabinets built-in back to back, consisting of a fitted wardrobe, chest of drawers, writing table, and each room had a bed and a chair. They were light and airy with light coloured paint [most service people recall dark green or brown paintwork and cream walls with a shudder!]. NCOs had rooms of their own and some places allowed curtains. The brown cork linoleum gave way to mats. Bathrooms and toilets were better arranged with easy-to-clean floors and plenty of basins.'

Myrtle Devine takes up the story and compares conditions today with when she first joined up in 1951.

'[There is] central heating and much more privacy in ablutions [now all in one building with plenty of showers and hot baths]. More electrical appliances are

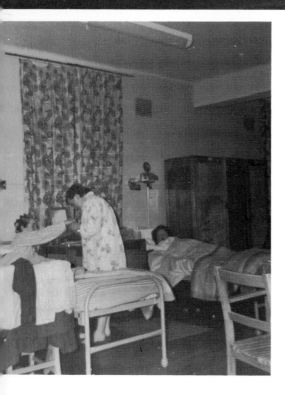

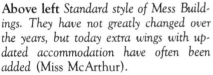

Above left Standard style of Mess Buildings. They have not greatly changed over the years, but today extra wings with updated accommodation have often been added (Miss McArthur).

Far left Large 4 to 6-bedded airwomen's room, usually for recent arrivals, who move to single rooms when vacant (Miss McArthur).

Left Airwomen's single bedroom, with built-in fitment and central heating (Miss McArthur).

Above Ablutions 1980 – showers, toilets and handbasins. SNCOs usually have bedroom handbasins (Miss McArthur).

Above right Ironing room with sink unit and drying room nearby (Miss McArthur).

Right Best-blue uniform, approved for WRAF Officers and airwomen 1954, from designs by Victor Stiebel. The air hostess-style hat introduced in the 1960s (Mrs Stevens).

supplied, like polishers, washing–machines and dryers. We now have civilian cleaners for the blocks, making it much easier for the airwomen.'

She thinks, however, that 'Number 1 uniform was much better when I joined up, perhaps not so glamorous, but it fitted and was of much better material. We did not have the open-neck, short-sleeved summer shirts, but we had grey lisle thread stockings [today's stockings are now grey to match the uniform], and flat, hard-wearing leather shoes, much better than those issued today. The 1960 air-woman air-hostess style hat does not stand up to everyday wear and shrinks when wet. I was issued with a hat with a brim and it did not matter if you had a thin or fat face, a brim always looked smart. I have seen three hat changes since 1951!'

In the 1960s, Kitt Voller discovered 'an almost complete change in uniform. We were allowed to wear court shoes and swap from brass to anodized buttons.' How many button-sticks now rest in honourable retirement!

Another great leap forward in the estimation of Doffy Watler was when 'from about 1947, we were allowed to wear "civvie" clothes off camp, when not on duty. I wore my first new coat for many years — a Dior Long Look — such luxury and glamour!'

Everyone with long experience of the WRAF agrees that food has vastly improved, perhaps due to the assistance of WRAF Catering Officers! Gone are the days when Pat King thought kippers and jam on one plate was a joke until she actually met them in 1950 at St Eval, and 'the Orderly Officer had the nerve to ask what we were complaining of!'. There is enough choice to bewilder the new entrant. The only complaints today are that many girls considering their figures, are asking for more health conscious foods, something Catering Officers have long advocated but not been able to implement in mixed dining restaurants because of the greater appetite of their airmen.

History was made for the WRAF in 1960 by Barbara Peters.

'I had become engaged to a Squadron Leader and made known my intention of retiring from my Permanent Commission. The Director, Dame Jean Conan-Doyle, was becoming very aware of the wastage of Officers and airwomen through marriage. During a staff visit, she asked me if I would consider delaying my retirement after marriage, so that the service could determine whether an In-Service marriage could work.

'To cut a long story short, I stayed on in the WRAF until 1963, and as the first serving married Officers, the original AMO was technically written about us. Needless to say, it was a most unusual situation for that time, and caused quite a lot of confusion and some extremely hilarious situations.'

As a result it is not unusual to meet married airwomen and Officers in the service. In fact the figure for married airwomen in 1984 was 41 per cent, of whom many live off as well as on camp, as can their unmarried sisters of today, if they wish.

Pay has also greatly improved. In the new WRAF of 1949, Doris McManus considered it 'very meagre. We were paid fortnightly and were not usually able to last out till next pay day.'. The outcome of the review of the National Board for Prices and Incomes on the pay of the armed forces, comparing service 24 hour

Off parachuting, 1975 (Mrs Stevens).

RAF Lawn Tennis Wimbledon Championship, 1979 (Miss Docherty).

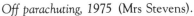

duties with civilian counterparts, was to introduce in 1970 the Military Salary. From then pay rose steeply, although such things as accommodation and food were no longer free. The idea of equal pay for women was taken on board to be introduced little by little. No longer were the women's services to be poor relations.

Working hours too changed for the better, though they did vary somewhat from station to station. Until the mid '50s, Wednesday afternoons were supposed to be set aside for sports, on which the RAF was most insistent and the girls less keen. In effect this often resulted on those who were good at sports taking part, with the others remaining at work. Work thus lost was done on Saturday mornings, and Saturday morning Working Parades lasted on some stations into the '70s.

Sport had therefore a somewhat chequered history, though no better facilities exist anywhere. PE Instructors work with infectious zeal, and sometimes teams travel around the world. Everything is on offer from netball, table tennis, squash, fencing, sailing, rifle shooting, mountaineering, parachuting, gliding, orienteering, athletics and swimming to the Nijmegen marches. WRAF regularly figure at Wimbledon. They also take part with the men in adventure training, expeditions and rescue teams. But enjoyment is the main criterion. The motto of one WRAF Officer was, 'Better to have played and lost than never to have played at all'.

Promotion sometimes was a bit of a puzzle. Elizabeth Jeffrey did not always consider it fair, 'as some airwomen [and RAF] were very good on the practical

Promotion: Just trying them out!

Below *A member of RAF Wyton Christian Fellowship Team wading to church in July 1957 to take the evening service* (Mrs Wigley).

Below right *A guest Dining-In Night in an Officers' Mess, 1987* (Mrs Boot).

part of their trade but could not write the theory'. As trade and education requirements became more important, personnel had to pass more tests before they could be considered. Unfortunately education tests contained mandatory mathematics, at which WRAF were notoriously weak.

WAAF Education Officers first appeared in 1946 to work alongside their RAF colleagues to mixed classes, but by the '60s, education was no longer compulsory, although it could be done in working hours if sections were willing. With the aid of small classes or RAF subsidised training, how many thousands of airmen and women, leaving school without qualifications, can now boast them! To Pat Arnold, 'the facilities are excellent for those who take advantage of them'.

Religion, too, has its place, though compulsory Church Parades are a thing of the past. The RAF Padres of various denominations are popular figures and they are available for advice whenever needed. 'If your knees knock, kneel on them' is a wartime saying, still valid today. Fellowships and societies are glad to welcome airwomen.

Pequita Campbell remembers social life in the Officers' Mess of the '50s 'as great fun, quite formal and very friendly. Formal occasions, however, were treated very seriously. No wife or WRAF Officer would dare to attend a cocktail party hatless or a ball without gloves. Nor would we dare to omit the required calls to leave our cards.'

Even in the '60s, these rules were disappearing, but one great event that has never changed, except in its frequency to once a month or even less, is the formal Dining In at both Sergeants' and Officers' Messes, when RAF in blue-grey and gold, and WRAF in long blue dresses, dine in candlelight with music and toasts, tended by white-gloved and coated stewards.

There were good times when girls were off-duty. Ivy Bailey recalls the dances

and get-togethers in the NAAFI, long realized as playing an essential part in the social life and meeting of airmen and women.

'We made our own entertainment and were far more happy with our lot than are people today.'

Audrey Tuck at North Weald was delighted to find that she had 'easy access to London and enjoyed the Service Clubs and theatres. The Sergeants' Mess was extremely good. We organized coach trips, dances and other things which were great fun. I helped to write, produce and take part in two revues. All the cast were men apart from myself. We did a spoof of Cinderella in uniform—Cinders an ACW2, the Ugly Sisters as Military Policemen, the Fairy Godmother an Administrative Officer and Cinders turning out to be the CO's long lost daughter. The proceeds went to the RAF Benevolent Fund.'

Indeed, good causes outside the station, at home and abroad, have always been important to the WRAF, who are usually busy collecting gifts, money and sometimes helping in such places as hospitals, schools, orphanages, homes for the sub-normal, handicapped and aged, as well as charities of all kinds. They also join in local activities, as when RAF Innsworth, after being given the Freedom of the City of Gloucester, contributed a float to their carnival, and in Cheltenham, four pretty airwomen were in their 1960 Carnival Queen contest and the Sketch Forces Pin-up competition. They are there, too, in the background giving support whenever the RAF is called to help in a disaster at home, such as the terrible flooding on the East Coast in 1953, or abroad, when RAF transport aircraft fly out relief supplies to such areas as the 1984 famine in Ethiopia.

Walk and cake for local charities to celebrate the WRAF 25th Anniversary, 1974 (Mrs Pleasant).

Edinburgh Floodlight Tattoo, 1959. The WRAF team, in the lighter coloured uniform, is in the middle directly behind the centre front sailors (Glasgow Herald & Evening Times).

It is a tradition for the RAF to take part in great public events. Rosemary Hodgkiss was in several service displays including the Royal Tournament at Earls Court in 1959.

'We had a naval instructor who taught us a club swinging sequence with wooden clubs which had torches on the ends with red, white and blue bulbs. We ended with a finale of club swinging in the dark, with the torches on, finishing in the shape of the Union Jack. It was pretty spectacular at the time.

'I went from the Tournament up to Edinburgh to learn Scottish country dancing for the Tattoo. From the Tattoo, I came down to RAF Uxbridge and performed the club swinging for the Festival of Remembrance at the Royal Albert Hall.'

When King George VI died, there was a great sense of shock and loss throughout the services, almost as if they had lost a well-loved member of their own family. A memorial service for the King, held in a hangar at RAF Odiham, has remained in Dorothy Gravell's memory ever since, and especially 'the solemn moment when we all repeated our vow of allegiance to Queen Elizabeth and her Heirs'.

The date for the Queen's Coronation Day was set as 2 June 1953, and Patricia

Brown was one of the airwomen marching in the procession.

'At last we were given the signal to move off. The RAF band played marching tunes for us to keep in step. Never in my life have I seen so many people. There were thousands; every window and roof was packed. My parents had invited various relatives to view the procession on TV with them — sets weren't quite so numerous as in recent years. When we'd marched about half-way round the route, orders came to halt the procession.'

Eve Myer was reserve parade commander for the WRAF Flight.

'I was not called upon, but then I acted as an usher in the Royal Enclosure — a really memorable day for me'.

At other Royal events, ceremonies and our own periodic celebrations and anniversaries, WRAF are usually represented. In 1965, Sally Wilkins was proud to be one of the airwomen selected to line the route for the State Funeral of Sir Winston Churchill.

The post-war years have seen the reduction of the RAF from 10 Home and three Overseas Commands in 1942 (Bomber, Fighter, Coastal, Army Co-operation, Balloon, Flying Training, Technical Training, Maintenance, Ferry, Northern Ireland and Middle East, India and Far East) to two Home and one Overseas in 1988 (Strike, Support and RAF Germany). 1964 saw the three service Ministries combined into the Ministry of Defence (MOD), hence Air Ministry Orders (AMOs) became known as Defence Council Instructions (DCIs). Such changes have meant a vast reduction in staffing levels, as the WRAF demonstrate: in 1988 they were around 6,000, whereas at their peak in 1943 they numbered approximately 182,000. Thus the old maxim of Lord Trenchard comes into play, 'Quality rather than quantity'. Sally Carter

Left *Books of Remembrance being given to St Clement Danes, London, the RAF Church, 1958 (Mrs Scott).*

Right *Senior Girls of the Warwickshire and Birmingham Air Training Corps (ATC) completing the 100 mile Nijmegen, March 1987 (Mrs James).*

appreciates this.

'The services are now in the Computer Age and you need more O and A levels to join up'.

To many it seems that the RAF requires a dedicated motivation increasingly hard to find.

Up to this point the WRAF have become RAF in every sense save flying. In most jobs, provided she is physically and mentally capable of doing them after the requisite training, the RAF considers a girl as interchangeable with a man. Women wanted parity and in almost all ways, including basic pay and, since 1968, ranks, they have gained it. For a ground career it is one of the most satisfying that can be offered to a girl today.

In the process girls have not become butch or loose-living. They have not lost their femininity but are still women in a man's world, outnumbered by 15 to one. Perhaps this very fact promotes RAF chivalry! The world they share with the RAF is a strange one of contrasts. On the one hand they are in a community within a community, making friendships closer and loyalties stronger. They are sheltered, guarded and guided in a law-abiding society in which everyone knows the rules, the limits and the penalties for breaking them. It is therefore up to a girl to make the most of what the RAF offers, be it in sport, social life or entertainment. As Hilary Trant comments, 'There is more in service life than just a job of work'.

On the other hand, though today there may be fewer restrictions and a more relaxed discipline (much deplored by many), the RAF has little patience with muddled thinking and uncertainty. As Muriel Trowbridge points out, 'I am amazed that so much responsibility was left in the hands of airwomen [and

Officers] sometimes as young as 19', often questions affecting life and death! This matures a girl far beyond her years. She learns to stand on her own feet, to sort out good from bad, to make decisions and act swiftly, to give as good as she gets. In this climate, inhibitions and shyness disappear. She knows her own worth.

The thought of flying is what attracts men and women to the RAF rather than any other service, but it is from this function that the WRAF are debarred. It is not from lack of ability — women in civil aviation have proved their worth — but for two reasons, emotional and economic. The first is that the RAF only recruits its pilots for front-line combat roles. Therefore, would the country be willing, in the unwelcome event of war, for its servicewomen to be aggressors? The second is whether the RAF dare risk losing a career girl through marriage or motherhood, when pilot training is so long and costly. A pregnancy would put a woman out of today's high velocity flying for too long for her to relearn her hard-won expertise.

The women of the ATA of the '40s show one possible compromise, though its feasibility is questionable with complicated modern aircraft. Testing is another thought, while flying transports is perhaps more realistic. But when the chips are down, is the person who prepares an aircraft any less responsible than the one who flies it?

Traditional attitudes change slowly. Thus it may be a long time, a last resort or never that women *in* the RAF, will be allowed to fly *for* it. Of course, it might be that the WRAF really do their best work in their posts on the ground.

Outside the regular RAF, some civil and ex-service women help in the Volunteer Reserve and give their time to train young boys and girls in the Combined Cadet Force or the Air Training Corps. They are to be found in most Commonwealth Air Force Services and Associations like New Zealand's famous 99. Joy Talbot joined the Women's Royal Auxiliary Air Force after the RAF.

'I was lucky enough to go to Gibraltar about six times to take part in the Annual Training Exercises and to Cyprus later. The next most exciting occasions were the six times I led my detachment of five airmen and five airwomen across the Royal Albert Hall during the Festival of Remembrance. I found it very moving to watch on television, but to take part is really something out of this world. Actually on my last visit I wondered whether I should line up with the Chelsea Pensioners!'

'What memories you brought back,' writes Marjorie Monckton of her service at the end of the '50s. 'Beautiful mornings on the airfield and cold dark nights in our wooden huts. But we did enjoy ourselves and worked hard but played hard as well.' Her feelings are echoed by Frances Patterson who, looking back a decade later, feels 'it is a way of life that teaches tolerance, self-reliance, self-discipline, responsibility towards one's neighbour and how to win through with hope — it really does impart the RAF's motto — "Through adversity to the Stars".'

The pride is there, if slightly confused, when Pat Sturgeon's three-year-old son, being very grown up, told a friend:

'My Grandpa was a sailor, my Daddy was a soldier and my Mummy was an airsick woman!'

Appendices

Appendix A Equivalent Ranks

Various trades and technical grades have further rank and name subdivisions in all services. Where no equivalent ranks exist, particularly among older ones, the nearest approximation is used, based on command responsibilities.

SHOULDER RANK BADGES	RAF	ARMY	NAVY	WRAF	WAAF	WRAF
1988	1988	1988	1988	AUG 1968	1942	AUG 1919
RAF						
	Marshal of the Royal Air Force	Field Marshal	Admiral of the Fleet			
	Air Chief Marshal	General	Admiral			
	Air Marshal	Lieutenant General	Vice Admiral			
	Air Vice Marshal	Major General	Rear Admiral			
RAF and WRAF						
	Air Commodore	Brigadier	Commodore	Air Commodore	Air Commandant	Commandant
	Group Captain	Colonel	Captain	Group Captain	Group Officer	Deputy Commandant
	Wing Commander	Lieutenant-Colonel	Commander	Wing Commander	Wing Officer	Assistant Commandant I
	Squadron Leader	Major	Lieutenant-Commander	Squadron Leader	Squadron Officer	Assistant Commandant II
	Flight Lieutenant	Captain	Lieutenant	Flight Lieutenant	Flight Officer	Administrator

SHOULDER RANK BADGES	RAF	ARMY	NAVY	WRAF	WAAF	WRAF
1988	1988	1988	1988	AUG 1968	1942	AUG 1919
	Flying Officer	Lieutenant	Sub-Lieutenant	Flying Officer	Section Officer	Deputy Administrator
	Pilot Officer	Second Lieutenant	Midshipman	Pilot Officer	Assistant Section Officer	Assistant Administrator
	Warrant Officer	Warrant Officer I Warrant Officer II	Warrant Officer	Warrant Officer	Warrant Officer	Senior Leader
	Flight Sergeant	Staff Sergeant	Chief Petty Officer	Flight Sergeant	Flight Sergeant	Chief Section Leader
	Chief Technician					
	Sergeant	Sergeant	Petty Officer	Sergeant	Sergeant	
	Corporal	Corporal Lance Corporal	Leading Seaman	Corporal	Corporal	Section Leader
	Junior Technician					Sub Leader
	Senior Aircraft-man		Able Seaman	Senior Aircraft-woman	Leading Air-craftwoman	
	Leading Air-craftman	Private	Ordinary Seaman	Leading Air-craftwoman	Aircraftwoman I	Member
	Aircraftman	Private	Ordinary Seaman	Aircraftwoman	Aircraftwoman 2	Member

Appendix B   Directors from 1918

Director	Date	Remarks	Died
WRAF 1 April 1918 – 1 April 1920			
Chief Superintendent Lady Gertrude Crawford	April 1918	Daughter of Earl of Sefton	1953
Lady Commandant The Hon Violet Blanche Douglas-Pennant	May 1918	Daughter of Lord Penrhyn	12 Oct 1945
Commandant Dame Helen Charlotte Isabella Gwynne-Vaughan GBE LLD DSc FLS	Sept 1918 – Dec 1919	Née Fraser	6 Aug 1967
WAAF 28 June 1939 – 31 January 1949			
WRAF 1 February 1949 – present			
Senior Controller later Air Commandant and after 1942 Air Chief Commandant Dame Katherine Jane Trefus-Forbes DBE LLD	1 Jan 1939 – 3 Oct 1943	Lady Watson-Watt (1966)	18 Jan 1971
Air Chief Commandant Lady Ruth Mary Eldridge Welsh DBE	4 Oct 1943 – 30 Nov 1946	Née Dalzell	25 June 1986
Air Commandant Dame Felicity H Hanbury DBE AE	1 Dec 1946 – 30 June 1950	Peake (1952)	
Air Commandant Dame Nancy M Salmon DBE AE	1 July 1950 – 9 Aug 1956	Snagge (1962)	
Air Commandant Dame Henrietta Barnet DBE	10 Aug 1956 – Mar 1960		11 Sept 1985
Air Commandant Dame Anne Stephens DBE	Mar 1960 – 31 Mar 1963		
Air Commandant Dame Jean Conan Doyle DBE AE	1 Apr 1963 – 12 Apr 1966	Lady Bromet (1965)	
Air Commandant Dame Felicity Hill DBE	13 Apr 1966		
Air Commodore Dame Felicity Hill DBE	1 Nov 1968 – 11 July 1969		
Air Commodore Philippa F Marshall CB OBE	12 July 1969 – 6 July 1973		
Air Commodore Molly G. Allott CB FBIM	7 July 1973 – 22 Oct 1976		
Air Commodore P Joy Tamblin CB BA CBIM FRSA	23 Oct 1976 – 18 Feb 1980		
Air Commodore Helen F Renton CB MA LLD	19 Feb 1980 – 30 Jan 1986		
Air Commodore Shirley A Jones ADC	31 Jan 1986		

Appendix C   Awards and Decorations from 1918

First World War WRAF 1918–20
DBE 1
CBE 1
OBE 7
MBE 16
BEM 1
Commendations 127

Second World War WAAF 1939–46
GC 2
DBE 2
CBE 3
OBE 20
MBE (Civil)   92
MBE (Military)   5
MM   6
BEM 90
BEM (Gallantry) 3
Commendations   8
Mentions in Despatches   2,497

Post-War WAAF and WRAF 1946 to the present
CB   4
DBE 6
CBE 5
OBE 17 (+ 1 Commonwealth)
MBE 53 (+ 4 Commonwealth)
BEM 105 (+ 11 Commonwealth)
Royal Victoria Medal (Silver) 1

Appendix D Strengths

WRAF, First World War and Post-war, 1918-20

Year	Date	Names	Officers		Airwomen		Totals
1918	Apr-July	From: QMAAC	67		6,738		6,805
		WRNS	46		2,821		2,867
		Women's Legion	–		496		496
	1 Aug	Women					15,433
	1 Sept	Women					17,728
	1 Oct	Women					20,505
	1 Nov	Women					24,190
	1 Dec	Women					24,659
1919	1 Jan	Women					23,825
	1 Feb	Women					22,952
	1 Mar	Women					23,057
	1 Apr	Women					21,744
	1 May	Women					19,234
	1 June	Women					18,791
	1 July	Women					14,857
	1 Aug	Women					14,567
			UK	O/seas	UK	O/seas	
	1 Sept	WRAF	295	31	12,460	1,003	13,789
	1 Oct	WRAF	177	23	4,440	800	5,440
	1 Nov	WRAF	80	17	1,332	358	1,787
	1 Dec	WRAF	20	6	566	142	734
1920	1 Jan	WRAF	13	5	339	120	477
	1 Feb	WRAF	9	5	335	79	428
	1 Mar	WRAF	9	4	302	61	376
	1 Apr	WRAF	0	0	0	0	0
1918	Apr-July	Total Service Transfers	113		10,055		10,168
1918-20	Total	Civilian Recruits	453		21,700		22,153
1918-20	Total	In/Out	566		31,755		32,321

WAAF, Second World War and Post-war, 1939-48

Date		Officers	Airwomen	Total
1939	3 Sept	234	1,500	1,734
1940	1 Jan	359	8,403	8,762
	1 Apr	520	8,420	8,940
	1 July	687	11,170	11,857
	1 Oct	1,170	16,194	17,364
1941	1 Jan	1,368	19,121	20,489
	1 Apr	1,547	25,497	27,044
	1 July	1,891	35,493	37,384
	1 Oct	3,012	61,297	64,309
1942	1 Jan	4,001	94,410	98,411
	1 Apr	4,041	106,787	110,828
	1 July	4,695	120,961	125,656
	1 Oct	5,379	136,088	141,467
1943	1 Jan	5,796	160,173	165,969
	1 Apr	5,940	174,119	180,059
	1 July	5,974	175,861	181,835
	1 Oct	5,880	174,459	180,339
1944	1 Jan	6,040	170,780	176,820
	1 Apr	6,090	169,578	175,668
	1 July	6,199	168,207	174,406
	1 Oct	6,276	164,968	171,244
1945	1 Jan	6,355	159,810	166,165
	1 Apr	6,316	153,306	159,622
	1 July	6,233	146,719	152,952
	1 Oct	5,256	119,193	124,449
1946	1 Jan	4,373	93,371	97,744
	1 Apr	2,973	66,128	69,101
	1 July	1,984	44,752	46,736
	1 Oct	1,448	31,142	32,590
1947	1 Jan	1,412	24,416	25,828
	1 Apr	1,283	23,113	24,396
	1 July	1,105	21,375	22,480
	1 Oct	713	20,117	20,830
1948	1 Jan	645	19,497	20,142
	1 Apr	611	17,607	18,218
	1 July	575	14,941	15,516
	1 Oct	526	13,564	14,090

WRAF, Post-war, 1949-85

Date		Officers	Airwomen	Total
1949	1 July	520	13,937	14,457
1950	1 July	536	9,531	10,067
1951	1 Aug	538	8,880	9,418
1952	1 Aug	583	9,648	10,231
1953	1 Aug	621	8,827	9,448
1954	1 Aug	613	7,759	8,372
1955	1 Aug	524	6,162	6,686
1956	1 Aug	470	4,827	5,297
1957	1 Aug	407	4,220	4,627
1958	1 Aug	366	3,950	4,316
1959	1 Aug	349	4,612	4,961
1960	1 Aug	340	4,964	5,304
1961	1 Aug	339	5,416	5,755
1962	1 Aug	375	5,470	5,845
1963	1 Jan	391	5,470	5,861
1964	1 Jan	446	5,469	5,915
	1 Dec	443	4,592	5,035
1965	1 Dec	415	4,392	4,807
1966	1 Dec	429	4,429	4,858
1967	31 Dec	449	4,521	4,970
1968	1 Dec	471	4,049	4,520
1969	31 Dec	448	3,996	4,444
1970	1 Dec	432	4,736	5,168
1971	1 Dec	442	5,268	5,710
1972	1 Dec	442	4,968	5,410
1973	1 Dec	365	4,312	4,677
1974	1 Dec	365	3,901	4,266
1975	1 Dec	308	3,989	4,297
1976	1 Dec	303	3,830	4,133
1977	1 Dec	337	3,766	4,103
1978	1 Dec	342	4,299	4,641
1979	1 Dec	391	4,883	5,274
1980	1 Dec	451	5,096	5,547
1981	1 Dec	546	4,793	5,339
1982	1 Dec	533	4,288	4,821
1983	1 Dec	534	4,611	4,945
1984	1 Dec	583	4,728	5,311
1985	1 Dec	624	4,806	5,430

Appendix E   WRAF Branches and Trades 1918-20

Officer Branches
Administration
Instructor
Technical
Wireless Experimental
Doctor (RAF Branch)

Airwomen Trades
Acetylene Welder
Assistant Armourer
By-product Woman
Camera Repairer
Carpenter
Clerk — General
Clerk — Pay
Clerk — Records Office
Clerk — Shorthand Typist
Clerk — Stores
Cook
Coppersmith
Domestic Worker (General)
Doper
Draughtswoman (Maps)
Electrician
Fabric Worker (Airships)
Fabric Worker (Sailmaker)
Fitter (Aero Engine)
Fitter (General)
Housemaid
Instrument Repairer
Laundress
Machinist

Magneto Repairer
Meteorologist
Motor Cyclist
Motor Transport Driver (General Duties)
Motor Transport Driver (Special Duties)
Nurse
Packer
Painter
Pantrywoman
Photographer
Pigeon Keeper
Rigger
Shoemaker
Signwriter
Storewoman (Technical)
Storewoman (non-Technical)
Tailor
Telephone Operator
Tinsmith and Sheet Metal Worker
Turner
Unskilled Worker
Upholsterer
Vegetable Woman
Vulcanizer
WRAF Patrol
Waitress
Washer (Motor car)
Wireless Mechanic
Wireless Operator

Appendix F   WAAF Branches and Trades 1939-45

Officer Branches
Accountant
Administrative
Catering
Code and Cypher
Equipment
Filter
Intelligence
Interception Controller
Medical and Psychological Assistant
Meteorological
Motor Transport

Movements Liaison
Operations 'B'
Operations 'C'
Orthoptist
Personnel Selection
Photographic Interpretation
Provost
Signals 'G'
Signals, Special Radar
Signals, Supervisory Radar
WAAF G (WAAF only)
Doctor (RAF Branch)

Airwomen Trades only
Administrative
Armament Assistant
Balloon Parachute Hand
Charging Board Operator
Clerk, Personnel Selection
Clerk, Special Duties, Watchkeeping
Dental Hygienist
Drogue Packer and Repairer
Fabric Worker (Balloon)
Fabric Worker, Rigger (Balloon)
Hairdresser
Instrument Mechanic
Orderly
Radio Assistant
Sparking Plug Tester
Tracer
WAAF Physical Training Instructor
WAAF Police
Wireless Telegraphy (W/T) Slip Reader

Airmen and Airwomen
Aircrafthand GD
Acetylene Welder
Air Movement Assistant
Aircraft Finisher
Armourer (Guns)
Balloon Operator
Batwoman
Carpenter I + II
Chiropodist
Cine Projectionist
Clerk, Accounting
Clerk, Equipment Accounts
Clerk, General Duties
Clerk, General Duties (Cypher)
Clerk, General Duties (Maps)
Clerk, General Duties (Postal)
Clerk, General Duties (Provisioning)
Clerk, General Duties (Technical)
Clerk (Movement Control)
Clerk (Signals)
Clerk, Special Duties (SD)
Cook & Butcher
Dental Clerk Orderly
Dispenser
Draughtsman Cartographer
Driver, Motor Transport

Electrician I
Electrician II
Embarkation Assistant
Equipment Assistant
Fabric Worker
Fitter II Aircraft
Fitter II Engine
Flight Mechanic (Aircraft)
Flight Mechanic (Engine)
Instrument Repairer I
Instrument Repairer II
Interpreter
Interpreter, Technical
Laboratory Assistant
Maintenance Assistant
Masseuse
Mess Steward
Meteorologist
Model Maker
Motor Transport Mechanic
Motor Transport Fitter
Nursing Orderly
Operating Room Assistant
Optician Orderly
Parachute Packer
Parachute Repairer
Pattern Maker (Architectural)
Photographer
Radar Mechanic (Air)
Radar Mechanic (Ground)
Radar Operator
Radar Operator (Computer)
Radiographer
Radio-telephone (R/T) Operator II
Radio-telephone (R/T) Operator IV
Safety Equipment Assistant
Safety Equipment Worker
Shoe Repairer
Tailor
Telegraphist II
Telegraphist—High-Speed
Telephonist
Teleprinter Operator
Vulcanizer
Waitress
Wireless Mechanic
Wireless Operator
Wireless Operator Mechanic

Appendix G   WRAF Branches and Trades 1985

Source: Publication 465

Officer Branches
Administrative — Catering
Administrative — Education
Administrative — Physical
   Education
Administrative, Secretarial Engineering
General Duties, Ground — Fighter
   Control
General Duties, Ground — Air Traffic
   Control
Provost
Photographic Interpretation
Supply
Legal*
Dental*
Medical*

*RAF Branches

Airwomen
Administrative
Administrative Clerk
Aerospace Systems Operator
Air Cartographer
Aircraft Mechanic (Airframe)
Aircraft Mechanic (Electrical)
Aircraft Mechanic (Propulsion)
Aircraft Mechanic (Weapons)
Aircraft Technician (Airframe)
Aircraft Technician (Electrical)
Aircraft Technician (Propulsion)
Aircraft Technician (Weapons)
Assistant Air Traffic Controller
Carpenter
Clerk (Catering)
Cook
Data Analyst
Dental Hygienist
Dental Surgery Assistant
Dental Technician
Dispenser
Electronics Engineering Technician
   (Flight Systems)
Electronics Mechanic (Air
   Communications)
Electronics Mechanic (Air Defence)
Electronics Mechanic (Air Radar)
Electronics Mechanic (Flight
   Systems)
Electronics Mechanic (Tele-
   communications)
Electronics Technician (Air
   Communications)
Electronics Technician (Air
   Defence)
Electronics Technician (Airfield)
Electronics Technician (Air Radar)
Electronics Technician (Flight
   Systems)
Electronics Technician (Synthetic
   Trainer)
Electronics Technician (Telecomm-
   unications)
Electrophysical Technician
Environmental Health Technician
General Mechanic (Electrical)
General Mechanic (Ground Support
   Equipment)
General Mechanic (Workshops)
General Technician (Electrical)
General Technician (Ground
   Support Equipment)
General Technician (Workshops)
Kennelmaid†
Laboratory Technician
Mechanical Transporter Driver
Mechanical Transport — Mechanic
Mechanical Transport — Technician
Medical Assistant
Mental Nurse
Operating Theatre Technician
Painter and Finisher
Photographer Ground
Physical Training Instructor
Physiotherapist
Plotter — Air Photography
Pupil Enrolled Nurse
Radiographer
Radio Operator (Voice)
RAF General Duties
RAF Police
Special Telegraphist

State Enrolled Nurse (Qualified)
Stewardess
Supplier
Survival Equipment Fitter
Telecommunications Operator

Telephonist
WRAF Shorthand Typist (Qualified)†
WRAF Typist (Qualified)†

WRAF only trade†

Appendix H   Airwomen in Main Trade Groups 1939-45
Ref: Form F 63510

Date	Aircraft Maintenance & Servicing	Armament	Ground Signals	MT	Medical	Balloon	Admin/ Domestic	Misc	TOTALS
1 Sept 1939									1,500
1 June 1940	707		1,381	695	311		4,861	1,162	9,117
1 Sept 1940	996		2,685	556	525	290	8,013	2,011	15,076
1 Sept 1941	2,989	44	6,525	1,227	1,975	1,859	34,019	4,128	52,766
1 Sept 1942	5,150	353	14,752	9,118	4,115	16,917	71,620	8,545	130,570
1 Sept 1943	16,366	670	26,070	15,156	4,568	7,973	94,260	9,767	174,830
1 Sept 1944	17,440	633	31,985	12,336	5,659	4,769	84,049	9,637	166,508
1 May 1945	15,576	575	29,646	10,959	5,146	3,464	77,089	8,553	151,008
1 Sept 1945	13,277	509	26,050	9,073	4,470	2,546	66,960	7,368	130,253

Appendix I   Approximate Distribution of Home Command WAAF 1944-45
Ref: Form F 63510

Home Commands	1 Oct 1944	1 Jan 1945	1 July 1945	1 Sept 1945
Air Ministry	497	485	488	454
Bomber	37,564	38,318	34,437	28,128
Fighter (inc AEAF/2TAF/BAFO)	40,911	40,177	37,290	28,477
Coastal	13,104	13,797	12,987	11,183
Irish	823	800	571	490
Balloon	8,584	3,184	–	–
Maintenance	12,994	13,006	12,509	11,876
Transport	5,694	6,930	9,801	13,798
Flying Training	20,477	21,709	18,506	15,169
Technical Training	26,730	23,761	20,029	20,147
Special Duty	22	25	32	40
Location Not Recorded	166	343	1,106	634

Appendix J   Strengths of RAF and WAAF — Home and Overseas 1939-45

Date	Home			Overseas			Service
	RAF	WAAF	Total	RAF	WAAF	Total	Grand Total
3 Sept 1939	158,718	1,734	160,452	13,857	–	13,857	174,309
1 Oct 1940	395,341	17,361	412,702	23,011	3	23,014	435,716
1 Oct 1941	667,051	64,259	731,310	103,952	50	104,002	835,312
1 Oct 1942	658,385	141,259	799,644	239,366	208	239,574	1,039,218
1 Oct 1943	655,786	180,000	835,786	330,607	339	330,946	1,166,732
1 Oct 1944	695,993	168,151	864,144	302,485	3,093	305,578	1,169,722
1 Sept 1945	653,243	130,396	783,639	285,953	5,495	291,448	1,075,087

Appendix K WAAF Overseas 1940-45

Ref: AP 3234 with amendments

		July/Dec 1940	July 1941	Dec 1941	July 1942	Dec 1942	July 1943	Dec 1943	July 1944	Dec 1944	Aug 1945	Dec 1945
Australia	Officers									3	3	3
	Airwomen											2
Austria	Officers											3
	Airwomen											13
Bahamas	Officers						7	7	9	9	5	—
Belgium	Officers									12	17	11
	Airwomen									77	1,185	208
Bermuda	Officers					4	4	4	4	4	3	2
Canada	Officers				13	22	26	27	26	28	28	24
Ceylon	Officers										26	11
	Airwomen										479	195
Denmark	Officers											1
France	Officers								3†		29	16
	Airwomen								10†		194	236
Germany	Officers										17	101
	Airwomen										72	1,063
Gibraltar	Officers								25	25	20	—
	Airwomen								5	5	5	—
Holland	Officers											1
India	Officers									9	88	86
	Airwomen									250	705	581
Italy	Officers								103	104	97	48
	Airwomen										13	144
Labrador	Officers						4	4	6	4	7	—
Malta	Officers								3	2	2	11
Middle East Area inc Egypt, Palestine, Aden, Cyprus, E Africa, Iraq and Syria	Officers		1	30	149	200	237	233	178	208	175	179
	Airwomen							*750	1,571	2,393	3,365	3,447
Newfoundland	Officers							4	4	4	4	—
Norway	Officers										1	1
	Airwomen										12	47
N W Africa	Officers							28	15	16	14	22
	Airwomen											847
Singapore	Officers											33
	Airwomen											167
Trinidad	Officers								1	—	—	—
USA	Officers	3	7	29	35	40	48	52	62	69	82	26

*Local Service Palestinians
†In September 1944

Appendix L   National Service and Volunteer WAAF 1939-45

Ref: Air Publication AP 3234

Period	Volunteers	National Service	Total
Sept 1939-Dec 1940	14,546	—	14,546
Jan-Dec 1941	81,928	—	81,928
Jan-Dec 1942	62,091	16,246	78,337
Jan-Dec 1943	11,144	17,192	28,336
Jan-Sept 1944	11,225	494	11,719
July-Dec 1945	2,383	—	2,383
Totals	183,317	33,932	217,249

Figures are approximate.

Appendix M   WAAF Casualties 1939-45

Ref: F 63510

Period	Died from natural causes	Wounded	Killed
3 Sept 1939-40	4	11	5
3 Sept 1940-41	8	21	11
3 Sept 1941-42	57	44	30
3 Sept 1942-43	74	100	33
3 Sept 1943-44	81	185	74
3 Sept 1944- Aug 1945	53	59	38
Totals	277	420	191

Nov 1949 Disablement Pensions to WAAF (eg Loss of hearing etc) 5,510
Commonwealth War Graves Commission WAAF — 24 Overseas, 144 Home

Appendix N   WRAF Overseas 1952-69

1952 August	1,074	1961 August	625
1953 August	968	1962 August	748
1954 August	1,094	1963 August	c800
1955 August	988	1964 August	827
1956 August	682	1965 1 December	775
1957 August	573	1966 1 December	664
1958 August	488	1967 1 December	506
1959 August	547	1968 1 December	545
1960 August	578	1969 1 December	587

Key to Abbreviations

ACW2	Aircraftwoman 2nd class (lowest rank)
ACSEA	Air Command South East Asia
AD	Air Depot
AHB	Air Historical Branch (RAF)
AMO	Air Ministry Order
AMP	Air Member for Personnel
AMSSO	Air Ministry Special Signals Office
AP	Air Publication
ARS	Aircraft Repair Shops/Section
ASD	Aeroplane Supply Depot
ASO	Assistant Section Officer
ATA	Air Transport Auxiliary
ATC	Air Training Corps
ATS	Auxiliary Territorial Service
AWOL	Absent without leave
BAFSEA	British Air Force South East Asia
BEM	British Empire Medal
BLA	Burma looms ahead
BP	Bletchley Park (Station X)
CBE	Commander of the Order of the British Empire
CBO	Charging Board Operator
CH	Chain Home (Radar)
CHEL	Chain Home Extra Low
CHL	Chain Home Low
C in C	Commander in Chief
CIU	Central Interpretation Unit (Photo)
CO	Commanding Officer (station)
Cpl	Corporal
CRT	Cathode Ray tube
CSL	Chief Section Leader
D-Day	Allied landings in Normandy 1944
DAF	Desert Air Force
DBE	Dame Commander of the Order of the British Empire
DCI	Defence Council Instruction
DF	Direction Finding
DH	de Havilland (Aircraft)
DI	Daily Inspection/Drill Instructor

DORA	Defence of the Realm Act
DP	Displaced Person
DWRAF	Director WRAF
DWAAF	Director WAAF
Enigma	German encoding machine
ENSA	Entertainments National Service Association
EPAS	Equipment Provisioning and Accounting Section
EVT	Educational and Vocational Training Scheme
FANY	First Aid Nursing Yeomanry (Women's Transport Service)
FEAF	Far Eastern Air Force
FFI	Free From Infection
Flashes	Trade/Nationality Badges
Flt	Flight (sometimes short for Flt Sgt)
Flt Lt	Flight Lieutenant
Flt Sgt	Flight Sergeant
FSPub	Field Service Publication
G	General
GC	George Cross
GCI	Ground Control Interception
GD	General Duties
Gee	Air Navigation Radar System
HMSO	Her Majesty's Stationery office
IC	In charge of
IOT	Initial Officer Training
JCP	Japanese Campaign Pay
KD	Khaki Drill (Hot weather uniform)
LACW	Leading Aircraftwoman
MBE	Member of the Order of the British Empire
Met	Meteorology/Meteorological
MM	Military Medal
MO	Medical Officer
MOD	Ministry of Defence
MP	Military Police/Minor Punishment

MT	Motor Transport		SIO	Station Intelligence Officer
			SIS	Special Intelligence Service
NAAFI	Navy, Army & Air Force Institute (Club for leisure and snacks)		SNCO	Senior Non Commissioned Officer (WO, Flt Sgt, Sgt)
			SO	Section Officer
NATO	North Atlantic Treaty Organization		SOE	Special Operations Executive
			S of (W)	School of (WRAF/WAAF)
NBC	Nuclear, Biological and Chemical		RT	Recruit Training
			Sqn	Squadron
NCO	Non Commissioned Officer (Cpl usually)		SSQ	Station Sick Quarters
			SWO	Station Warrant Officer
OASC	Officer and Aircrew Selection Centre		2TAF	2nd Tactical Air Force
			TDS	Training Depot Station
OBE	Officer of the Order of the British Empire		TME	Telecommunications Middle East
OC	Officer Commanding (Section)			
OCTU	Officer Cadet Training Unit		U-boat	German submarine
Ops	Operations (Flying)		UK	United Kingdom
			Ultra	Intelligence information
Padre	Service Chaplain		US	Unusable (out of order)
PE	Physical Education		USA	United States of America
POW	Prisoner of War		USAAF	United States Army Air Force
PSI	President of the Service Institute (Welfare Fund)		USSR	Union of Soviet Socialist Republics (Russia)
PT	Physical Training		UT	Under Training
PTI	Physical Training Instructor			
			V-1	German pilotless flying bomb
QMAAC	Queen Mary's Army Auxiliary Corps		V-2	German pilotless rocket
			VAD	Voluntary Aid Detachments
			VIP	Very Important Person
RADAR	Radio Detection and Ranging		VE day	Victory in Europe Day
RAF	Royal Air Force		VJ day	Victory over Japan Day
RCM	Radar Counter Measures			
RDF	Radio Direction Finding		WAAC	Women's Army Auxiliary Corps
RFC	Royal Flying Corps		WAAF	Women's Auxiliary Air Force
RNAS	Royal Naval Air Service		Wingco	Wing Commander
ROM	Radar Operator Mechanic		WO	Warrant Officer
RT	Radio Telephone/ist/y		WRAF	Women's Royal Air Force
			WRNS	Women's Royal Naval Service
Sally Ann	Salvation Army		WT	Wireless Telegraphy
SARD	Scientific Aeronautical Research Depot			
SCAF	Supply Control and Accounting Flight		X	Station, Bletchley Park
SD	Special Duties			
Sgt	Sergeant		Y	Radio listening stations
SHAPE	Supreme Headquarters Allied Powers Europe		YWCA	Young Women's Christian Association

Select Bibliography

Books about the WRAF/WAAF

Babington Smith C. *Evidence in Camera* (David & Charles, 1957)
Baker E. R. *WAAF Adventure* (Lonsdale, 1946)
Beauman K. B. *Partners in Blue* (Hutchinson, 1971)
Beauman K. B. *Wings on Her Shoulders* (Hutchinson, 1943)
Carne D. *The Eyes of the Few* (P. R. Macmillan, 1960)
Chauncey A. *Women of the Royal Air Force* (WRAF Old Comrades Association, 1922)
Clayton A. *The Enemy is Listening* (Hutchinson, 1980)
Collett-Wadge D. *Women in Uniform* (Sampson Low, 1946)
Derbyshire *Shirley Joins The WRAF* (Bodley Head, 1955)
Douglas-Pennant V. *Under the Searchlight* (Allen & Unwin, 1922)
Farson & Paris* *Bombers' Moon* (V. Gollancz Ltd, 1941)
Joubert P. de la Ferté *The Forgotten Ones* (Hutchinson, 1961)
Forbes & Portal *Book of the WAAF* (Amalgamated Press Ltd, 1942)
Garth S. *With the WAAF* (R. Tuck, 1942)
George G. A. *Eight Months with the WRAF* (Heath Cranton Ltd, 1920)
Gwynne-Vaughan H. *The Junior Leader* (Hutchinson & Co, 1943)
Hall A. *We Also Were There* (Merlin Books, 1985)
HEB, *WAAF in Action* (Adam & Chas Black, 1942)
Izzard M. *A Heroine in Her Time* (Macmillan, 1969)
Korwin M. *In Spite of Everything* (Dunlop & Drennan, 1942)
Masson M. *Christine* (Hamish Hamilton, 1975)
Macmillan N. *Sir Sefton Brancker* (Heinemann, 1935)
Mitchell D. *Women on the Warpath* (J Cape, 1965)
Nicholson J. **Kiss the Girls Goodbye* (Hutchinson, 1944)
Noble V. *Girls You Amaze Me* (Allen, 1943)
Powys-Lybbe U. *The Eye of Intelligence* (Kimber, 1983)
Priestley J. B. *British Women Go to War* (Collins, 1943)
Reynolds V. & Others *Service Women WRNS, WRAC, WRAF* (Educ Explorers, 1977)
Ross C. **The Colours of the Night* (M Joseph Ltd [Magnum 1981], 1962)
Ross C. **Battledress* (Eyre & Methuen Ltd [Magnum 1980], 1979)
Scott P. *They Made Invasion Possible* (Hutchinson, 1944)

Settle M. L. *All the Brave Promises* (Heinemann, 1966)
Taylor L. *Airwomen's Work* (Pitman, 1943)
Warren P. M. *The Best of Enemies* (Howard Baker, 1986)
WRAF *Women of the Royal Air Force on the Rhine* (Bachem, Cologne, 1919)
WRAF *Handbook for WRAF* (Gale & Polden, 1919)
Worrall A. *Lambs in Blue* (New Horizon, 1983)
Wyndham J. *Love is Blue* (Heinemann, 1986)
*Novels

Books on the RAF
Adkin F. J. *Through Hangar Doors* (Airlife, 1985)
Adkin F. J. *From the Ground Up* (Airlife, 1983)
Bishop E. *The Debt We Owe* (Longmans, 1969)
Bowyer C. *Royal Air Force Handbook 1939-45* (Allan, 1984)
Boyle A. *Trenchard* (Collins, 1962)
Beaton C. Air of Glory (—, 1941)
Congdon P. *Behind Hangar Doors* (Sonik Books, 1985)
Donne & Fowler *Per Ardua ad Astra* (F. Muller Ltd, 1982)
Gander T. *Encyclopaedia of the Modern Royal Air Force* (Patrick Stephens, 1984)
Gossage *The Royal Air Force* (Hodge & Co Ltd, 1937)
Hammerton J. *ABC of the RAF* (Amalgamated Press Ltd, 1942)
Hering P. *Customs & Traditions of the RAF* (Gale & Polden, 1961)
Jackson R. *The RAF In Action – Flanders to Falklands* (Blandford, 1985)
Jones H. A. *War in the Air* (Oxford Clarendon Press, 1937)
Kinsey G. *Bawdsey – Birth of the Beam* (Terence Dalton, 1983)
Longmate E. N. *The Royal Flying Corps* (Chatto & Windus, 1981)
Lumley E. A. *Army and Air Force Doctor* (London, 1971)
Morris A. *The Balloonatics* (Jarrolds, 1970)
RAF BF *A Life Time of Service 1918-83* (Seagull, 1983)
Reader *Architect of Air Power* (Collins, 1968)
Richardson A. *Wingless Victory* (Odhams, 1950)
Royle T. *The Best Years of Their Lives* (Michael Joseph, 1986)
Smith *The Royal Air Force* (Blackwell, 1963)
Taylor J. W. R. *Best Flying Stories* (Faber & Faber, 1956)
Taylor, Moyes & Bowyer *Pictorial History of the RAF Vol I & II* (Allan, 1980)
Terraine J. *Right of the Line* (Hodder & Stoughton, 1985)
Ed Walbank F. A. *Wings of War* (Batsford, 1942)

Other services
Air Ministry *Story of the Air Training Corps* (Air League of Brit Empire, 1946)
Bidwell S. *Women's Royal Army Corps* (Leo Cooper Ltd, 1977)
Birdwell R. *Women in Battledress* (Fine Editions Press NY, 1942)
Boase W. *The Sky's The Limit* (Osprey, 1979)
Talbot Booth *Ranks & Badges in the Navy, Army, RAF & Auxiliaries* (Philip & Son Ltd, 1940)
Cheeseman E. C. *Brief Glory* (Harborough Pub Co Ltd, 1946)
Cowper J. M. *The Auxiliary Territorial Service* (War Office, 1949)
Curtis L. *The Forgotten Pilots* (Nelson & Saunders Ltd, 1985)
Dorling H. T. *Ribbons & Medals* (G. Philip, 1940)
Dupays P. *Anglaises en Uniforme* (Ed de la Critique, 1951)
Goldsmith M. *Women at War* (Lindsay Drummond Ltd, 1943)

Gwynne-Vaughan H. *Service with the Army* (Hutchinson, 1942)
Marwick A. *Women at War 1914-18* (Fontana, 1977)
King A. *Golden Wings* (Pearson, 1956)
Lomax J. *Women in the Air* (J. Murray, 1986)
Mason U. S. *WRENS 1917-77* (Educational Explorers, 1977)
Popham H. *FANY 1907-84* (Secker & Warburg, 1984)
Stradling A. H. *Customs of the Services* (Gale & Polden, 1966)
Warner & Sandilands *Women beyond the Wire* (Joseph, 1982)
Williams H. *Immortal Memory* (Bamber & Co Ltd)

Other sources
Anderson V. *Spam Tomorrow* (Hart-Davis, 1956)
Battle *War Brides* (Star Paperback USA, 1983)
Calvocoressi P. *Top Secret Ultra* (Cassell Ltd, 1980)
Costello J. *Love, Sex and War* (Collins, 1985)
Daily Mail *The War Despatches 1939-45* (Marshall Cavendish, 1977)
Davidson B. *Special Operations Europe* (Gollancz, 1980)
Dorrie V. *Daughters of Britain* (G. Ronald, 1950)
Foot M. R. D. *SOE in France* (HMSO, 1966)
Foot M. R. D. *SOE 1940-46* (BBC, 1984)
Foot M. R. D. *Resistance* (Eyre & Methuen, 1976)
Gwynne-Vaughan H. *The Discipline of Learning* (Birkbeck, 1954)
Hinsley F. H. Vol I, II & III *British Intelligence in the Second World War* (HMSO, 1979)
Lewin R. *Ultra Goes to War* (Hutchinson, 1978)
Maugham *Lies as Allies* (OUP, 1941)
Miller H. *Service to the Services* (Newman Neame Ltd, 1971)
Waller & Vaughan-Rees *Women in Wartime* (Optima, 1987)
Wavell A. *Generals & Generalship* (Penguin Special, 1941)
Yass M. *This Is Your War* (HMSO, 1983)
10-14 Anniversary *Battle of Britain* (RAFA, 1950-54)
Roof over Britain 1939-42 (Ministry of Information, 1943)
Women in Industry No 22 (Bibliographies, House of Commons Library, 1947)
The Labour Woman 1939-45 (Labour Party, 1945)
Service Overseas Gp 454 (HMSO, W. P. Lord Ltd, 1942)
Manpower 1943 (Ministry of Labour, 1943)
We Speak from the Air (HMSO, 1942)

WRAF/WAAF Strengths, AHB

Monthly Return of Personnel of RAF in British Isles and Overseas		1918-20
AP 3234	*Women's Auxiliary Air Force Appendix 2*	1939-45
AP 3234	*Ch. 18 Appendix*	1945-51
WRAF *Director's Letters*		1951-69
Stats 510	*Annual Digest of RAF Statistics* (Part D excludes PM, Med & Dent Offs)	1951-69
Stats 1204	*Monthly Record Office Statement of Establishment & Mustered Strength of Ground Personnel by Trades*	1950-66

Stats 1204	*Monthly Record and Pay Office Statement of Established & Mustered Strength of Ground Personnel by Trades*	1967-71
Stats 1204	*Monthly Personnel Management Centre Return of Establishment & Mustered Strength of Ground Personnel by Trades*	1972-84
Stats 216	*Monthly Messing Return of Officers by Branch Rank and Type of Commission*	1969-78
Stats 1316	*Monthly Personnel Management Centre, Return of Officers Pay by Branch etc*	1979-84
	Tri-Service Manpower Statistics	1970s

Articles from Magazines & Journals etc

Air Force Magazine
WRAF Officers Association Gazette
The Airman
Officer
Royal Air Force Quarterly
Royal United Service Institution Journal (RUSI)
Royal Air Force Journal
Flight International
Illustrated London News
Picture Post
The Legion
Provost Parade
MTE Journal
The Aeroplane
Air Clues
Meteorological Magazine
Newspapers
RAF News

Other sources
Hansard (HMSO)
Handbooks of Britain (HMSO)
Whitaker's Almanacks
Atlas of World Affairs (Boyd-Methuen)
Encyclopaedia Britannica

RAF Material

Branch Histories
Station handbooks
Arrival briefs, various
Dateline
News releases
MOD Letters
Press Cuttings
Files (DWRAF, AHB, War Office etc)
AMWOs
AMOs
DCIs
GAIs
Air Force Lists
Air Publications
Career Pamphlets
PAM 103s
Personal papers
etc.

Index